#984082

T4-ABM-257

621370E

604.2 Mor
Morris, George E
Technical illustrating

WITHDRAWN
TOLEDO-LUCAS COUNTY
PUBLIC LIBRARY

JUL 2 2 1980

SANGER

TOLEDO-LUCAS COUNTY
PUBLIC LIBRARY

Technical Illustrating

GEORGE E. MORRIS

PRENTICE-HALL, INC., Englewood Cliffs, New Jersey

Library of Congress Cataloging in Publication Data

MORRIS, GEORGE E   1937–
    Technical illustrating.

    1. Technical illustration.   I. Title.
T11.8.M67   604'.2   74-13565
ISBN 0-13-898155-8

It all has to begin somewhere.
To my mother, ISABELLA MARIE

© 1975 by Prentice-Hall, Inc.
Englewood Cliffs, New Jersey

All rights reserved. No part of this book
may be reproduced in any form or by any means
without permission in writing from the publisher.

10 9 8 7 6 5 4 3 2 1

Printed in the United States of America

PRENTICE-HALL INTERNATIONAL, INC., *London*
PRENTICE-HALL OF AUSTRALIA, PTY. LTD., *Sydney*
PRENTICE-HALL OF CANADA, LTD., *Toronto*
PRENTICE-HALL OF INDIA PRIVATE LIMITED, *New Delhi*
PRENTICE-HALL OF JAPAN, INC., *Tokyo*

Contents

Part I Projection Schemes 1

1 Multiple View Orthographic Projection 3

  A Auxiliary Planes
  B Section Views

2 Axonometric Projection 10

  A Isometric Projection: position of axes, box method for construction, center line layout method for construction, inclined or oblique surfaces, sections, angles, curves, circles, ellipse construction, ellipse guides, spheres, dimensioning
  B Dimetric Projection: points of view, position of axes, construction, circles
  C Trimetric Projection: axes and scales
  D True Axonometric Projection

3 Oblique Projection   60

   A Receding Axis Angle
   B Length of Receding Lines
   C Positions of Objects
   D Offset Measurements
   E Construction Methods
   F Circles and Angles
   G Sections and Dimensions
   H Clinographic—A Special Case

4 Perspective   75

   A Use of Perspective Drawings
   B Terminology and Concepts: projectors, shapes, sizes, measurements, horizons, vanishing points
   C Perspective Systems: one-point perspective, two-point perspective, three-point perspective

5 Shades and Shadows   94

   A Definitions: shadow, shade, light, direction of light
   B Principles: parallel lines, lines that cast shadows, planes that cast shadows
   C Multiple View Drawings
   D Pictorial Drawings: direction of light
   E Closure

Part II Tools of the Trade   111

6 Essential Equipment   113

   A Pens: technical fountain pens, other inking pens
   B Lettering Devices: Leroy sets, Koh-I-Noor Rapidoguides
   C Compasses: lead compass, nibs-type inking compass, drop-bow compass, beam compass, Koh-I-Noor compasses
   D Miscellaneous: triangles, irregular and ship curves, pencils, pencil pointers, erasers, straightedge, T square, drafting machines, cutout templates, ink, paper

E Specialty Items: ultrasonic cleaners, camera lucida, visualizer, ink dryer, reducing lens, lamps, proportional dividers, logarithmic spiral curve, pantograph
F Incidental Equipment and Supplies

Part III Using Skills and Tools   143

7 Styles   151

A Freehand
B Mechanical: Leroy lettering, typeset lettering, the formula approach to sizing
C Closure

8 Techniques and Media for Shading   165

A Rulings
B Acetate Sheets
C Hand Stipple
D Stipple Board
E Scratch Board
F Ink Wash
G Airbrush
H Tint Screen
I Closure

9 Projection Slides   197

A Format
B Letter Sizes and Line Widths
C Black and White or Color 2×2 Slides: colored lines on a black background, black lines on a colored background, white lines on a colored background, colored lines on a colored background
D Black and White or Color $3\frac{1}{4} \times 4$ Slides: colored lines on a black background, white lines on a colored background
E Notes Concerning Slides: choosing a format, detail on a slide, use of duplicate slides, typewritten copy for slides, legibility of copy, slide titles, ideas per slide, projection of slides, use of dark slides

Part IV Appendices 209

A Reproduction Processes 211

B High Contrast Photography 215

C Typography 217

D Typographic Measure 223

E The Greek Alphabet 224

F International Standard Prefixes 225

G Symbols and Abbreviations 227

H Objects to Draw 230

Preface

Thoughts on Fundamentals

Each of us, whether we are a teacher, a student, a beginning illustrator, or an accomplished illustrator, wishes to learn a new subject or technique as rapidly as possible and as thoroughly as possible. Often we are asked to believe that shortcut methods are a means by which we can acquire knowledge rapidly. If we stop for a moment and examine the proposition, we will see that shortcut methods and thoroughness usually are not compatible. *Nothing* can or will replace an understanding of fundamental concepts.

Let us retrace a part of our life—from birth to the present—and our growing knowledge of communication during that period. Our initial method of communicating to our parents that we were hungry and that our diapers were in need of change was to cry. We expressed satisfaction by gurgling, smiling, and laughing. Later we pleased Mom and Dad, Grandmother, and a host of relatives by forming the sound of their name. The next step was to put our unrelated storehouse of words into unintelligible phrases. Finally we mastered the art of sentence formation. By this time we were ready to begin the formal education process.

In Kindergarten we learned the ABC's and word associations. Later we learned, in progressive steps, the use of nouns, verbs, adjectives, and the other parts of speech. Then we were taught how to "put it all together"—how to construct sentences, paragraphs, and stories. With not too much imagination we can observe a similar path in learning to be a technical illustrator.

Technical Illustrating does not present shortcut methods that might lead to questionable results. The teacher and student will find no discussion of isometric or perspective printed grids. Why? Because the student learns nothing about the projection scheme if he has these printed crutches to lean upon. After, and *only* after, a student has the fundamental concepts of a technique in mind, he may wish to attempt to use methods other than those basic to the technique. Then he will understand the limitations of such shortcuts.

Treatment of Topics The usual scheme of presentation in a graphics book is to first discuss lettering, line weights, and equipment necessary to make drawings. *Technical Illustrating* departs from this historic approach. We assume that anyone interested in graphics will be able to print intelligibly and to know how to hold a pencil. He must also recognize how to use a T square and triangle. As a result of this assumption, we begin discussion with projection techniques.

Following projection schemes are discussions of equipment and uses of equipment and skills. In 15 years of illustrating, the author has found the items discussed to be of major importance. Appendices are no less important and give the student a ready reference.

To the Instructor It is my sincere desire that the material here will provide you with methods and information to *assist* you in training illustrators. My confidence in the techniques presented and uses thereof are founded upon experience—they have served me well. The figures used have been chosen and executed carefully. In many cases you will be able to use the figures effectively as a study guide. Students may be assigned the task of explaining what projection technique, what shading media, and what other techniques were used for a particular figure. Figure captions include many of these data and are important. Encourage your students to read captions and study figures.

Appendix H provides 75 objects that you may assign for home study or home plates. Because the figures in the appendix are general in nature, they may be assigned while you are studying axonometric, oblique, or perspective. The purpose of letting you choose from the list is simple: each student may have a different rate of learning. By selecting figures less difficult for those who are not progressing as rapidly, you give him more practice—the only way he will learn.

Chapters 7 and 8 are extremely important. Each gives the student exposure to the real world of illustrating. I encourage you to assign problems of the kind that require the student to use each of the media discussed. He can redraw a figure from this text or another text, using a different technique from the original. Have them shade spheres and other solids by stippling. Again, the watch word is practice. He can learn in no other way.

I welcome comments about *Technical Illustrating* and will be indebted to you for errors you find and point out to me.

To the Student

You are either beginning a course of study that might be your life's work or you are enlarging upon your skills attained prior to studying technical illustrating. I wish you every success in years to come and sincerely hope that you find this book an asset to your education.

The liberal use of illustrations in *Technical Illustrating* will give you examples that will be of value to you for years to come. Remember, and remember well, examples give rise to ideas. Ideas lead to good illustrations. Practice and the implementation of your ideas will make you a good illustrator.

GEORGE E. MORRIS
Champaign, Illinois

Acknowledgements

Whereas most of us will read the text of a book, seldom will we read the preface and acknowledgements. These items are considered to be vehicles for the authors to be a philosopher (preface) and to thank his wife for her thoughtful support during the excruciatingly painful ordeal of writing a book (acknowledgements). All authors are, of course, philosophers of sorts. The preface material is included to project his basic reasons for writing the book in the manner he did. It is his one opportunity to defend his approach. Acknowledgements take two forms: politically motivated (thanking a department head or dean) and sincere thanks to the *many* people who contribute to the book.

The idea for me to write this book came from Dennis P. Curtin, a friend and a talented editor. Had Denny not suggested that I engage the project, I would never have done so. Thanks, Mr. C.

Nick Holonyak, Jr., has been an inspiration by allowing me to associate with him. He has given me a rare opportunity: to illustrate his papers, which are always on the frontier of new science. His philosophy on life and his instatiable desire to excel is contagious.

Publishers are many. *Good* publishers are few. Prentice-Hall has been good to me, and is, to my way of thinking, *numero uno*. My association with such professionals as Nick Romanelli, Marv Warshaw, Jim Bacci, Virginia Huebner, Leon Ligouri, Rosalie "Meg" Herion, Rusty Hockett, Eileen Thompson, Bob Duchacek, Nancy Baker, Maureen Wilson, Margaret McAbee, and Ken Wisman has made me aware of what the production staff of a publisher contributes to the publication of a book.

The last of these people, Ken Wisman, was production editor for this book. As every author discovers, his interest in his book flags at certain times during production. During these times Ken was there to prod and nag—as we had agreed for him to do. He kept the book on schedule, did an excellent job keeping track of details, and, most importantly, was a joy to work *with*.

The name Betty Adam, the lady who copyedited a horribly rough manuscript, will always have a special meaning to me—meticulous.

Before ending this note, I wish to make a few general acknowledgements to people who have *always* been a help—whether in support of writing or whatever the chore.

> Carl Larson, Roger Hayward, Bob MacFarlane, Doug Sanford, Jack and Jackie Gladin, Rich Desselman, Alice Prickett, Karol Goebel, Pat, Gene, Terry, and Steph Walsh, Stella Goodenough, Walt Wood, Susan Lutz, Phil Mason, Jeff Sund, Dave Hildebrand, and John Dean.

A special friend deserves special mention. Some of my drawings appear in physics journals in the U.S.S.R. I thank Zhores Alferov for fond memories and for using my drawings.

Now, back to the old saw of thanking your wife. Shirley typed this manuscript at least six times, while at the same time caring for the needs of our four children (George, Jr., Brian, John, and Anna), keeping the house from looking like a disaster area, washing the clothes, and performing myriad other chores. She is also my star typesetter for SCIENTIFIC ILLUSTRATORS (*our* agency), my confidant, and lover. How can you describe the contribution your wife makes to a book you write? You can't. It's like everything a married couple does: It happens and we take it for granted. Thanks, Shirl.

Part I

Projection Schemes

An illustrator is called upon to draw box diagrams, electrical circuit diagrams, graphs, and objects. To execute box diagrams and other simple line drawings and produce an effective illustration, he must choose a style suited to the work and then execute the work with skill. When asked to draw an object, he also must choose a suitable style and do professional work but, further, he must *think in three dimensions and draw in two dimensions*. Engineering draftsman may argue that what is commonly called orthographic projection does not require this "think 3-D, draw 2-D" process. We caution them to remember that a three-dimensional object is being represented by the orthographic projection and although plane views of the object are being used, the process is indeed valid.

Before venturing into discussions of projection schemes, we will make a distinction between *projection* and *drawing*. Strictly speaking, projection implies the use of intersecting lines to locate points, as shown in Fig. I.1(a). As an alternative method to using intersecting lines, we may measure a distance and transfer this measured distance with a scale, Fig. I.1(b): a construction called *drawing*. Most graphic artists, illustrators, draftsmen, engineers, and scientists use the

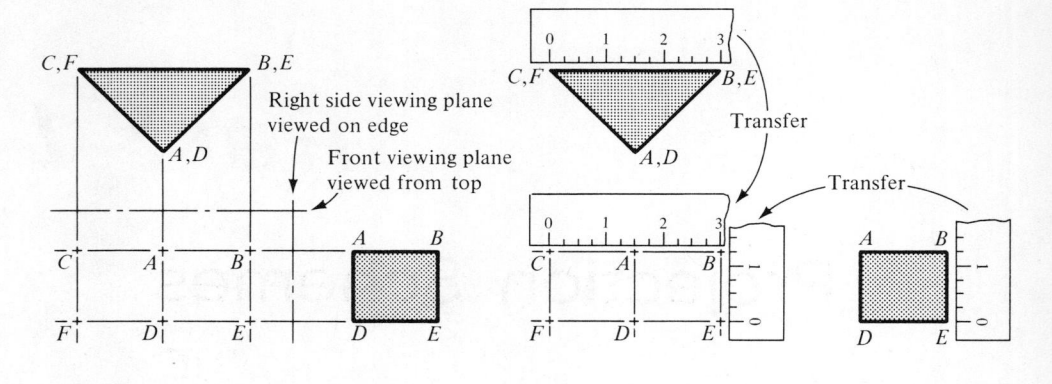

(a) Intersecting lines = projection   (b) Transferring dimensions = drawing

Figure I.1 Comparing (a) projection to (b) drawing. In (a), a front view is determined by projecting points from the two given views, whereas in (b) a scale or dividers are used to transfer distances to contruct the front view.

words *drawing* and *projection* interchangeably, but we suggest that the *distinction* between projection and drawing be kept in mind. In most cases we are called upon to make drawings and not projections.

Consider an illustrator employed by a company that manufactures complex machinery. If he were to submit an isometric or perspective drawing of a part to the shop foreman as a guide from which the part was to be manufactured, he would likely find the shop foreman an unpleasant man to deal with. By the same token, if a manufacturer were to provide a complex shop drawing (orthographic projection) as assembly instructions for Santa, the customer would be less then happy. Clearly, a multiple view orthographic drawing is called for in Case 1 and a pictorial (axonometric, oblique, or perspective) drawing is called for in Case 2.

Because we will not be concerned to a large extent with shop (engineering) drawings in this book, less attention will be devoted to multiple view orthographic projection than to the other schemes. Many texts are available on this one facet of drawing and the reader is encouraged to consult them for detailed considerations. For our purposes, we must be aware of the general method and understand the principles of the projection scheme. These principles are important to learning other schemes.

1

Multiple View Orthographic Projection

Figure 1.1 illustrates the essential features of multiple view orthographic projection: we observe a three-dimensional object from as many positions necessary to see all lines in true measure. Examining the figure, we find that (1) lines projected from the object pierce the viewing planes at right angles; in other words, the lines are ORTHOGONAL to the planes; and (2) the projection lines from the object to any one viewing plane are parallel because we are viewing the object from an infinite distance. These two facts *define* orthographic projection.

Note that if an infinite number of points between points 1 and 2 and points 1 and 3 on the object are projected normal to the viewing planes, lines *AB* and *AC* are defined. It would, however, be time-consuming and unnecessary to project an infinite number of points to define a line when we have merely to recall from plane geometry that two points in a plane determine a straight line in that plane.

In orthographic projection we will use several mutually perpendicular viewing planes to describe the object. By placing three views in the standard format shown in Fig. 1.1 the object can be described completely, even though the left-side, rear, and bottom views of the object have been omitted. Herein lies a major rule to observe when using multiple view

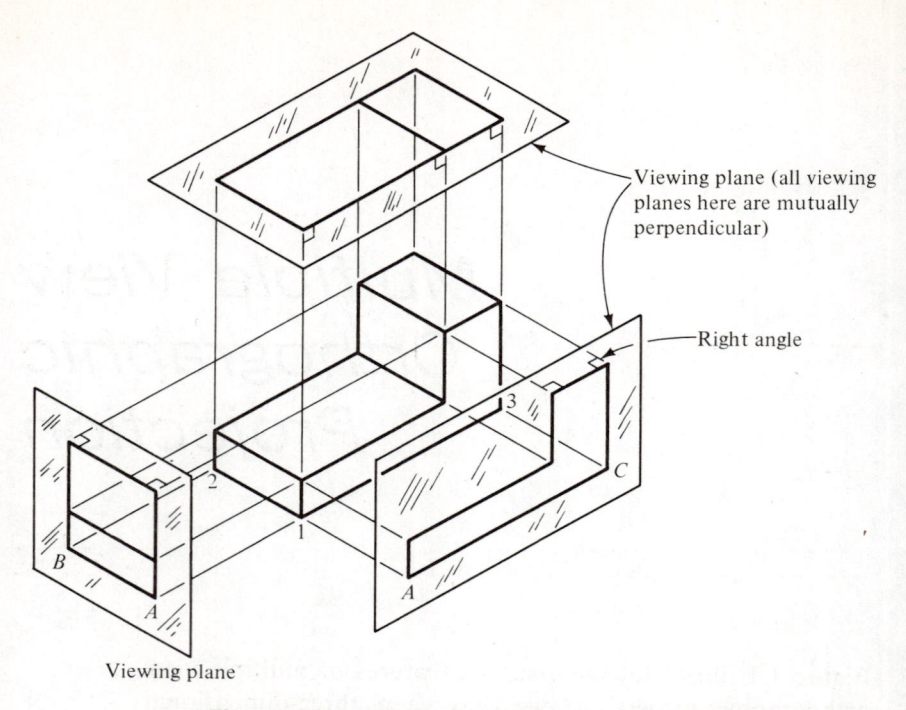

Figure 1.1 For each view, the observer stands an infinite distance from the object. Lines of sight are thus parallel. The observer is also positioned such that lines of sight strike viewing planes at right angles.

orthographic projection: *Use only those views necessary to describe the object completely.* Time and effort, which are costly commodities, are wasted if an illustration is made up of more views than are necessary, not to mention the complications introduced.

To illustrate the basic views in multiple view orthographic projection, assume the role of a photographer assigned to photograph the object shown in Fig. 1.2 from the top, front, bottom, rear, right side, and left side.* After snapping the pictures, we develop the film and arrange the negatives as shown in Fig. 1.3. With imagination, we can think of the negatives as the sides, top, and bottom of an unfolded box.

From Fig. 1.3 we see that the rear, left-side, front, and right-side views are aligned horizontally and are the same *height*. In similar fashion, the top, front, and bottom views

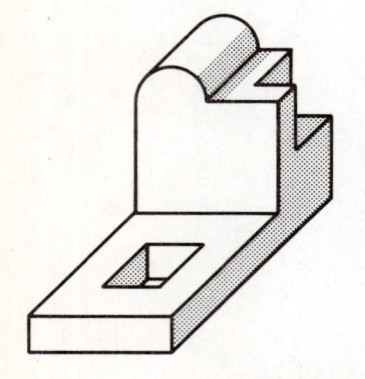

Figure 1.2 The object shown here in oblique is to be photographed from the six sides described.

*Remember that the photographer must position the camera lens axis normal to each face he is photographing. The film in the camera is a viewing plane.

4

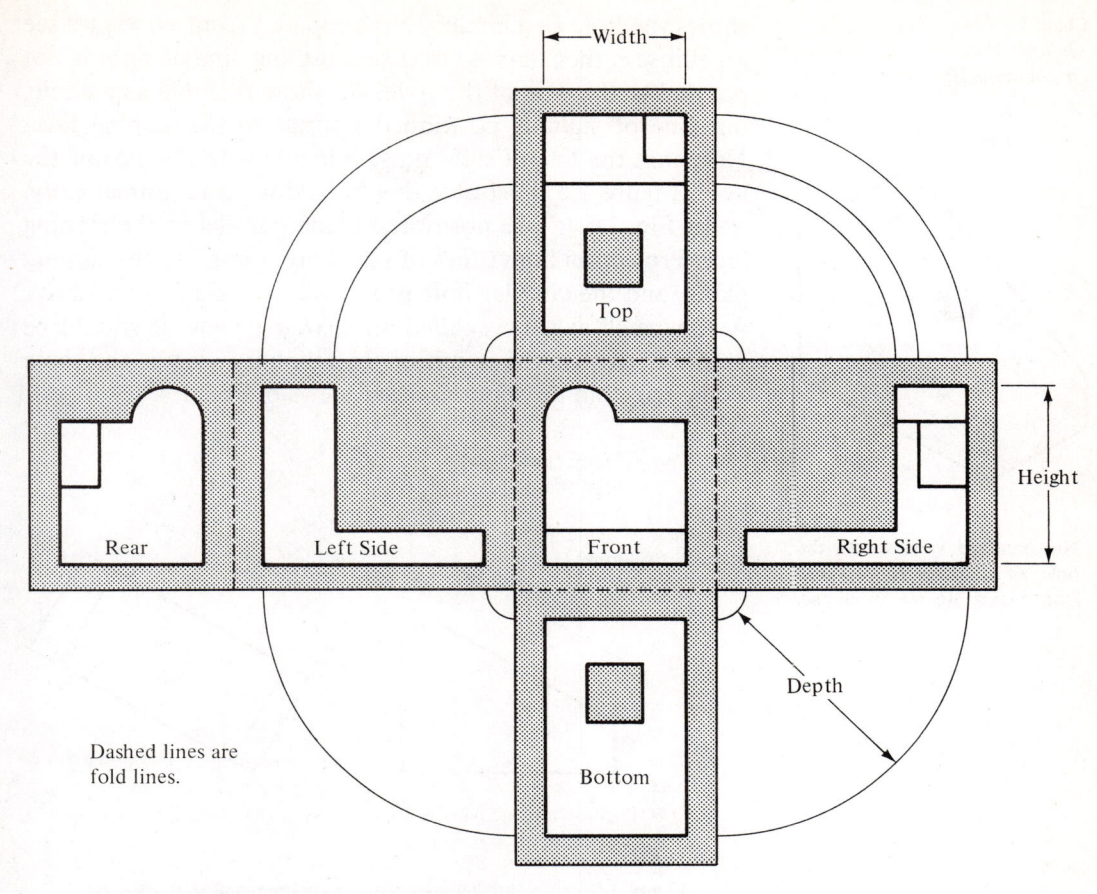

Figure 1.3 Negative box unfolded to show relationships among views.

are aligned vertically and are the same *width*. The circular construction lines illustrate another important feature of this scheme: The top, right-side, bottom, and left-side views are equidistant from their respective fold lines and are the same *depth*. Keeping in mind which views correlate with other views, we have a method by which dimensions (height, width, and depth) can be transferred among the views when lines lie in or parallel to principal planes.

Now, consider how to represent in true length the faces of an object that do not lie in, but are at some angle to the principal planes. In Fig. 1.4 an object with a sloping front face is pierced by a circular hole. No standard view

1A
Auxiliary Planes

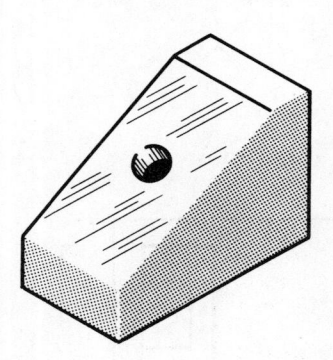

Figure 1.4
No standard view shows the hole as a circle. In top and front views, we see an ellipse.

shows the hole as a circle: In the top and front views, we see an ellipse rather than a circle because our line of sight is not parallel to the axis of the hole. To show the hole as a circle, our line of sight is positioned normal to the sloping face. Note that the line of sight must coincide with the axis of the hole. Figure 1.5 illustrates this procedure diagrammatically.

In Fig. 1.5 (a) we position a plane parallel to the sloping face. Projection lines (lines of sight) are normal to the sloping plane, and the circular hole projects as a circle in Fig. 1.5(b). A view such as this is called an *auxiliary* view. It should be pointed out that the width of the auxiliary view is the same as the width in the front and top views of Fig. 1.4.

(a) Position a plane parallel to the sloping face

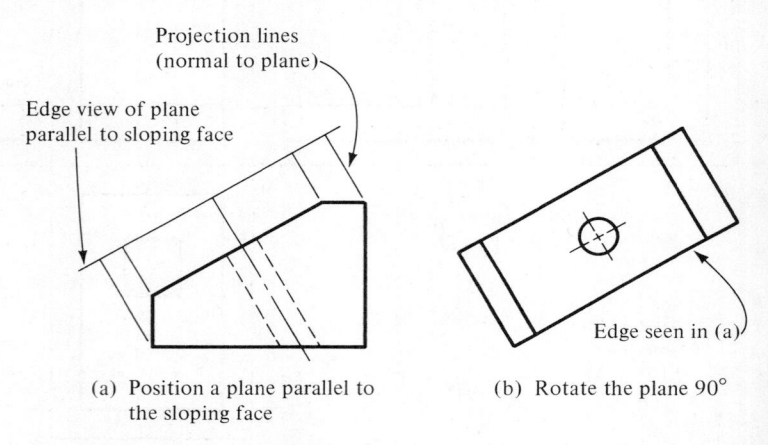

(b) Rotate the plane 90°

Figure 1.5 Procedure by which an auxiliary plane is positioned parallel to a nonprincipal plane and then rotated into plane of paper to show features in true length and shape.

1B
Section Views

In some instances we will attempt to show an intricate or complex structure inside an object. Hidden lines will not always do the trick so we are forced to find another solution. In Fig. 1.6(a) an object has been cut in half to determine the contents. This operation reveals features we would not have guessed to be there had hidden lines been used as shown in Fig. 1.6(b).

As stated earlier, our attention will be focused mainly on illustrating techniques, not engineering drawings. Multiple view orthographic projection remains primarily the property of engineering draftsmen, who are not interested in aesthetics as a first consideration. Their objective is the same, however:

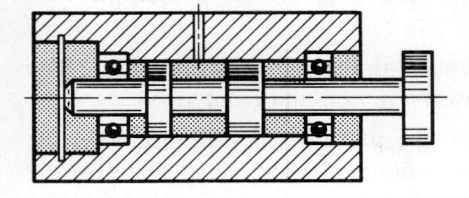

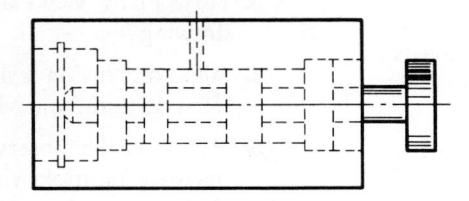

(a) Section view. Note that circular shaft is not cross sectioned. This is standard procedure.

(b) View of same assembly shown in (a) using hidden lines to delineate internal components.

Figure 1.6 The use of a section view to show internal structure and components.

to tell a story to a selected audience. Further consideration of this valuable projection scheme is left to the individual reader.

The list of references that follows will provide him ample material from which to study,

REFERENCES

1. W. Luzadder, *Fundamentals of Engineering Drawing* (6th ed.). Englewood Cliffs, N.J.: Prentice-Hall, Inc., 1971.
2. T. E. French and C. L. Svensen, *Engineering Drawing and Graphic Technology* (11th ed.). New York: McGraw-Hill Book Co., 1972.
3. A. S. Levens, *Graphics, Analysis and Conceptual Design* (2nd ed.). New York: John Wiley & Sons, Inc., 1968.
4. R. P. Hoelscher, C. H. Springer, and J. S. Dobrovolny, *Graphics For Engineers*. New York: John Wiley & Sons, Inc., 1968.
5. D. Fuller, *Functional Drafting For Today*. Boston, Mass.: Industrial Education Institute, 1966.
6. H. E. Grant, *Engineering Drawing with Creative Design* (2nd ed.). New York: McGraw-Hill Book Co., 1968.
7. C. L. Martin, *Design Graphics* (2nd ed.). New York: The MacMillan Company, 1968.
8. J. R. Walker and E. J. Plevyak, *Industrial Arts Drafting*. Chicago: The Goodhart-Willcox Co., Inc., 1960.

QUESTIONS

1. Describe briefly the two defining concepts of multiple view orthographic projection.
2. How many *standard* views describe an object? Name the views.

3. How many views are required to execute a multiple view drawing?

4. What dimension is identical in the rear and front views? The left-side and front views? The top and front views?

5. Where is the observer (the illustrator) positioned when he makes a multiple view orthographic drawing? Describe the position exactly.

6. When is it necessary to use auxiliary views?

7. Why should auxiliary views be used?

8. When and why are section views used?

9. Why do you think multiple view orthographic projection is an important (or unimportant) technique?

10. What are two limitations of multiple view orthographic projection?

PROBLEMS

1. Make a multiple view orthographic drawing of the block in Fig. P1.1 using the minimum number of views to describe the object completely. Include all dimensions, which are given in inches.

2. Make a multiple view orthographic drawing of a circular cylinder 8 in. tall. The cylinder has an outside diameter of 3 in. and a wall thickness of $\frac{3}{32}$ in. A $1\frac{1}{2}$-in. diameter hole is bored 5 in. from the bottom. On the top face of the cylinder, four equally spaced slots ($\frac{1}{4}$ in. wide × $\frac{1}{8}$ in. deep) are cut. Include all dimensions necessary to make the piece.

3. Make a multiple view drawing of your T square. *Note*: It may be necessary to use geometry to determine the size of certain radii.

4. The isometric drawing shown in Fig. P1.2 is a piece to be manufactured. Make a multiple view drawing suitable for use in a machine shop. *Note*: Two auxiliary views are required. The rectangular hole is $\frac{1}{2}$ in. deep and is centered in the sloping face. The circular hole is also centered in the sloping face. All dimensions are in inches.

5. Make a multiple view drawing of the part with the following description, employing a cross-section view as well as the necessary multiple views. The object consists of a circular cylinder 2 in. in diameter by 4 in. long. (The cylinder is bored with a $1\frac{1}{2}$-in. diameter hole $2\frac{1}{2}$ in. deep.) Attached to the

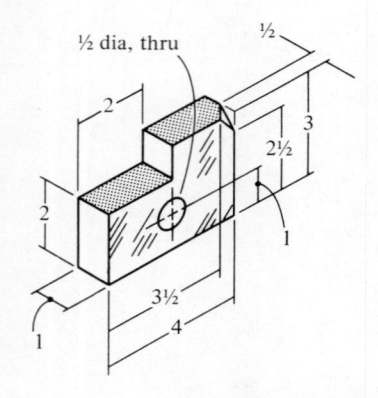

Figure P1.1

cylinder 1½ in. from the bored end by means of a ⅜-in. diameter thread is a square-shaped rod ½ in. on a side by 2½ in. long. The cylinder has a ⅛-in. wide groove ⅛ in. deep, 1 in. from the open end of the cylinder cut on the cylinder circumference. Sketch this object before drawing.

6. Problems as assigned by instructor from Appendix H.

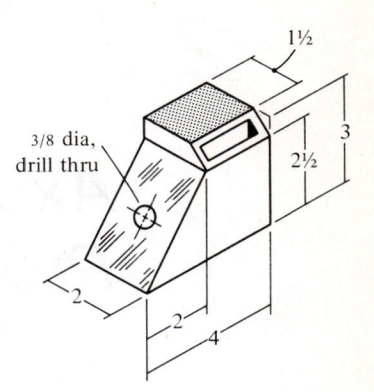

Figure P1.2

2

Axonometric Projection

Plane oblique to three principal axes

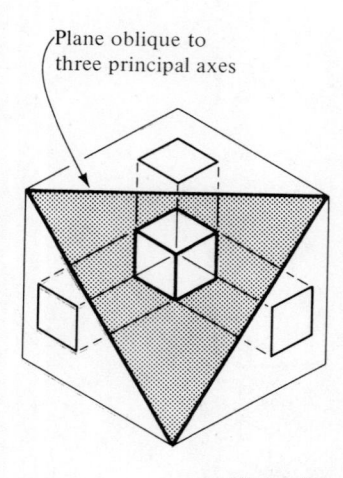

Figure 2.1

In multiple view orthographic projection our ability to present a picture to an audience is limited because we must assume that the audience possesses great imagination, which may or may not be the case. To assemble plane views in the mind's eye is difficult, even for the expert. For this reason, pictorial illustrations, in which three faces of the object are shown simultaneously in one view, are often used rather than multiple view orthographic drawings. One projection scheme for such pictorial representations is called *axonometric*.

An axonometric projection is the projection of an object onto a plane that is oblique to three principal planes of the object (see Fig. 2.1). Because this definition places no restriction on positioning the object in relation to the viewing plane, other than being oblique to three principal planes, an infinite number of different views exists. Fortunately, three relatively simple subschemes of the axonometric scheme have been devised and standardized: (1) isometric, (2) dimetric, and (3) trimetric.

Before discussing any of the axonometric projection schemes, we will point out that as the scheme becomes more difficult to execute (isometric → dimetric → trimetric), distortion inherent to the scheme becomes less prominent. Diagram A illustrates this statement.

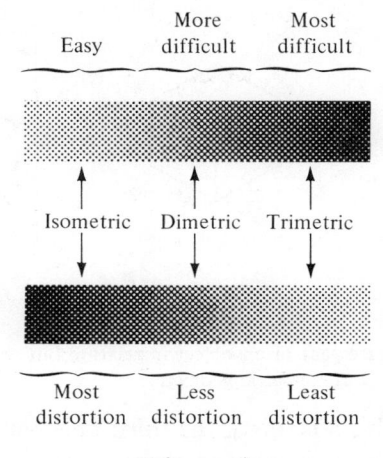

Diagram A

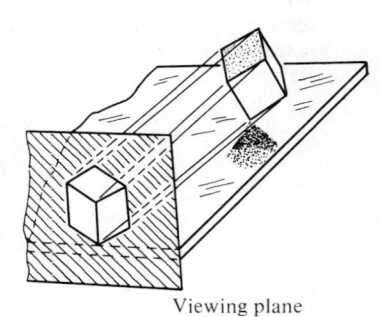

If we wish to use an axonometric projection scheme that can be executed rapidly and if we are not interested in reducing distortion, we will use isometric. On the other hand, if we wish to reduce distortion and are not concerned with ease of execution, we would use trimetric.

Isometric* projection is used widely in technical illustrating. Referring to Fig. 2.2, we observe that isometric projection is another orthographic projection. The observer (the illustrator) is an infinite distance from the object,† thus projection lines are parallel. In addition, the observer stations himself such that lines of sight pierce the viewing plane normally. Recall that orthographic projection was described the same way.

The object is rotated through an angle of 45° about a vertical axis, placing two faces of the cube in positions such that each face will show in the viewing plane. In addition, the object is tilted toward the viewing plane such that the angle of tilt (35°16′) will produce equal angles (120°) among the three projected edges OX, OY, and OZ as shown in Fig. 2.3(b). Note

2A
Isometric Projection

Figure 2.2
Axonometric projection

---
*Iso means equal; metric means measure—equal measure.
†In theory only is the illustrator infinitely far from the object. In practice, infinity is a "fur piece down the road."

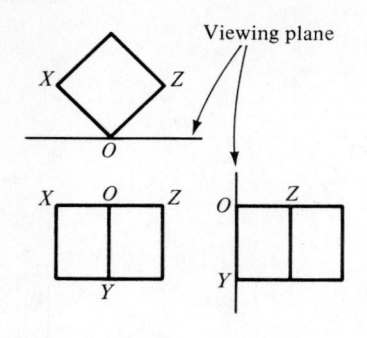

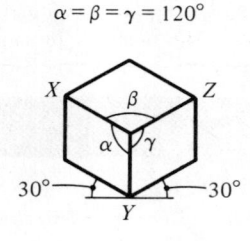

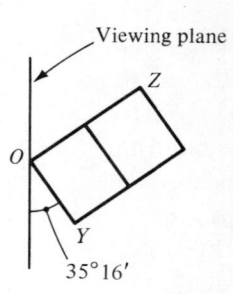

(a) Object is rotated 45°

(b) Object is tilted 35°16'

Figure 2.3 Placement of an object in relationship to a viewing plane to arrive at isometric geometry.

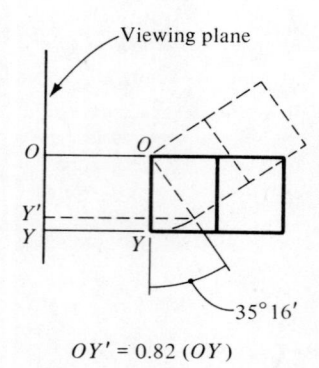

$OY' = 0.82\,(OY)$

Figure 2.4 When the object is tilted (dashed line position), distance OY is forshortened to OY'.

that when the object is tilted, the third face comes into view.

When an object is rotated through 45°, no changes in height, width, or depth result: We merely change our view. When the object is tilted, changes in dimensions occur as shown in Fig. 2.4: Object measurements are multiplied by $\sqrt{2/3}$ or 0.82 to become isometric measurements.

These foreshortened values are used by the purist, i.e., the illustrator who wishes to be exact and use either isometric projection or a special scale. In practice, the use of a special 82-percent-of-size scale is a waste of time. The smarter illustrator will reason that because changes are *uniform*, no one will know whether he used a full-size or an 82-percent-of-size scale. He merely enlarges the illustration when he uses the full-size scale and must call it an isometric drawing rather than an isometric projection. Figure 2.5 illustrates relative sizes of the isometric projection and the isometric drawing. We can only suggest that the isometric drawing be used. For the purist, Fig. 2.6 illustrates the construction of an isometric scale.

POSITION OF AXES

We are not limited to the one view* used here to illustrate the basic concepts of isometric projection. Isometric axes may be positioned in any one of as many positions as there are headings on the compass—an infinite number. The simplest rule concerning presentation of an object is: *Choose*

*The orientation of axes is shown by drawing the three axes in position.

a viewing position that best describes the object. The question is: Just how should an illustrator decide which view is best for a particular object? Applying a mixture of common sense and knowledge about the object can help to answer the question.

First of all, decide how the object is seen in everyday circumstances. For example, we usually see a book either on a horizontal surface or standing on a bookshelf, as shown in Fig. 2.7. We would not expect to view a book from below, unless it were on a high shelf, Fig. 2.7(c). Note the position of isometric axes in this figure. Objects with which we lack familiarity will pose problems. In these cases, we are obliged to confess our ignorance and ask the person for whom we are working to point out the feature(s) to be emphasized. Then we must sketch, discuss, and illustrate.

Always remember, if we are familiar with the object and no special features should be emphasized, the object is drawn as we would ordinarily see it. If special features must be brought to light, consider axes orientation. Remember also that the isometric axes may be oriented to our liking, as long as a 120° angle between adjacent *projected* axes is maintained.

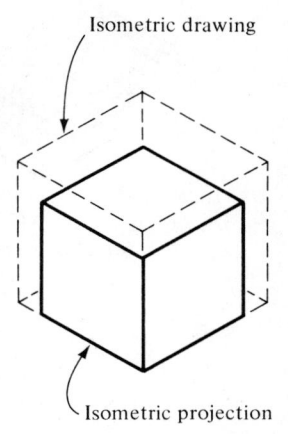

Figure 2.5
An isometric projection (solid lines) and an isometric drawing (dashed lines) of a cube are superimposed to show relative size. The projection is 82 percent as large as the drawing.

BOX METHOD FOR CONSTRUCTION

Before constructing objects in isometric, we will discuss terms used in describing the construction. Projection axes make angles of 120° with each other and are defined as *isometric axes*. Any line that is parallel to an isometric axis is an *isometric line*, whereas lines that are not parallel to isometric axes are *nonisometric lines*. These definitions may

Steps to construct an isometric scale

1. Draw a base line.
2. Draw a line at 45° to the base line, and mark it off in full size increments.
3. Draw a line at 30° to the base line.
4. Project points vertically downward from the 45° line to the 30° line.
5. Cut the isometric scale out and mount it to a piece of heavy paper or thin cardboard.

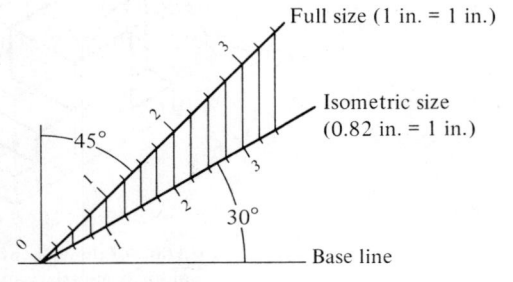

Figure 2.6 Following the procedure shown here, an isometric scale may be constructed.

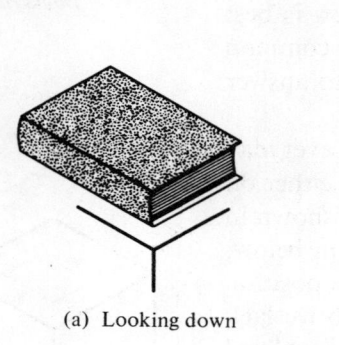

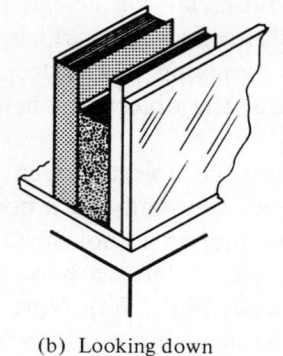

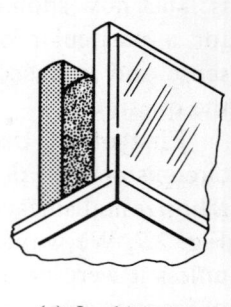

(a) Looking down   (b) Looking down   (c) Looking up

Figure 2.7 Positions from which a book is usually viewed. Isometric axes are shown as heavy lines.

be extended into three-space terminology to define *isometric* and *nonisometric planes*.

In Fig. 2.8(a) we find a multiple view drawing of an

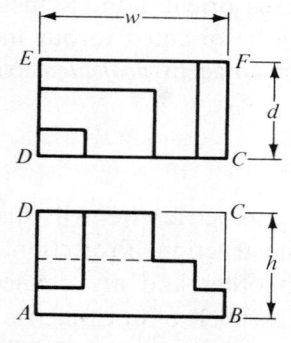

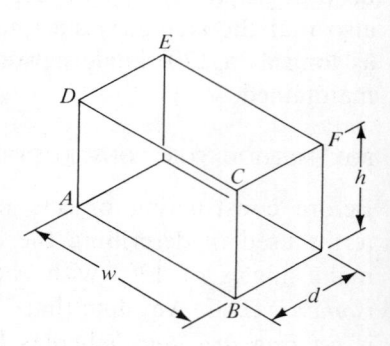

(a) Multiple view drawing that uses *minimum* number of views to describe the object.

(b) Minimum size box that encloses object

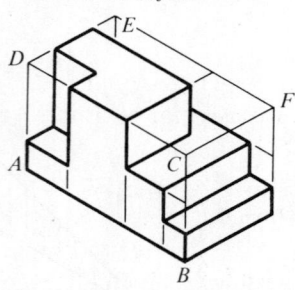

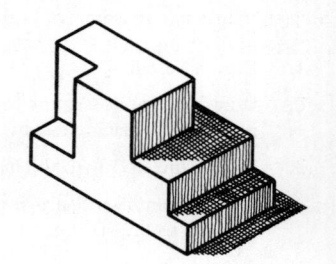

(c) Transfer dimensions from (a) along isometric axes and lines.

(d) Shade and remove construction lines to complete the drawing.

Figure 2.8 Example of box method for construction.

object on which all faces form right angles with their intersecting faces. A first impression is that it will be a formidable task to make an isometric drawing from the multiple view drawing. Let's see how easily the parts fall in place using box construction.

The first step is to choose a viewing position. Important features (depressions) can be seen best from a downward-directed view. Note that we have chosen to look downward from the right, although we could just as correctly have chosen a downward-from-the-left view. Next, a minimum-size box of dimensions h (height), w (width), and d (depth) that encloses the object is constructed. From this point to completion we transfer dimensions from the multiple view drawing to the isometric drawing, noting that dimensions must be transferred along isometric lines or axes. Study Fig. 2.8 carefully. Box construction is a powerful tool and is used often, even by experts.

CENTER LINE LAYOUT METHOD FOR CONSTRUCTION

Although any object may be drawn in isometric using the box method, drawings of objects made up mostly of circular shapes may be constructed more easily using the center line layout method. In Fig. 2.9(a) a flanged pipe to be drawn in isometric is shown in a multiple view drawing.

We start with point A and draw a center line, which is an isometric line, and then locate points B and C along this center line. Points D, E, F, and G (the centers of circles) are located and marked. Then, using ellipse guides, the circular surfaces are drawn to give the completed isometric as shown in Fig. 2.9(b).

INCLINED OR OBLIQUE SURFACES

Because all surfaces in Fig. 2.8 are normal to intersecting surfaces, transferring measurements is simple: We recall that transfers are made along isometric lines or axes. On many objects, all surfaces do not intersect normally but at some angle greater or less than 90°. To make isometric drawings of these objects, a procedure much like that used in drawing orthogonal surface intersections is followed. In Fig. 2.10, note the viewing position that shows clearly the inclined surfaces S_1 and S_2 and the use of box construction.

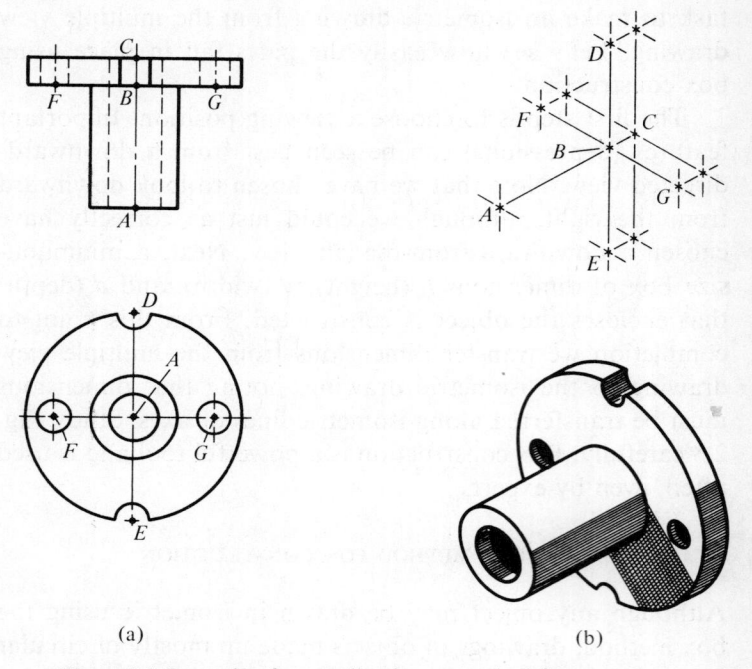

Figure 2.9 Example of center line layout method for construction.

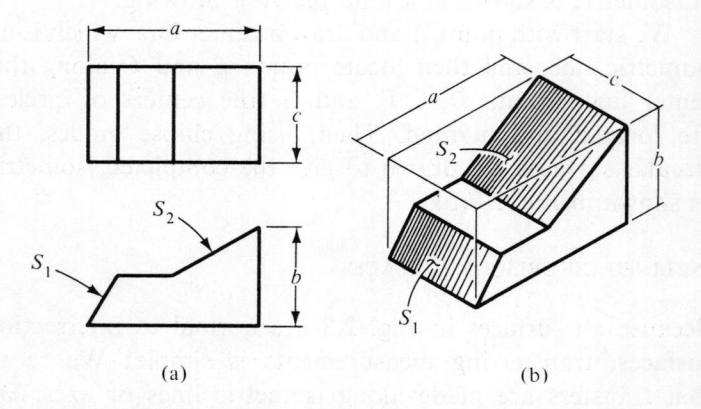

Figure 2.10 Example of inclined surfaces intersecting isometric planes.

In Fig. 2.11(a), surfaces oblique to and inclined to isometric planes are shown. A natural question to ask, after we see both inclined and oblique surfaces, is: What is the difference between the two types? The distinction is simple.

When a surface inclined to an isometric plane intersects the plane, the intersection is an *isometric line*. When a surface oblique to an isometric plane intersects the plane, the intersection is a *nonisometric line*.

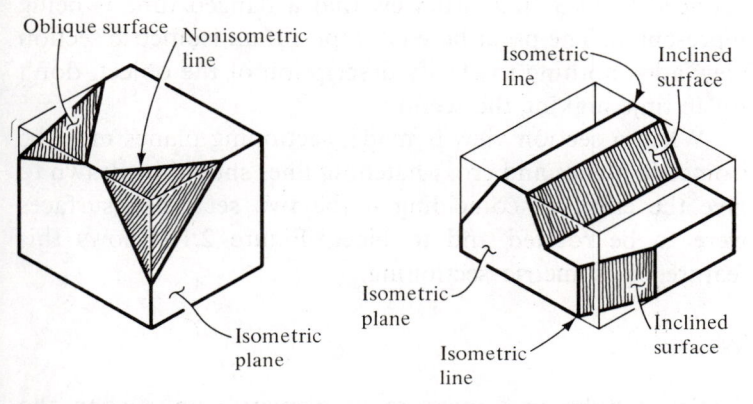

(a) Oblique surfaces intersecting isometric planes

(b) Inclined surfaces intersecting isometric planes

Figure 2.11 Nonorthogonal surface intersections with isometric planes.

SECTIONS

It is impossible in some cases to show the interior construction or arrangement of an object or assembly unless either exploded views or section views are used. Let us consider an object such as the one shown in Fig. 2.12(a). Here the reader may very well become confused by overlapping

(a) View using hidden lines to show internal structure

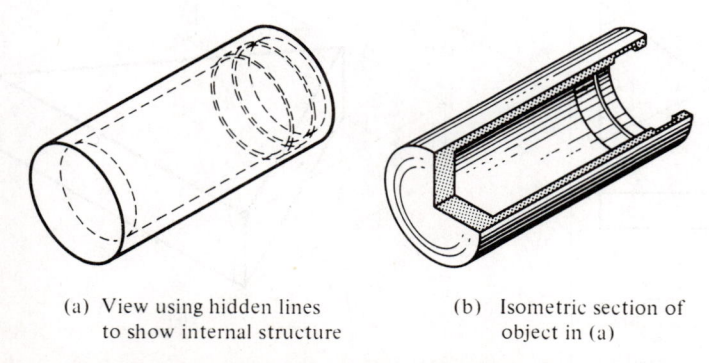

(b) Isometric section of object in (a)

Figure 2.12 Comparing the use of an isometric section to using hidden lines to show internal parts of an assembly.

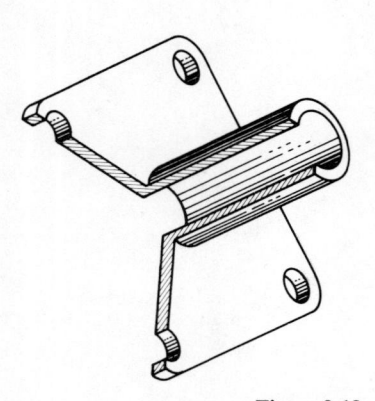

Figure 2.13
The illustration of the object shown sectioned is no more descriptive than the object shown not sectioned. Note that the center line layout method for construction was used here.

circular elements. The only feature we are sure of is the circular cylinder. The section view in Fig. 2.12(b) removes confusion. Internal features are now clear.

In Fig. 2.13 an object has been sectioned but it is clear that the section view adds nothing but work: We could have deduced from a standard view that a flanged tube is being represented. The point here is simple: If an isometric section view adds nothing to clarify description of the object, don't waste time making the section.

When a section view is made, sectioning planes must be isometric planes and cross-hatching lines should be drawn to give the effect of coinciding if the two sectioned surfaces were to be rotated and to meet. Figure 2.13 shows this feature of isometric sectioning.

ANGLES

Angles will be true measure in isometric only when the plane in which the angle lies is parallel to the viewing plane. Any other angle will appear larger or smaller than true measure. Because surfaces in isometric are for the most part inclined to the viewing plane, most angles in isometric are not true measure. For example, the angles in the top view in Fig. 2.14(a) are equal and true measure. When an isometric drawing of the object is made in Fig. 2.14(b), none of the angles is true measure: Two angles (α and β) appear smaller and one angle (γ) appears larger than the true measure angles in Fig. 2.14(a).

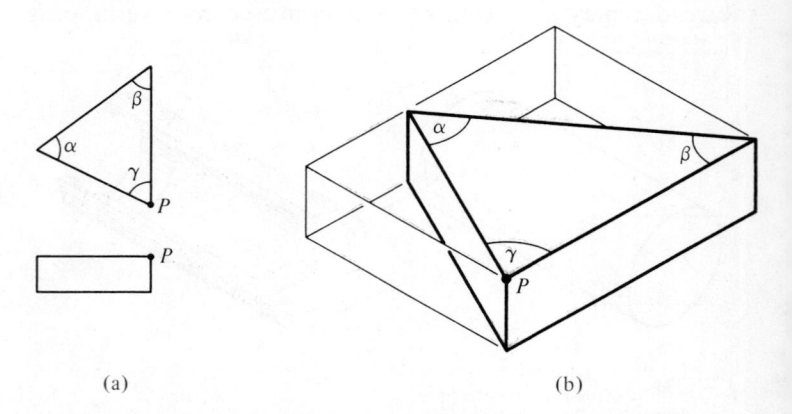

(a)   (b)

Figure 2.14 An example of how angles in isometric distort from true measure values.

The object in Fig. 2.14 is simple. We will now consider a more complex object. In Fig. 2.15(a) a multiple view drawing is shown and from it the isometric drawing in Fig. 2.15(b) is made. Because we are familiar with the concepts of orthographic projection, we know that only angle γ in the front view of Fig. 2.15(a) is true measure. (Can you explain why?) After using box construction to make the isometric drawing in Fig. 2.15(b), we find that none of the angles is true measure. This fact has an important bearing upon construction procedure involving angles.

Offset measurements (NOT ANGULAR MEASUREMENTS) are used when drawing objects with planes intersecting at angles. The angles are, in a manner of speaking, converted to linear measurements, which are made along isometric lines or axes. Study Fig. 2.14 and 2.15 carefully to be certain the conversion from angular to linear measurements is understood.

CURVES

An illustrator is often called upon to make isometric drawings of objects that do not have plane-surface contours: One or more surfaces may be curved. Let us examine a plane

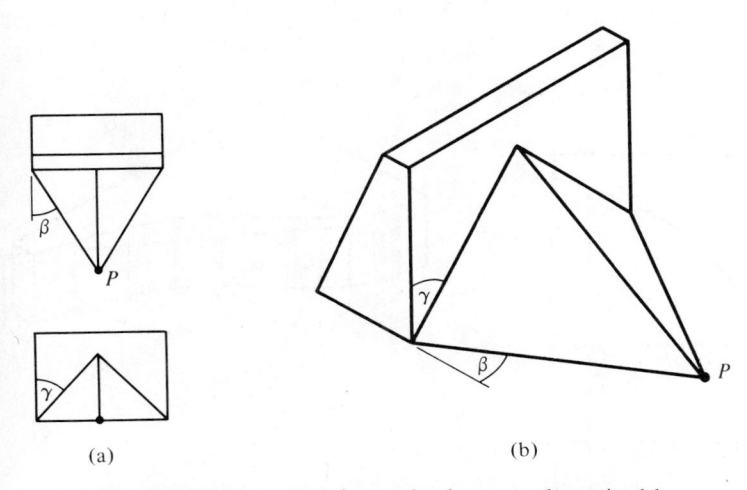

Figure 2.15 Position of nonisometric planes are determined by offset measurements. Angles β and γ in (a) are not equal to angles β and γ in (b). For that reason dimensions A, B, and C are transferred from (a) to (b) to show the angles properly.

surface intersected at 90° by a curved surface as in Fig. 2.16. Note that two views in Fig. 2.16(a) completely describe the object and, as stated earlier, more views would be wasted effort.

Again the box method for constructing the isometric is used and again the viewing position to best describe the object is chosen. The first step in constructing the curved surface is to pass a series of planes through the multiple view drawing at *more or less* equal-interval spacing. Equal-interval spacing is not required or desired because in areas of rapidly changing curvature (see Fig. 2.16) we may wish to use more points for plotting the curve than equally spaced planes would generate.

Next, a minimum-sized rectangular volume that contains the object is constructed. Then, in successive steps, planes of height h normal to the left receding axis are drawn at the same intervals as in the multiple view drawing and the distances from line PR (an isometric axis) to the curve are transferred from the top view in Fig. 2.16(a) to the isometric drawing. An irregular (French) curve is used to smooth in the curved surface boundaries.

The principle used to construct the drawing in Fig. 2.16 can similarly be applied to constructing an object made up of curved surfaces intersecting with curved surfaces. Such an object is shown in Fig. 2.17. The procedure is identical

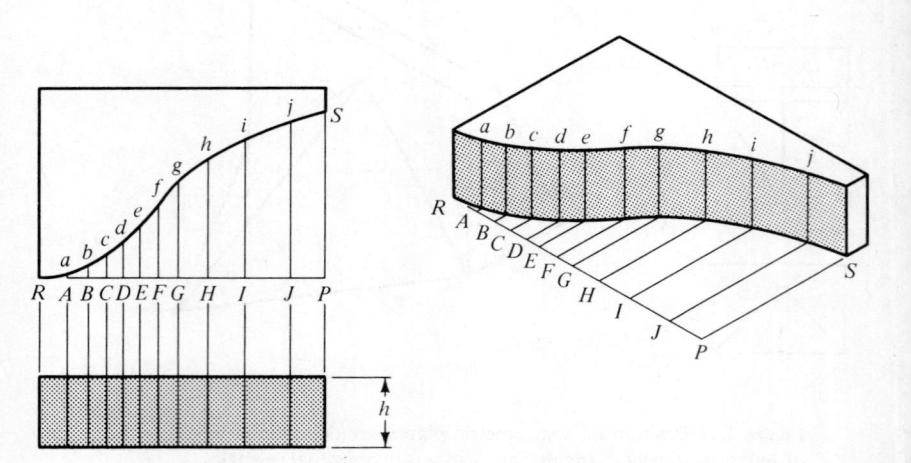

Figure 2.16 An object composed of curved surface intersected by plane surfaces is constructed using the box method.

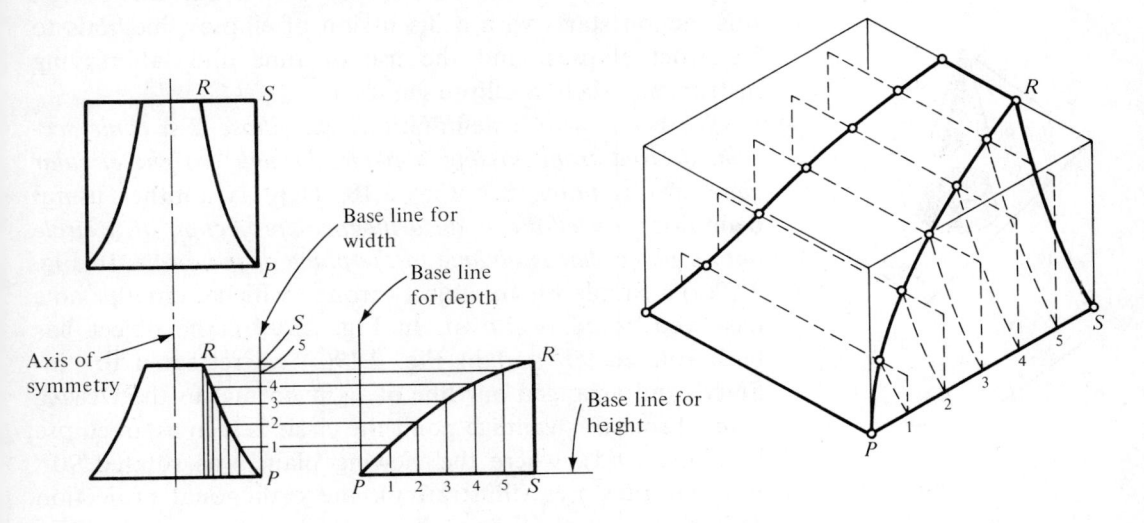

(a) Orthographic views from which measurements for width, depth, and height are taken

(b) Isometric drawing showing the transfer of width, depth, and height from (a)

Figure 2.17 Box construction is used here to make an isometric drawing of an object composed of intersecting curved surfaces. Careful "bookkeeping" is essential. Note the use of an axis of symmetry.

here, except that we must acknowledge changes in width, depth, and height at each sectioning plane.

The object in Fig. 2.17 has a laborsaving feature—an axis of symmetry. When we locate a point to the right of the axis, we also locate a point to the left of the axis. Note the use of box construction and several sectioning planes. From point P, depth measurements are made along the receding isometric axis. Width and height measurements are made from the receding axis. For each point on the curve PR, we must find a width, a depth, and a height. The process is time-consuming, requires accuracy and care, but is simple.

CIRCLES

Even though we use the word *circle* in isometric, we seldom see a circle in an isometric drawing. What is circular in multiple view orthographic drawing is elliptical in an isometric drawing, unless the plane in which the circle lies in the isometric is parallel to the viewing plane. For this reason this section starts with a discussion of ellipses, methods to construct ellipses, and the use of time and laborsaving instruments such as ellipse guides.

We begin with a defininition: *An ellipse is a conic section, derived from passing a plane through a right circular cone of revolution.* See Fig. 2.18. Here is another useful definition: *An ellipse is an orthogonal projection of a circle onto a plane that is oblique to the plane of the circle.* In Fig. 2.19(a) a simple square object through which a circular hole has been bored is shown. In Fig. 2.19(b), the object has been rotated 90° and in Fig. 2.19(c) we retreated to "infinity" and arranged our line of sight normal to the *viewing plane.* From this vantage point the circle is seen as an ellipse in Fig. 2.19(d), where the viewing plane was rotated 90°. For our purposes (illustrating), the orthogonal projection definition is best. When ellipse guides are discussed (see p. 25), the importance of this definition will become evident.

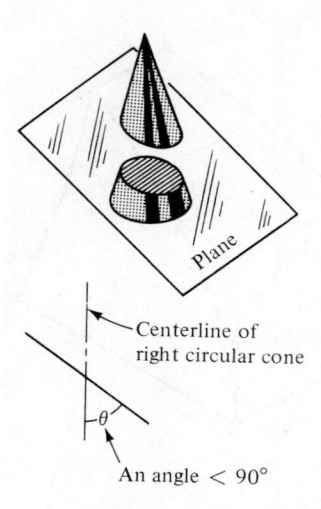

Several features of an ellipse must be defined so we can converse in the language of illustrators. First of all, we should realize by now that even though an ellipse *represents* a circle in certain projections, an ellipse is an ellipse and nomenclature associated with a circle *does not* apply to an ellipse. In some books the minor- and major-axis lengths are referred

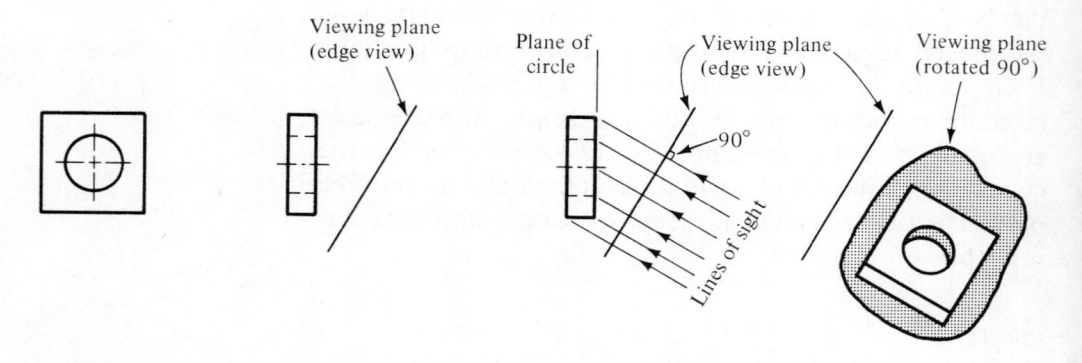

Figure 2.18 A plane has been passed through a right circular cone at some angle less than 90° to the cone center line. The resulting cross section of the cone is an ellipse.

(a) Front view of object (b) Side view of object (c) Establishing lines of sight (d) The final product

Figure 2.19 An ellipse as the orthogonal projection of a circle onto a plane oblique to the plane of the circle.

to as minor and major *diameters*. Such names for the axes of an ellipse are misnomers and are to be avoided. From Fig. 2.20, along the long axis, distance AB is the major-axis length and along the foreshortened axis, distance CD is the minor-axis length. Points E and F are called *foci* (*focus* is the singular term).

ELLIPSE CONSTRUCTION

Mathematicians define an ellipse as the locus of points moving such that the sum of the distances from two points (the foci) is a constant equal to the length of the major axis. If we were to use a piece of string, two thumb tacks, and a pencil, as shown in Fig. 2.21, we could generate a crude ellipse based on the mathematical definition. Try this experiment, but don't expect a perfect ellipse.

To draw a large ellipse or an accurate ellipse at some non-standard viewing angle (an angle not included in a collection of ellipse guides), we must construct the ellipse. Many methods exist but only three will be shown here. Additional methods are described in the reference texts listed at the end of Chapter 1. First we will use the four-center method shown in Fig. 2.22.

$\overline{AB}$ = Major axis length
$\overline{CD}$ = Minor axis length
a = ½ $\overline{AB}$, locates foci E and F

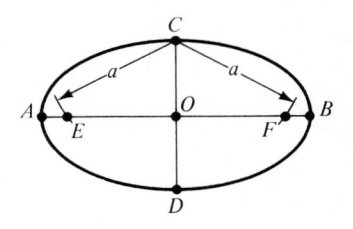

Figure 2.20
Parts of an ellipse.

$\overline{AB} = \overline{EP_2} + \overline{P_2F}$
   $= \overline{EP_1} + \overline{P_1F}$

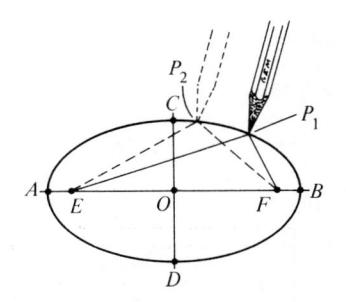

Figure 2.21
An ellipse may be constructed according to a mathematical definition.

Radius R is used between points a and c and b and d.

Radius r is used between points c and b and d and a.

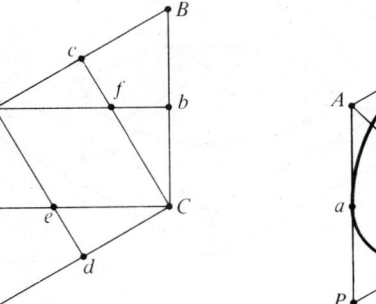

(a) The first three steps in constructing an ellipse are incorporated in this diagram. Refer to text.

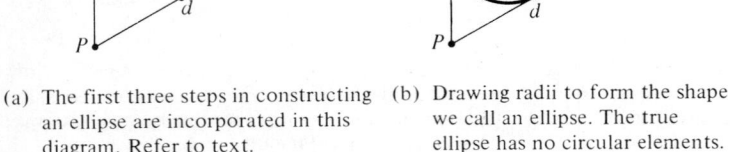

(b) Drawing radii to form the shape we call an ellipse. The true ellipse has no circular elements.

Figure 2.22 Constructing an ellipse using the four-center method.

24 / Chap. 2
Axonometric Projection

1. Draw an isometric square *PABC* that will enclose the ellipse.
2. Find the midpoints *a*, *b*, *c*, and *d* of the four sides of the square.
3. Connecting lines *Ab, aC, Ad,* and *cC* intersect to locate points *e* and *f*.
4. Radii of the sizes shown (*R* and *r*) are drawn to complete the ellipse.

The method described above is straightforward, executed easily, and gives results satisfactory for most pictorial illustrations. The method, however, is not completely accurate.

If an accurate ellipse is desired, a point-by-point plot is one answer. The method used here is identical to that used to construct Fig. 2.17(b); i.e., planes are passed through the object and offset measurements locate points on the ellipse. Accuracy of the final shape is a function of the number of planes used: Few planes equal least accuracy; many planes equal most accuracy. The ellipse shown in Fig. 2.23 is constructed using offset measurements. An irregular (French) curve is used to draw the smooth ellipse curve.

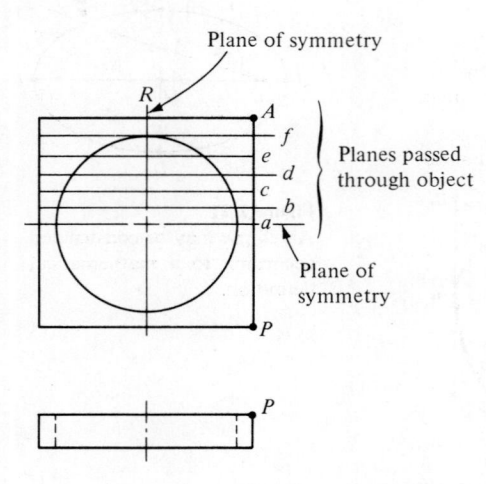

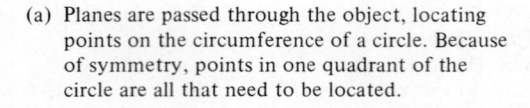

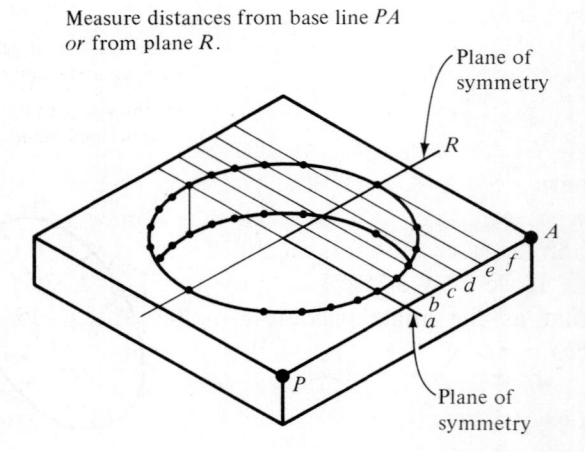

(a) Planes are passed through the object, locating points on the circumference of a circle. Because of symmetry, points in one quadrant of the circle are all that need to be located.

(b) Planes *b, c, d, e,* and *f* have mirror images below plane *a*, which is a plane of symmetry. Thus, by locating four points in the quadrant shown, we locate points in the other three quadrants.

Figure 2.23 Constructing an ellipse point-by-point.

The third method illustrated is a simple but accurate one called the *diagonal* method (Fig. 2.24). Here we construct an isometric square and proceed as follows

1. Draw a semicircle on one side of the "square" and, with a 30–60° triangle, divide the circle into six equal parts.
2. Project the points of intersection on the semicircle back to line $O-O$.
3. Draw the horizontal lines and the diagonal OP in the square.
4. Draw in vertical lines passing through the horizontal line–diagonal intersection points, locating points a through l.
5. Using an irregular curve, draw the ellipse.

ELLIPSE GUIDES

Because the ellipse is used so frequently in isometric and other pictorial schemes, it becomes important to find an accurate yet rapid method to draw ellipses. From previous discussion it is clear that construction methods that can be executed rapidly are least accurate and those that are accurate are time-consuming to execute. Our dilemma is solved in many cases by using ellipse guides (templates). By using these thin plastic sheets with elliptical cutouts, we have at hand a rapid *and* accurate method to draw ellipses.

When we are making an isometric pictorial drawing and have need to represent a circle, we can use either of two types of ellipse guides: angle or isometric. A natural question to ask is, "What is the difference between the two types?"

If we view a circle as shown in Fig. 2.25(a), we will see that as the angle becomes smaller, the minor-axis length becomes smaller. The circle projection at each angle has definite proportions. Plastic cutout guides made to corresponding proportions are called *angle ellipse guides*. A complete set of angle ellipse guides is shown in Fig. 2.25(b). Note carefully that angle ellipse sizes are major-axis lengths. This is *not* the case with isometric ellipse guides.

An isometric ellipse guide is actually an angle ellipse guide for which the angle is 35°16′. The isometric angle, however, is not the only difference. An isometric guide may

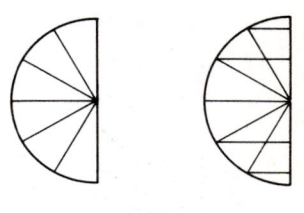

Step 1 Step 2

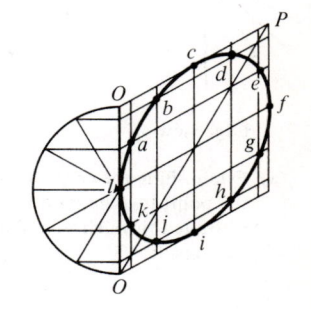

Steps 3, 4, and 5

Figure 2.24
Constructing an ellipse using the diagonal method.

Position number
Angle to line of sight
5(90°)
4(60°)
3(45°)
2(30°)
1(15°)
0(0°)

Edge view

Front view

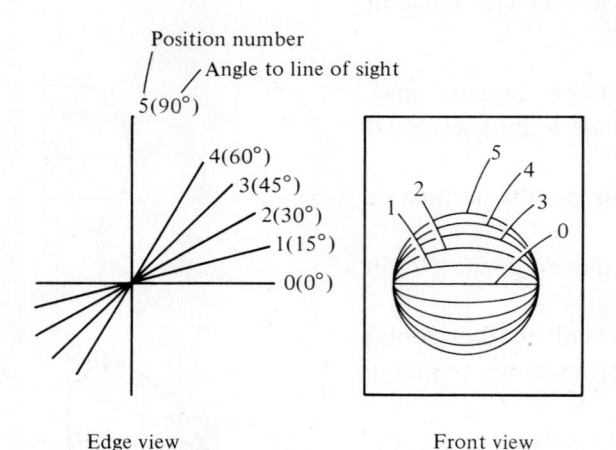

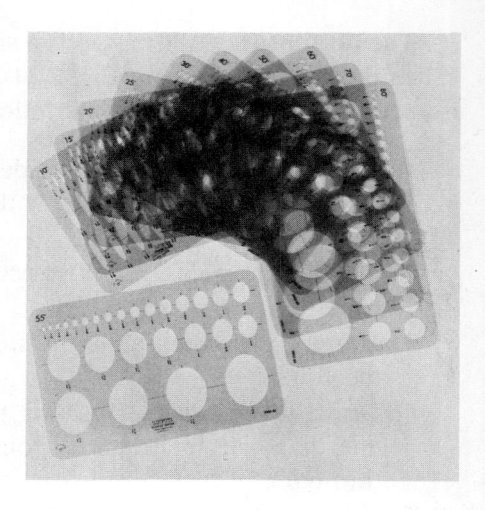

(a) Establishing the center of the circle (position 5) as the point to align with the line of sight, the circle is rotated through 90°. Ellipses shown in the front view result.

(b) A set of angle ellipse guides. In the upper left corner of each guide is the angle we see in part (a). (Photograph by R. T. Gladin)

Figure 2.25 The origin of the name *angle* ellipse.

be used to draw ellipses on an isometric plane *only*. In addition, sizes printed on isometric guides *do not* refer to major-axis lengths but to a length along an isometric axis. Thus a 1-in. ellipse on an isometric guide is equivalent to a 1.22-in. angle ellipse guide. (Recall that an isometric projection is 0.82 smaller than an isometric drawing or a drawing is $1/0.82 = 1.22$ larger than a projection.)

A typical isometric ellipse guide is shown in Fig. 2.26. Because no advantage is gained by using isometric ellipse guides, we suggest using angle ellipse guides exclusively. The 16′ difference in viewing angle is of no consequence. Before passing to other considerations, we must not forget to mention the most important facet of using an ellipse guide, i.e., proper alignment. Examine Fig. 2.27(a) and (b) closely. In each case an ellipse has not been aligned properly and each view is distorted. In the second view of each object the ellipses have been aligned properly and give a pleasing, undistorted view. A simple rule should be committed to memory at this point: To properly align the guide, *the minor axis of the ellipse must always be positioned to coincide with the center line of the circular shape.* This rule applies to the use of ellipse guides in any pictorial projection scheme.

Sec. 2.A / 27
Isonometric Projection

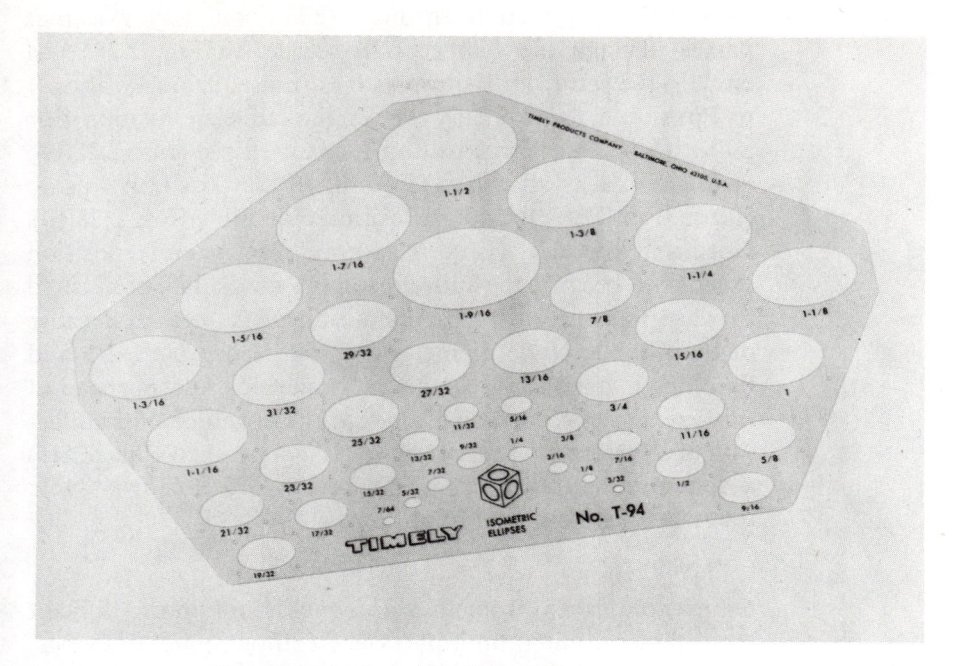

Figure 2.26 An isometric ellipse guide.

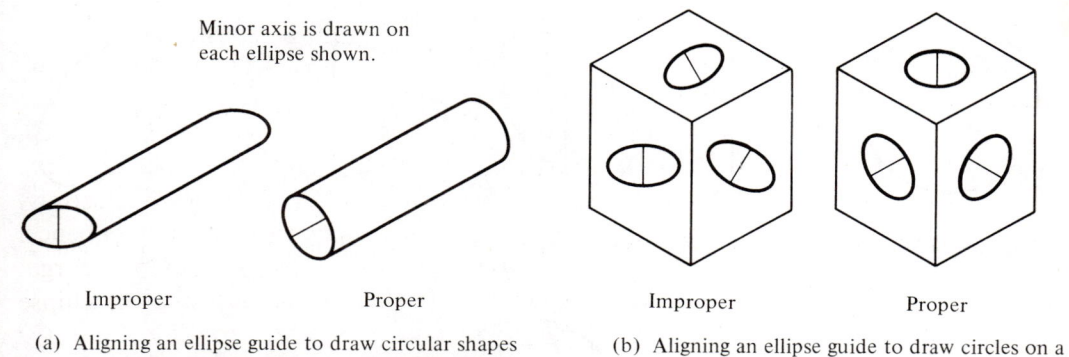

Minor axis is drawn on each ellipse shown.

Improper   Proper   Improper   Proper

(a) Aligning an ellipse guide to draw circular shapes on a cylinder. The minor axis aligns (properly) with an isometric line—the centerline.

(b) Aligning an ellipse guide to draw circles on a plane. The minor axis aligns (properly) with an isometric line.

Figure 2.27 Alignment of ellipse guides.

The rule is simple to follow because on quality ellipse guides the minor- and major-axis lines are designated. We have merely to draw a central axis and superimpose the minor-axis tic marks.

SPHERES

A sphere is defined here as a volume of revolution resulting from revolving a circle through 180° about any axis that passes through the center of the circle. In Fig. 2.28(a), a circle is viewed from the top as it is rotated from Position 1 to Position 5. In isometric we see the circle in Position 1 as a line [Fig 2.28(b)], at Position 2 as an ellipse [Fig. 2.28(c)], at Position 3 as an ellipse [Fig. 2.28(d)], at Position 4 as an ellipse [Fig. 2.28(e)], and at Position 5 as a line [Fig. 2.28(b)]. Note that the circle is seen as an ellipse in *every* position except two because the entire revolving model has been tilted forward to conform to the definition of isometric. Because of the tilt, the circle diameter is forshortened by $\sqrt{2/3}$ and becomes a major-axis length in isometric. The purpose of this exercise is to demonstrate that the envelope of a collection of ellipses representing circles is a sphere. In Fig. 2.28(f) a sphere with traces from positions 1 to 5 is shown. Note the intersection point P of all traces.

DIMENSIONING

Dimensioning an isometric drawing is no more difficult than dimensioning multiple view orthographic drawings. Certain ground rules must be established, however, to assure

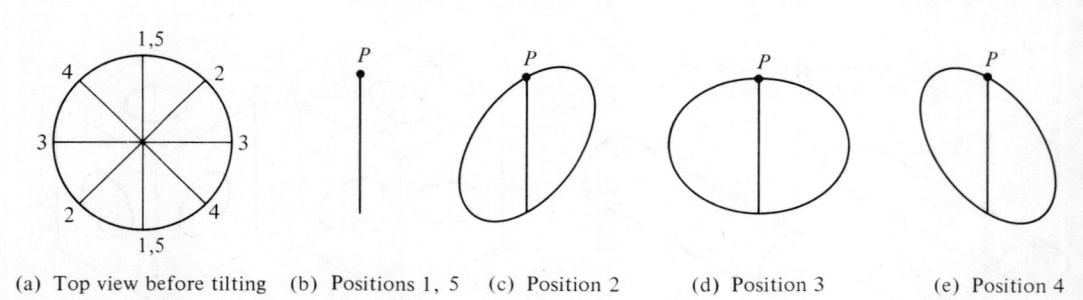

(a) Top view before tilting (b) Positions 1, 5 (c) Position 2 (d) Position 3 (e) Position 4

(f) Complete sphere

Figure 2.28 If a circle is rotated through 180°, a sphere is generated.

consistency. One unbendable rule is that all dimension lines must be isometric lines; i.e., dimension lines must lie in isometric planes. Figure 2.29(a) illustrates a common error that is corrected in Fig. 2.29(b). Cover Fig. 2.29(b) and study Fig. 2.29(a). It is difficult to see that the dimension lines and the dimension are in the plane of the sloping face until we see the correct version in Fig. 2.29(b). It should be obvious that in Fig. 2.29(a) the dimension line, although it is *drawn* vertical, does not lie in an isometric plane nor is it the height of the object.

Two conventions for lettering are acceptable—aligned and unidirectional (see Fig. 2.30). In either convention, all

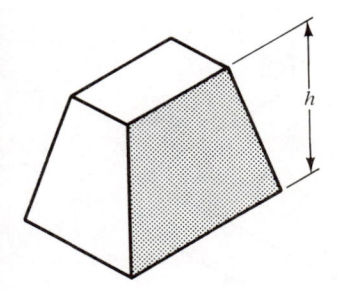

(a) The dimension line shown here is not in the proper plane. The height shown is greater than the actual height, because it is measured on a diagonal.

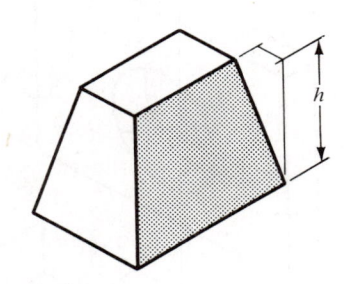

(b) In this view the dimension line is properly positioned. As a result, h is shown true measure.

Figure 2.29 Dimension lines in isometric.

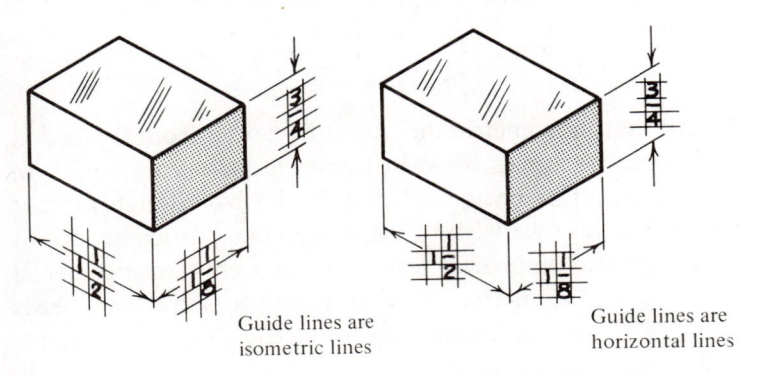

Guide lines are isometric lines

Guide lines are horizontal lines

(a) Aligned convention

(b) Unidirectional convention

Figure 2.30 Lettering conventions. Either (a) or (b) can be used. Never use a combination of the two conventions.

lettering should be vertical (read by holding the printed page as you are holding this page). Why ask a reader to crank his head to an angle to read? Note that guidelines for lettering in Fig. 2.30(a) are parallel to isometric axes and that in both (a) and (b) the base of each arrowhead is parallel to an isometric axis. Although either method is acceptable, a mixture of the two is not. Figure 2.31 illustrates dimensioning an object using the unidirectional convention.

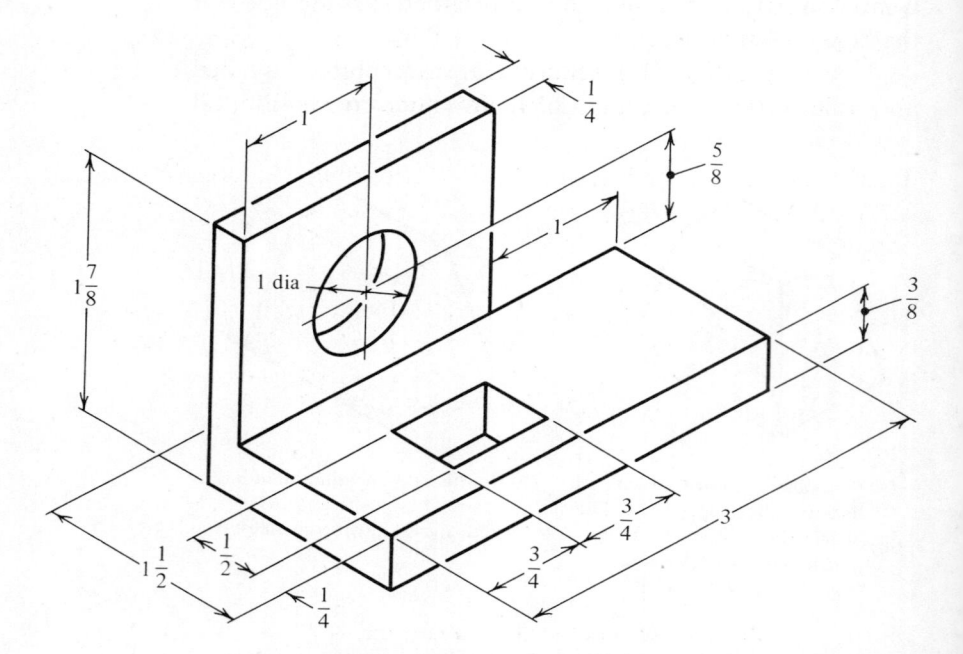

Figure 2.31 Dimensioning an object represented by an isometric drawing.

2B
Dimetric Projection

Recall that in isometric the object is viewed from a position such that the angles between isometric planes are equal. In many cases this scheme will not be flexible enough for our needs. Suppose we wish to emphasize one particular face of an object and emphasize less a face that contains no special features. An isometric drawing will not serve our needs here* so we turn to another axonometric projection scheme called *dimetric*.

In the dimetric scheme two of the three projected principal

*In isometric, all faces are emphasized equally.

axes make equal angles with the viewing plane, whereas the third axis makes an angle different from the other two, as shown in Fig. 2.32. As a result of the angular relationship among axes, a similar relationship exists among axis scales: Two axes are foreshortened a different amount. We now see the rationale for the name dimetric: Two (*di*) scales are needed to measure (*metric*) distances.

The simple exercise shown in Fig. 2.33 gives us a "mind's eye" approach to dimetric, as opposed to strict geometric considerations. In Fig. 2.33(a) and (b) we view the top of a cube from two different directions. (Note that the cube has not been tilted with respect to the viewing plane.) In Fig. 2.33(a) we view the cube head on, whereas in (b) we view from an angle. An important feature of dimetric is demonstrated here: Lines of sight are parallel because we view from infinity.

If we now tip the cubes toward the viewing plane and show the top faces, we have, effectively, produced dimetric views of the cubes. See Fig. 2.33(c) and (d). Be aware that the views shown here are two of many positions that we could choose and still conform to the defining criteria for dimetric

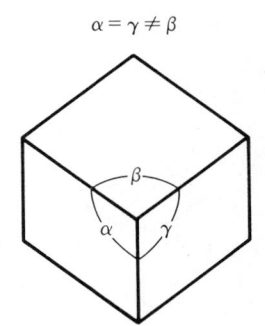

Figure 2.32
In dimetric, two angles are equal; the third is unequal ($\neq$) to the other two.

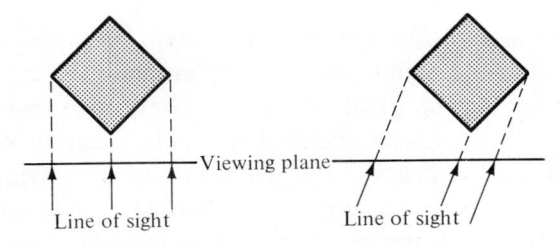

$\alpha = \gamma \neq \beta$

(a) Top view of a cube before the object is tilted, establishing relationship of viewer, object, and viewing plane.

(b) Same as (a), but from a different viewing position.

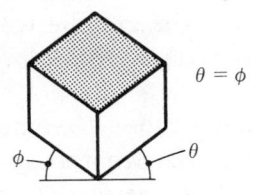

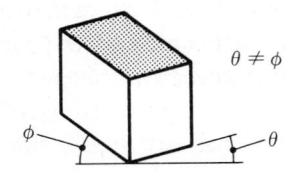

(c) A dimetric drawing resulting from viewing position in (a). $\theta = \phi$

(d) A dimetric drawing resulting from viewing position in (b). $\theta \neq \phi$

Figure 2.33 Examples of dimetric viewing positions.

32 / Chap. 2
Axonometric Projection

drawings: Two projected axis angles must be equal. Before considering the implications of this more sophisticated axonometric scheme, we caution the reader to a drawback of dimetric.

When dimetric is the chosen scheme, the drawing will be more difficult to make than will an isometric drawing. The use of two scales and two angles for receding axes complicates our bookkeeping system. As a plus factor, we are pleased to find that distortion in the scheme is less than in isometric. In other words, the drawing is more realistic.

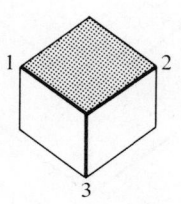

POINTS OF VIEW

One major advantage of executing a drawing in dimetric rather than isometric is that the illustrator can control emphasis of object features. By choosing a proper set of axes he can

1. Emphasize one of the three principal planes in the object, while at the same time subordinate the other two planes as shown in Fig. 2.34.
2. Emphasize two planes equally and subordinate the third as shown in Fig. 2.35.

Two facts of importance are noted by examining Fig. 2.34 and 2.35 carefully. First of all, emphasis is the same as exposed area; i.e., planes are emphasized by exposing more of them. A second point noted is that by rotating the set of axes (labeled 1, 2, and 3) 90° clockwise (CW) a symmetrical dimetric becomes an asymmetrical dimetric.* Although in each figure a downward-directed view was chosen, we could just as easily have chosen an upward-directed view as shown in Fig. 2.36. With just as much ease we could have rotated the axes counterclockwise (CCW) rather than CW and have emphasized the same two planes. The exercise that follows gives an idea of the number and variety of points of view available from one set of axes.

To begin with, let us examine a cube—a geometric solid that has six faces. Starting with the front face, we label faces as follows: front face, A; right-side face, B; rear face,

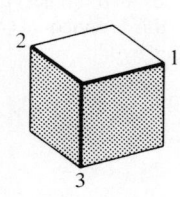

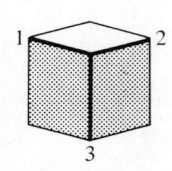

(a) Symmetrical

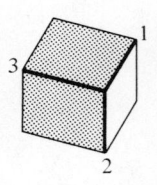

(b) Asymmetrical

Figure 2.34
Emphasizing one plane by choosing axes.

(a) Symmetrical

(b) Asymmetrical

Figure 2.35
Emphasizing two planes by choosing axes.

*A symmetrical dimetric drawing is one in which receding axes recede at the *same* angle. An asymmetrical dimetric drawing is one in which the receding axis angles are *unequal*.

C; left-side face, O; top face, E; bottom face, F. Then we choose as set of dimetric axes as shown in Fig. 2.37(a), labeled 1, 2, and 3. From Fig. 2.37(a) to (c) we see that the chosen axes can be arranged in three downward-directed positions. Parts (d) to (f) show three upward-directed positions. Thus we have six basic axes arrangements.

Now let us inscribe a simple object within the rectangular volume—using box construction—as shown in Fig.

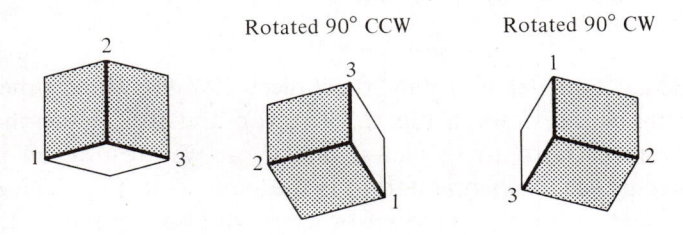

(a) Symmetrical (b) Asymmetrical

Figure 2.36 Upward-directed view of a cube.

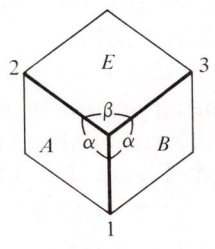

(a) Dimetric axes 1, 2, 3 chosen. Front (A), top (E), right side (B) faces are chosen.

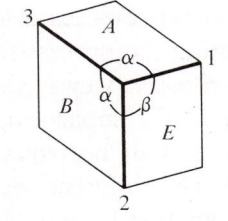

(b) Axes in (a) rotated 90° CCW

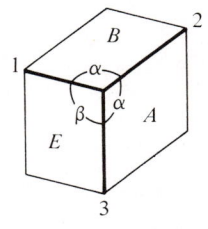

(c) Axes in (a) rotated 90° CW

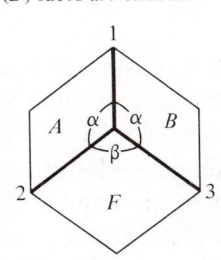

(d) Dimetric axes 1, 2, 3 chosen. Front (A), top (E), right side (B) faces are chosen.

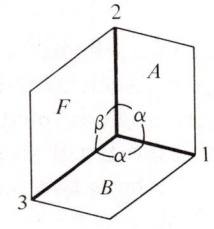

(e) Axes in (d) rotated 90° CW

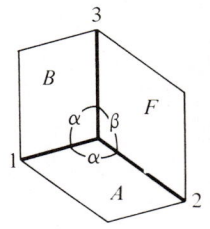

(f) Axes in (d) rotated 90° CCW

Figure 2.37 Six basic arrangements of axes 1, 2, and 3 in a dimetric drawing.

34 / Chap. 2
Axonometric Projection

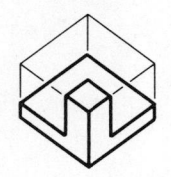

(a) The object and chosen axes.

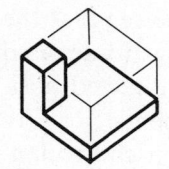

(b) Rotate (a) 90° CW

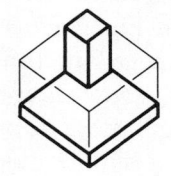

(c) Rotate (b) 90° CW

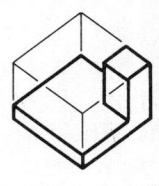

(d) Rotate (c) 90° CW

Figure 2.38 Rotating an object to obtain four different dimetric views.

2.38(a); then let us rotate the object CW 90° three times, giving us the views in Fig. 2.38(b), (c), and (d). Remember that in each of these views, the object was resting on its bottom face. Axes orientation is the same as in Fig. 2.37(a).

Next, using the same set of axes, suppose we repeat the revolving process with the object lying on its right-side face. We would see four views different from those with the object on its bottom face. If we were to repeat the complete process, placing each of the four remaining faces on the bottom, we would see 16 different views of the object, or a total of 24 different views for axes oriented as in Fig. 2.37(a).

Repeating the process for Fig. 2.37(b) to (f), we can see that 144 *different* views of *one* object using *one* set of axes is possible. By comparison, isometric allows us only 48 different views. Our horizons are enlarged. Figure 2.39 illustrates the 144 different views possible using one dimetric axes combination.

POSITION OF AXES

In the dimetric scheme, axes are positioned such that any two angles between axes are equal (but greater than 90°) and the third angle is unequal to the other two. In addition, axes are foreshortened so that two different scales must be employed. We have two parameters (angle sizes and scales), therefore from which to choose to start a dimetric drawing.

If we begin by choosing convenient angles (15, 30, or 45°), we must determine scale factors by graphical means.*

---

*This graphical construction is shown in our discussion of trimetric projection (see p. 43).

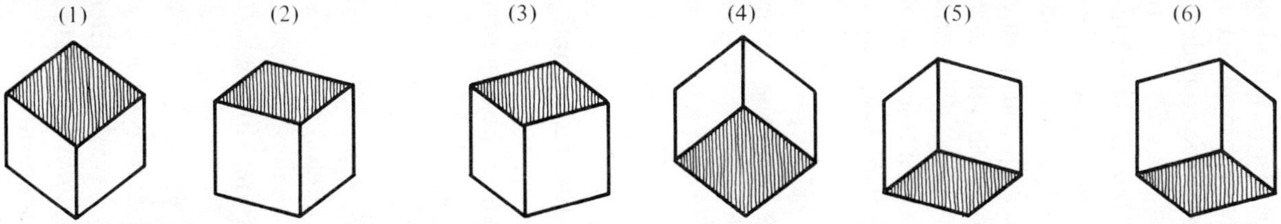

Axes are positioned as shown in (1)–(6). For each position, the object may be placed on each of six faces and rotated 90° CCW as shown in columns (a)–(d). For each position of axes, we show 24 *different* views of the object. Six axes positions yield 6 × 24—or 144 different views. Choosing a different set of axes results in a completely different set of 144 views.

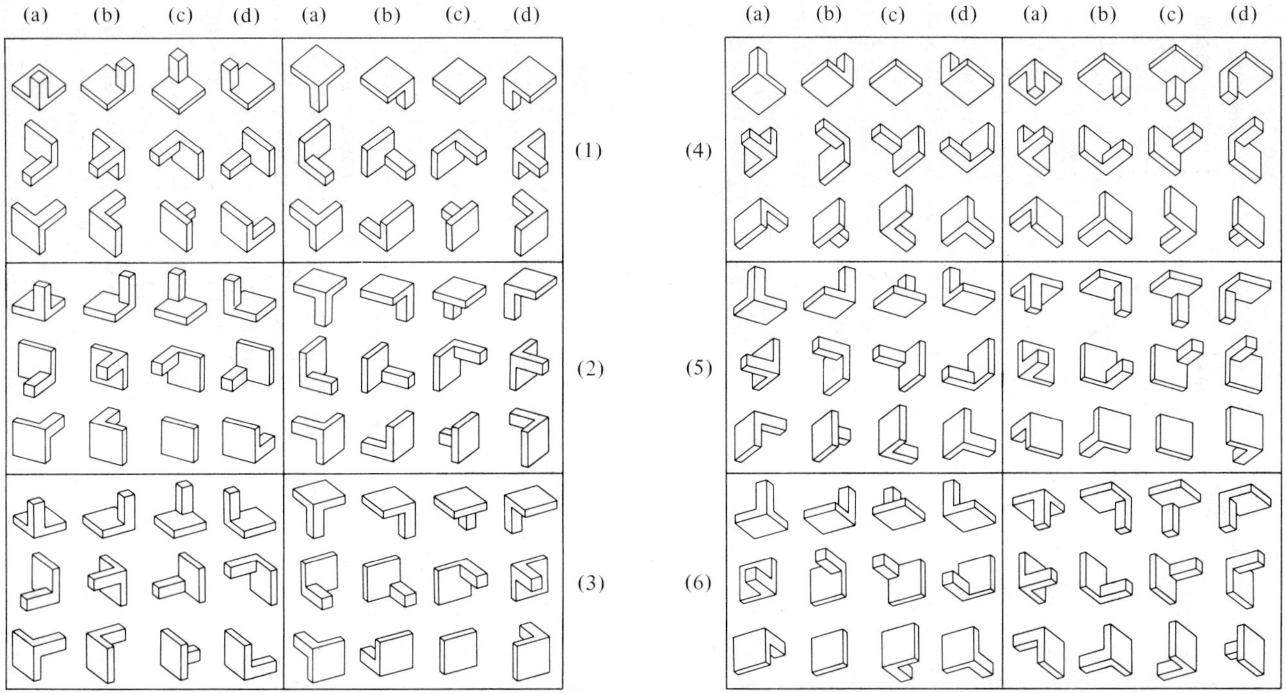

Figure 2.39 The 144 different views of an object in dimetric using *one* set of axes for *one* object.

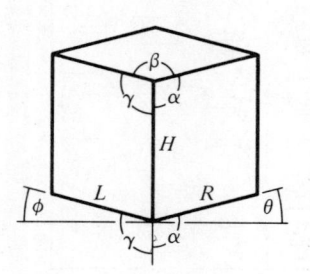

Figure 2.40
The geometry for dimetric projection.

$\theta = \alpha - 90°$
$\phi = \gamma - 90°$

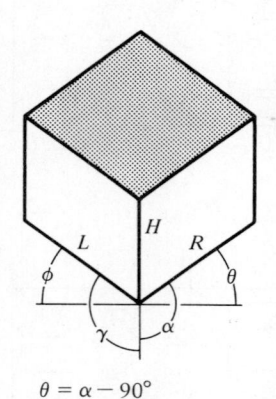

Figure 2.41
A symmetrical dimetric cube: $\theta = \phi$, $L = R = 1$, and $H = \frac{3}{4}$.

In addition to determining scale factors, we will discover that for convenient angles the scales are *not* convenient. For example, if we choose to draw a symmetrical dimetric with 30° receding axis angles, we will be using a scale of 0.82 in.= 1 in. Clearly, such a scale factor is difficult to use so an alternative to choosing angles first must be considered.

Referring to Fig. 2.40, we see that α, β, and γ are the angles the axes L, R, and H make with the viewing plane when projected into it. Remember that two of the three angles are equal and two of the three axes (R, L, H) are equal in length. Because we wish to choose scale values arbitrarily, choices must be reasonable. One of the two scales, therefore, is chosen to be unity—the simplest choice of all. The other scale is designated to be fraction of unity, but a fraction easy to deal with: Fractions such as $\frac{1}{3}$, $\frac{1}{2}$, $\frac{5}{8}$, $\frac{2}{3}$, and $\frac{3}{4}$ fit the description.

From the trigonometric relationship below and simple geometric relationships, the angles α, β, γ, θ, and φ are found. See Fig. 2.40.

$$\cos \sigma = -\frac{\sqrt{2E^2 - U^2}}{2E}$$

where σ = one of the two equal angles (desired quantity)
E = one of the two equal scales
U = the third scale, which is unequal to the other two

As an example, we will determine a set of axes and angles from the formula and geometric relationships. In Fig. 2.41 the cube is a symmetrical dimetric; i.e., $\theta = \phi$ and L scale $= R$ scale. Remembering that scales (not angles) are chosen arbitrarily, let the L and R scales be unity and the H scale be $\frac{3}{4}$. Substituting into the trigonometric relationship and solving, σ = 127°.

From Fig. 2.41, $\theta = \alpha - 90°$ and $\phi = \gamma - 90°$. Because σ = α = γ, we know that $\theta = \phi$ and, therefore, $\theta = \phi =$ 127° − 90° = 37°. The scales and angles have been determined quickly and although the 37° angle is not "standard," it is easier to work with than nonstandard scales are.

We will not usually want to use mathematics to determine scales and angles. Figure 2.42 provides us with a graphical means to find the same two parameters. The steps involved in using the graph are

$$\cos \sigma = -\sqrt{\frac{2E^2 - U^2}{2E}}$$

E = one of the equal scales
U = the other scale

1. Choose scales for the two equal axes and the third axis.
2. If the drawing is symmetrical ($\theta = \phi$) and the vertical scale is unity (1), find θ from Curve A.
3. If the drawing is symmetrical ($\theta = \phi$) and the vertical scale is not unity ($\neq 1$), find θ from Curve B.
4. If the drawing is asymmetrical ($\theta \neq \phi$) and the left receding scale is unity (1), find θ from Curve A.
5. If the drawing is asymmetrical ($\theta \neq \phi$) and the left receding scale is not unity ($\neq 1$), find θ from Curve B.

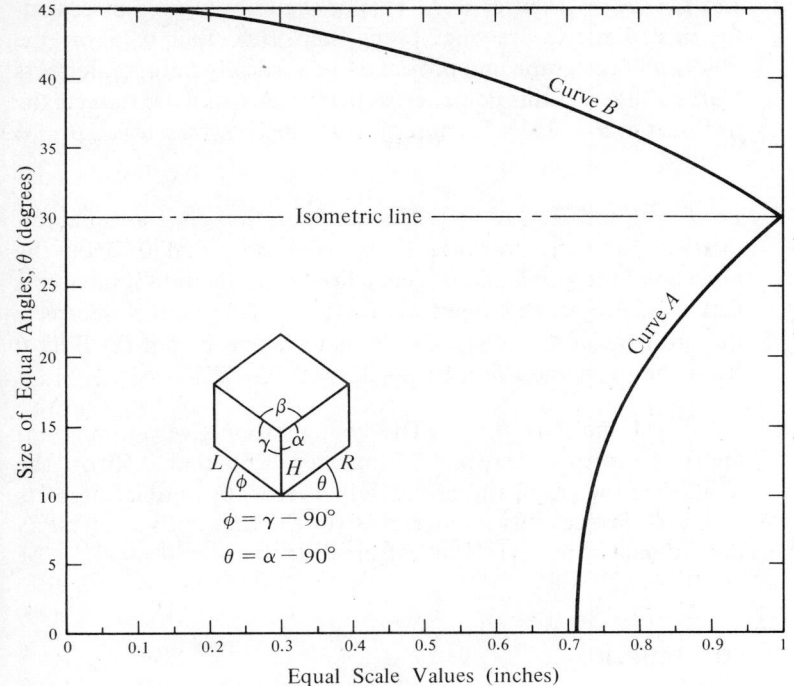

Figure 2.42 Curve used to find angles θ and ϕ for a dimetric drawing when axis scale values are given.

1. Choose scales for the two equal-length axes and the third (unequal) axis.
2. If the drawing is symmetrical ($\theta = \phi$) and
   (a) $H = 1$, find θ from Curve A.
   (b) $H \neq 1$, find ϕ from Curve B.
3. If the drawing is not symmetrical ($\phi \neq \theta$) and
   (a) $L = 1$, but $R = H < 1$, find ϕ from Curve A. Then $\theta = 90° - 2\phi$.
   (b) $L \neq 1$, but $R = H = 1$, find ϕ from Curve B. Then $\theta = 90° - 2\phi$.

To be certain that the use of the graph is understood the following examples are provided.

Example 1

Let $L = R = 1$ and $H = \frac{3}{4}$. This configuration gives us a symmetrical dimetric drawing. Using step 2(b), find 0.75 on the abscissa of the graph and project a line vertically until it intersects Curve B. Project this point across (to the left) until it intersects the ordinant at $\theta = 37°$. Because the drawing is symmetrical, $\theta = \phi = 37°$.

Example 2   Let $L = R = \frac{3}{4}$ and $H = 1$. This configuration gives us a symmetrical dimetric drawing. Using step 1(a), find 0.75 on the abscissa of the graph and project a line vertically until it intersects Curve *A*. Project this point across (to the left) until it intersects the ordinant at $\theta = 13\frac{1}{2}°$. Because the drawing is symmetrical, $\theta = \phi = 13\frac{1}{2}°$.

Example 3   Let $L = 1$ and $R = H = \frac{3}{4}$. This configuration gives us an asymmetrical dimetric drawing. Using step 3(a), find 0.75 on the abscissa of the graph and project a line vertically until it intersects Curve *A*. Project this point across (to the left) until it intersects the ordinant at $\phi = 13\frac{1}{2}°$. (Note that we find ϕ, not θ.) Find θ from the expression $\theta = 90° - 2\phi = 90° - 27° = 63°$.

Example 4   Let $L = \frac{1}{2}$ and $R = H = 1$. This configuration gives us an asymmetrical dimetric drawing. Using step 3(b), find 0.50 on the abscissa of the graph and project a line vertically until it intersects Curve *B*. Project this point across (to the left) until it intersects the ordinant at $\phi = 41°$. Find θ from the expression $\theta = 90° - 2\phi = 90° - 82° = 8°$.

CONSTRUCTION

In the section on isometric two powerful methods for construction were presented—the box and center line layout methods. Each method is applicable in dimetric, but words of caution are offered. In executing a drawing in dimetric, we must remember that two scales are used and that if offset measurements are made in a plane in which two scales are called for, *two* scales must be used. In Fig. 2.43 a

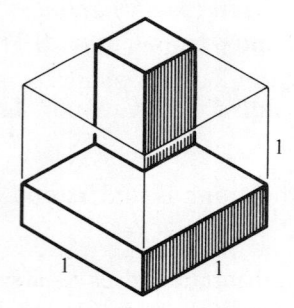

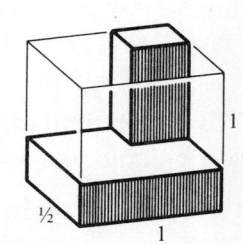

(a) Isometric—all scales are equal   (b) Dimetric—two scales are used

Figure 2.43 The use of box construction (a) in isometric and (b) dimetric. One scale is used throughout in isometric but in dimetric two scales are employed.

simple object is drawn in isometric and dimetric using box construction. Note that in dimetric the left receding scale is one-half the right receding and vertical scales.

If a drawing is executed in dimetric and the center line layout method is employed, we are obliged to remember that two scales are being used. Until we consider choosing ellipse guides (or ellipse construction methods) for dimetric, the same techniques used in isometric drawing may be applied to dimetric drawing.

CIRCLES

In the section on isometric we learned that circles usually project as ellipses and that the simplest way to draw an ellipse is with an ellipse guide. The same is true in dimetric, with a slight variation. Because we use two different angles and two different scales in dimetric, two different angle ellipse guides are used to draw ellipses in dimetric planes. A natural response to this statement is, "How do I determine the angles for ellipse guides?"

One method is to determine a major- and minor-axis length for each ellipse and then, by trial and error, to find the ellipse guide that matches these lengths. Another method uses graphical means to find the ellipse angle value. Then, using an ellipse with a major-axis length equal to the diameter of the circle we are representing in dimetric, draw the ellipse.

To demonstrate the use of a graphical procedure to find angle ellipse values, we will follow the example in Fig. 2.44. Note that we use the values $R = H = 1$, $L = \frac{3}{4}$. From Fig. 2.42, $\theta = 37°$ and $\phi = 15°$. Rather than finding three values for ellipse guides, we will first find the correct guide for the top face.

1. Draw axes L, R, and H at the proper angles.
2. Locate point A at some arbitrary distance from point O along axis R. Then construct line AB perpendicular to the extension of axis H.
3. Construct BC perpendicular to the extension of axis R and AC perpendicular to the extension of axis L.
4. Now draw line gg through point O, parallel to AB.
5. Find the midpoint of line dC; using the midpoint,

40 / Chap. 2
Axonometric Projection

draw a semicircle of diameter *dC*. This locates point *h* on line *gg*.

6. Draw dashed line *dh*. Angle *Bdh* (measured with a circular protractor) is the angle ellipse guide value for face I, i.e., 27°30′.
7. Repeat the steps above to find the ellipse value for face III. Face II, because of symmetry, uses the same ellipse value as does face I.

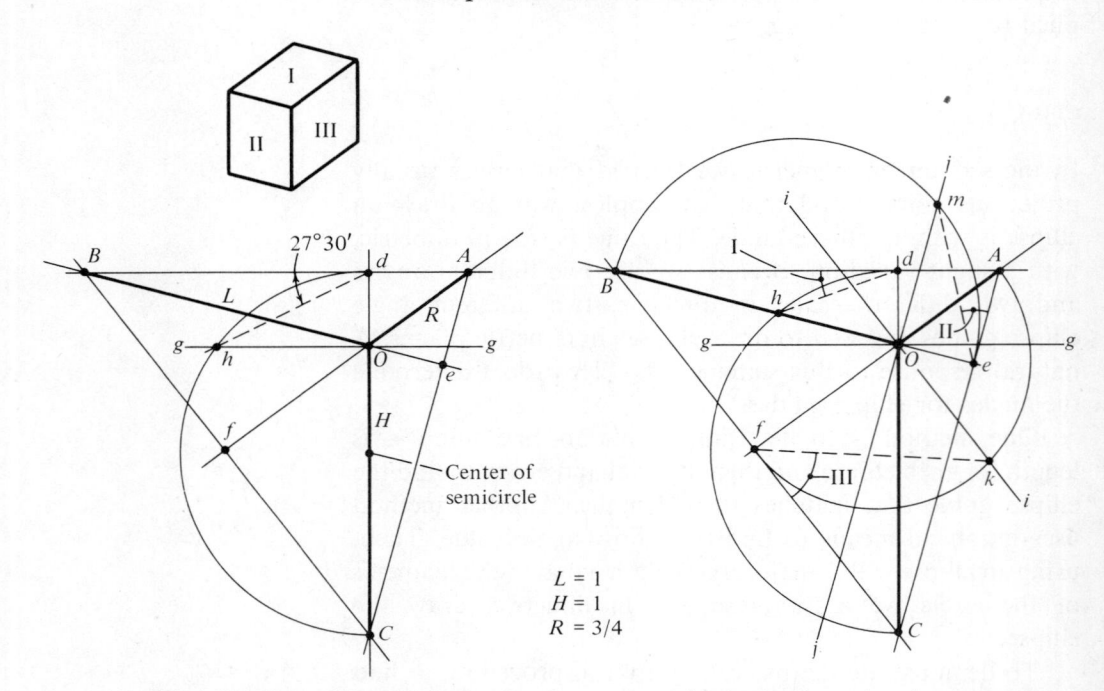

(a) Angle ellipse guide value for face I

(b) Angle ellipse values for all three faces

Figure 2.44 Graphical determination of angle ellipse values for dimetric drawings. Follow procedure carefully.

Two important facts should be noted here. First, a *circular* protractor is used to measure angles *Bdh*, *Afm*, and *Cfk*. Second, the 27°30′ value found in step 6 is not practical. Ellipse guides are not available at that angle. Most guides progress from 15 to 60° in 5° increments. Because the difference of 2 to 3° is small, a 25 or 30° guide is used for ellipses on faces I and II.

It should be noted that the ellipse values determined are not exact. What we have found is an ellipse that is *close* to the desired value and one that will look correct when employed in the designated planes. If accuracy is demanded, construction methods described earlier must be used.

The construction procedure above was presented to illustrate that the trial and error method is obsolete and that the reader can perform simple construction to find the appropriate angle ellipse guides.

There are those who do not, or would not, wish to use the construction methods necessary to determine angles for ellipses. For these illustrators Table 2.1 is provided. Accompanying this table are the twelve parts of Fig. 2.45, which will give the reader a visual concept of what entries in the table produce. These twelve axes orientations will meet nearly every need.

Table 2.1. DIMETRIC AXIS ANGLE AND ELLIPSE GUIDE SELECTION.

Refer to Fig. 2.45	Scale Values L	R	H	Axis Angles ϕ (degrees)	θ (degrees)	Ellipse Guide Values* I (degrees)	II (degrees)	III (degrees)
part (a)	1	1	$\frac{1}{2}$	41	41	60	20	20
(b)	1	$\frac{1}{2}$	1	7	41	20	60	20
(c)	$\frac{1}{2}$	1	1	41	7	20	20	60
(d)	1	1	$\frac{5}{8}$	39	39	55	25	25
(e)	1	$\frac{5}{8}$	1	11	39	25	55	25
(f)	$\frac{5}{8}$	1	1	39	11	25	25	55
(g)	1	1	$\frac{3}{4}$	37	37	50	30	30
(h)	1	$\frac{3}{4}$	1	15	37	30	50	30
(i)	$\frac{3}{4}$	1	1	37	15	30	30	50
(j)	$\frac{3}{4}$	$\frac{3}{4}$	1	15	15	15	45	45
(k)	$\frac{3}{4}$	1	$\frac{3}{4}$	60	15	45	15	45
(l)	1	$\frac{3}{4}$	$\frac{3}{4}$	15	60	45	45	15

*Used *only* on dimetric planes.

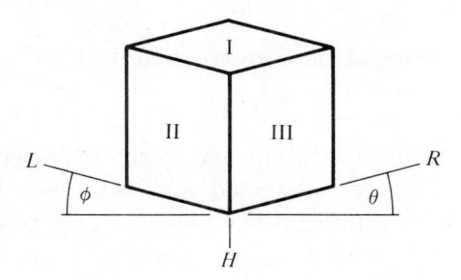

Occasionally, an object will have a circular feature on a nondimetric plane, in which case Table 2.1 is of no use. For these cases, we must resort to trial and error fitting of ellipse guides to the dimetric box in which the circle fits.

(a) $L = R = 1, H = 1/2$
$\theta = \phi = 41°$

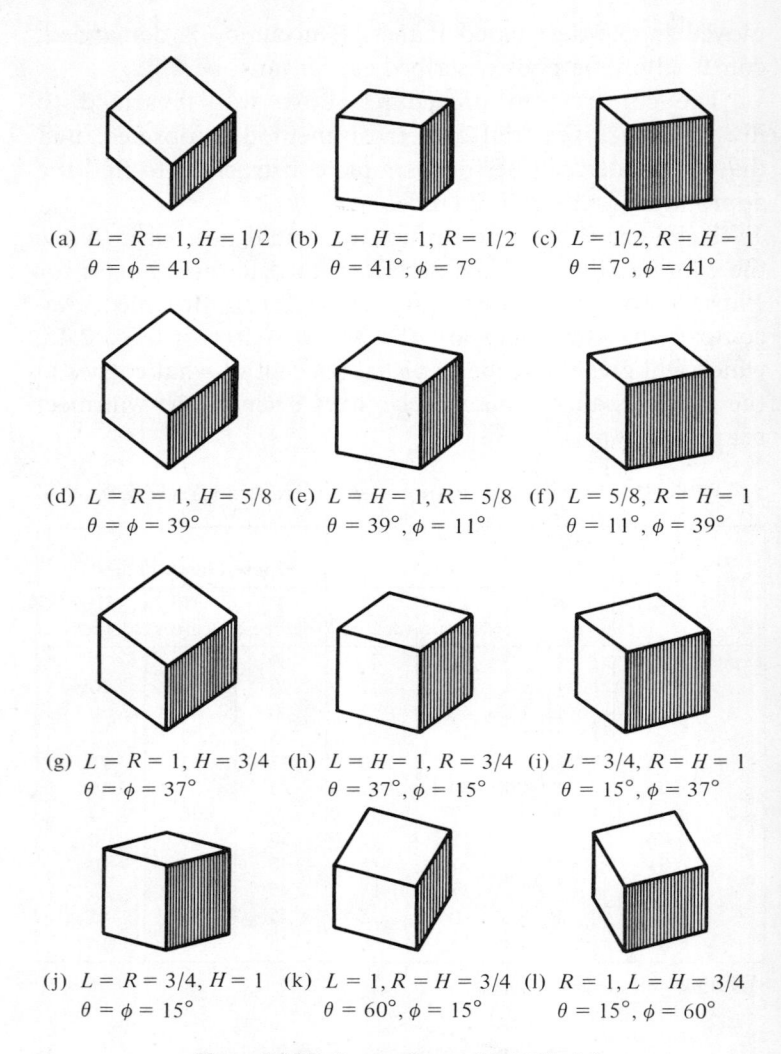

(b) $L = H = 1, R = 1/2$
$\theta = 41°, \phi = 7°$

(c) $L = 1/2, R = H = 1$
$\theta = 7°, \phi = 41°$

(d) $L = R = 1, H = 5/8$
$\theta = \phi = 39°$

(e) $L = H = 1, R = 5/8$
$\theta = 39°, \phi = 11°$

(f) $L = 5/8, R = H = 1$
$\theta = 11°, \phi = 39°$

(g) $L = R = 1, H = 3/4$
$\theta = \phi = 37°$

(h) $L = H = 1, R = 3/4$
$\theta = 37°, \phi = 15°$

(i) $L = 3/4, R = H = 1$
$\theta = 15°, \phi = 37°$

(j) $L = R = 3/4, H = 1$
$\theta = \phi = 15°$

(k) $L = 1, R = H = 3/4$
$\theta = 60°, \phi = 15°$

(l) $R = 1, L = H = 3/4$
$\theta = 15°, \phi = 60°$

Figure 2.45 Reference figures for Table 2.1.

2C
Trimetric Projection

A trimetric projection is an axonometric projection of an object that has been positioned such that none of the projected axes form equal angles with each other. See Fig. 2.46.

Because the three angles are unequal, three unequal, foreshortened scales must be used to make measurements along or parallel to principal axes. The use of three scales is the major disadvantage of trimetric drawing: It is time-consuming and, to a beginner, confusing. In most cases, the advantage gained in reducing distortion by using this projection scheme will not outweigh the disadvantage of more time required to make the drawing.

There will be cases, however, in which a trimetric drawing will be worth the time and effort. The object shown in Fig. 2.47 is such a case. In Fig. 2.47(a) an isometric drawing of a bracket-like object is shown. Note that oblique face does not show in the isometric but in Fig. 2.47(b), the trimetric drawing, the face is shown. In general, the trimetric drawing shows the object better than the isometric does.

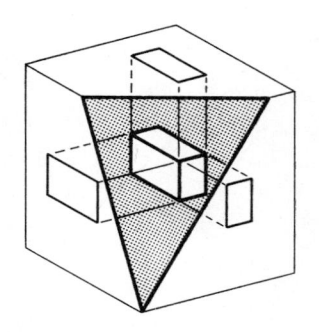

AXES AND SCALES

In both isometric and dimetric drawings, position of axes and choice of scales are simple considerations. The same simplicity is not a part of the trimetric scheme. Figure 2.48 shows a cube intersected by a plane parallel to the projection plane. In passing through the cube the plane forms triangle ABC. Examine this figure carefully, and note that

1. Angle AOB, by definition, is a right angle.
2. The legs of triangle ABC, formed by the intersection, are true length in the projection plane; i.e., $A_pC_p = AC$, $A_pB_p = AB$, and $B_pC_p = BC$. (The subscript p denotes *projected*.) This is so because parallel lines in parallel planes are equal length.

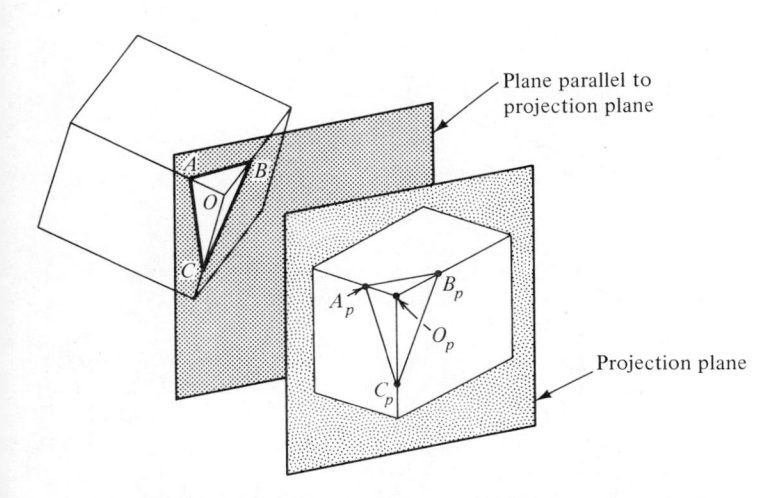

Figure 2.46
Trimetric projection.

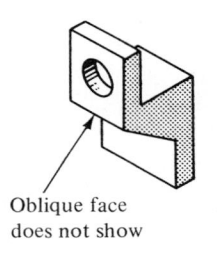

Oblique face does not show

(a) Isometric drawing

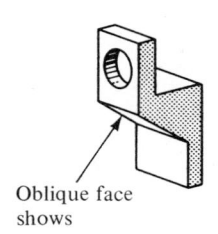

Oblique face shows

(b) Trimetric drawing

Figure 2.47
A case in which trimetric is used to show a feature that isometric will not show.

Figure 2.48 Trimetric projection axes and scales are determined by using geometry arising from this figure.

3. Lines AO, BO, and CO are foreshortened in the projection plane; i.e., $A_pO_p \neq AO$, $B_pO_p \neq BO$, and $C_pO_p \neq CO$.

The three facts above allows us to construct scales to measure distances along the three trimetric axes. Recall the definition of a trimetric drawing—one in which the three projected axes form unequal angles in the projection plane (see Fig. 2.46). For any choice of angles θ and ϕ, a method for constructing scales is given below. (Refer to Fig. 2.49.)

1. Choose angles θ and ϕ such that $\theta \neq \phi \neq \psi$ ($\neq$ means not equal to).
2. Locate point A and construct AB perpendicular to the extension of OC.
3. Construct AC perpendicular to the extension of OB.
4. Draw BC. (Note that BC is automatically perpendicular to the extension of OA.)
5. Find the midpoints of lines AB and AC.

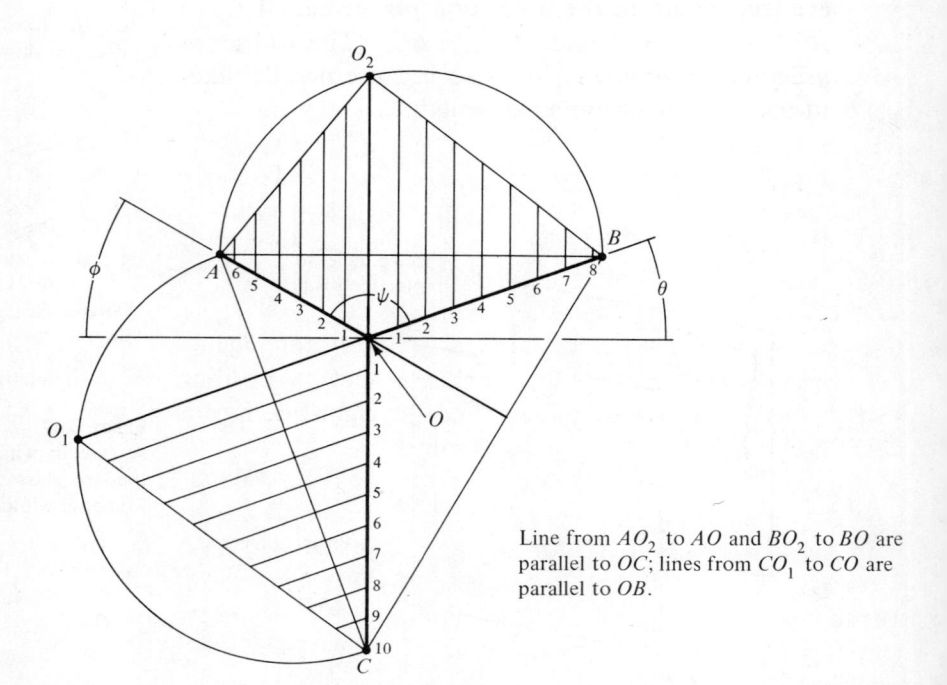

Line from AO_2 to AO and BO_2 to BO are parallel to OC; lines from CO_1 to CO are parallel to OB.

Figure 2.49 Construction of trimetric scales.

6. Using the midpoints as centers, draw semicircles of radius $\frac{1}{2} \cdot (AB)$ and $\frac{1}{2} \cdot (AC)$.
7. Extend OB and OC to intersect the semicircles, locating points O_1 and O_2, respectively.
8. Mark off full scales along lines AO_2, BO_2, and CO_1. These lines are *true length*.
9. Project the full scales back to the lines OA, OB, and OC. Scales thus projected are foreshortened the proper amount.
10. Mount the three scales on a piece of thin plastic or stiff paper and trimetric scales for the chosen angles are ready to use. See Fig. 2.50 for the proper mounting alignment.

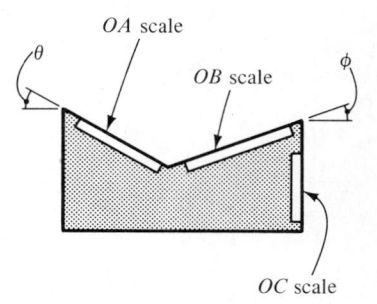

Figure 2.50
Trimetric scales constructed by the procedure in Fig. 2.49 may be used as straightedges when mounted on a stiff cardboard or plastic.

Scales used in trimetric drawings are dependent on the choice of two angles, θ and ϕ. Although a great number of angles are available, by choosing the pair of angles carefully, we will be selecting a view of the object that shows it to best advantage.

Most objects to be drawn have prominent features on one or more faces. As an exercise to illustrate choosing angles, we will draw the same object, shown in Fig. 2.51(a), using several different pairs of angles.

By studying this one figure carefully, we can begin to see the relationships that exist between a trimetric drawing and the choice of pairs of angles. In Fig. 2.51(b) and (c) the values of angles θ and ϕ have been interchanged resulting in a change of emphasis of surfaces on the cube. In (b) the front face is largest (emphasized most), the top face is the next largest face (emphasized secondarily), and the right-side face is the smallest face (emphasized least). Interchanging the angles in (c) results in a change in viewing position so that the left-side face is shown and the right-side face is not. Emphasis on faces remains the same.

Figure 2.51(d) through (g) show the same cube with the left axis receding at the same 10° angle in each case, but with the right axis receding at angles ranging in size from 20 to 60°. Scanning this row of figures we see that the result of progressively enlarging the one angle is a shift in secondary emphasis. In (d), the 10–20° pair, the right-side face is emphasized secondarily, whereas in (g) the top face is emphasized secondarily. In all cases, (d) to (g), the front face is

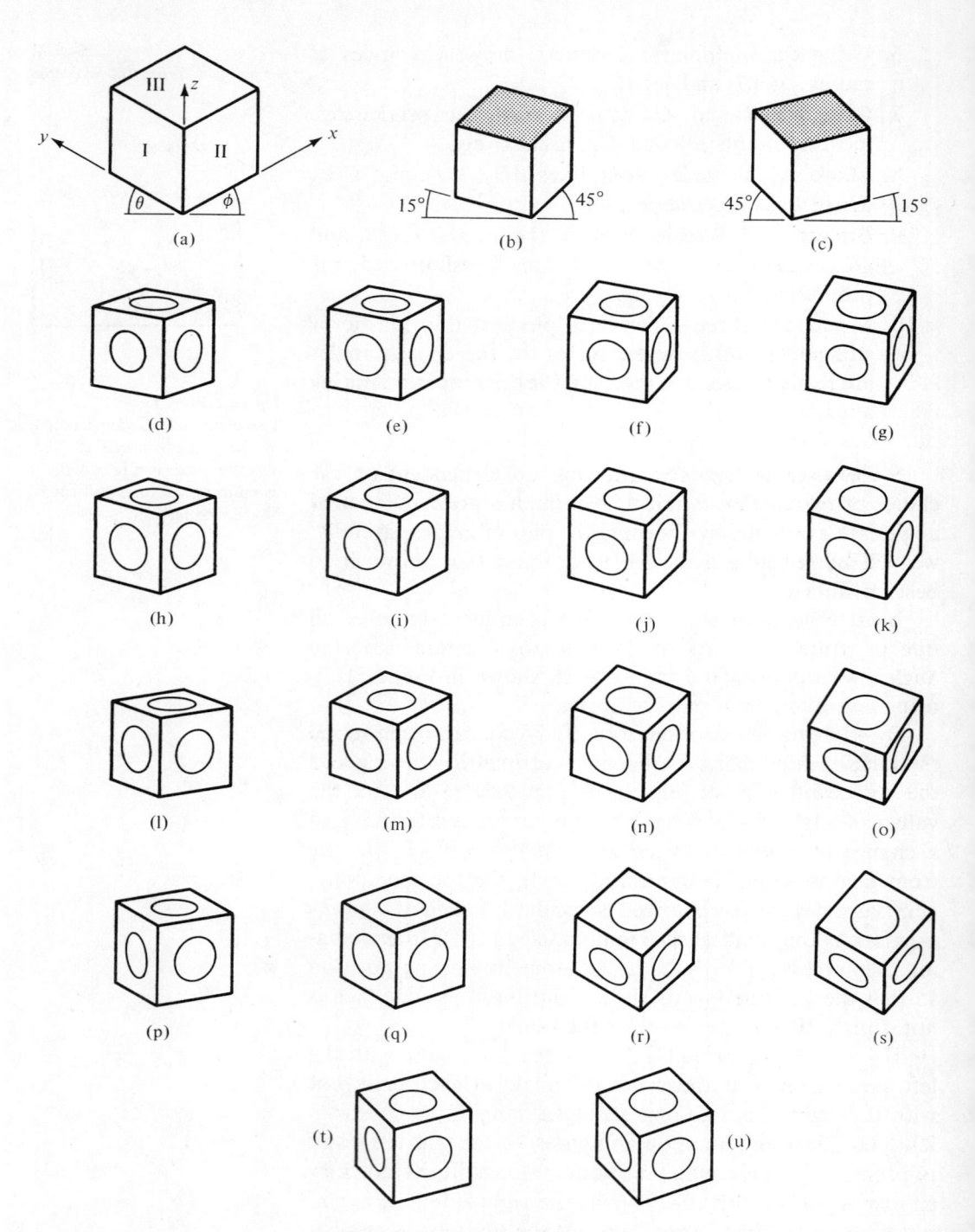

Figure 2.51 Trimetric drawings of an object employing different pairs of angles θ and ϕ show trends and relationships.

emphasized most. The other rows of drawings illustrate the same trends using different pairs of angles.

Another fact illustrated in the series of drawings in Fig. 2.51 is that ellipses are more nearly circular on faces exposing larger areas: In other words, the angle ellipse value in degrees is larger. As an example, examine Fig. 2.51(d). The largest exposed area is on the front face and a 50° ellipse is used here. The right-side and top faces, which expose the second and third largest areas, use 35 and 15° ellipses, respectively.

We learned earlier, in the section on dimetric, that scales and ellipse guide values to use with chosen axis angles are determined by a graphical construction. To eliminate this time-consuming construction, Table 2.2 is presented. Used in conjunction with Fig. 2.51, this table gives all necessary values for axis angles, axis scales, and ellipse guides.

Each row in Table 2.2 (from left to right) gives us values for receding axis angles (columns 1 and 2), values for each axis scale (columns 3, 4, and 5), values for angle ellipse guides (columns 6, 7, and 8), and a reference picture from Fig. 2.51 (column 9). To illustrate using Table 2.2, we will now make a trimetric drawing of the object shown in Fig. 2.52.

Note that circular features of the object lie on the front face, one circular boss lies on the top face, and the side view is simple and contains no circular features. As a result of these findings, we should choose a pair of angles for receding axes that will emphasize the front face most, the top

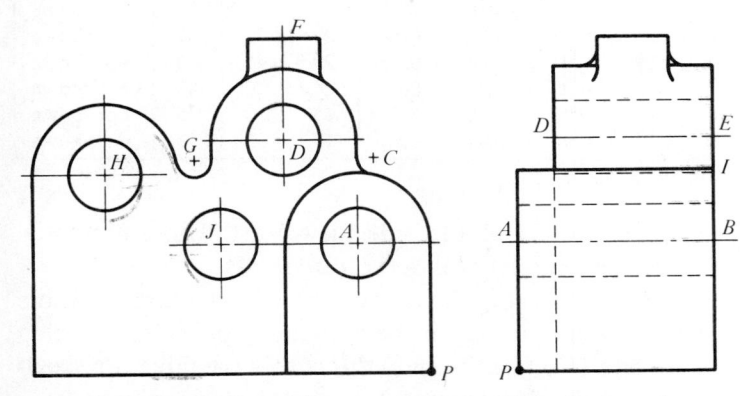

Figure 2.52 Multiple view drawing of an object to be drawn in trimetric.

48 / Chap. 2
Axonometric Projection

Table 2.2. Trimetric Axis Scales and Ellipse Guide Selection.

Receding Axis Angles (Degrees)		Axis Scales (Percent of Full Size)			Angle Ellipse Values (Degrees)			Example from Fig. 2.51
θ	φ	x	y	z	I	II	III	
10	20	0.60	0.84	0.96	50	35	15	part (d)
10	30	0.56	0.88	0.94	55	25	20	(e)
10	50	0.56	0.94	0.88	55	20	25	(f)
10	60	0.60	0.96	0.84	50	15	35	(g)
15	20	0.68	0.78	0.95	45	40	20	(h)
15	30	0.65	0.86	0.92	50	30	25	(i)
15	45	0.65	0.92	0.86	50	25	30	(b), (j)
15	55	0.68	0.95	0.78	45	20	40	(k)
20	10	0.84	0.60	0.96	35	50	15	(l)
20	15	0.78	0.68	0.95	40	45	20	not shown
20	25	0.72	0.80	0.90	45	35	25	not shown
20	30	0.72	0.84	0.88	45	35	25	(m)
20	40	0.72	0.88	0.84	45	25	35	not shown
20	45	0.72	0.90	0.80	45	25	35	(n)
20	55	0.78	0.95	0.68	40	20	45	not shown
20	60	0.84	0.96	0.60	35	15	50	(o)
25	20	0.80	0.72	0.90	35	45	25	not shown
25	45	0.80	0.90	0.72	35	25	45	not shown
30	10	0.88	0.56	0.94	25	55	20	(p)
30	15	0.86	0.65	0.92	30	50	25	not shown
30	20	0.84	0.72	0.88	35	45	25	(q)
30	40	0.84	0.88	0.72	35	25	45	not shown
30	45	0.86	0.92	0.65	30	25	50	(r)
30	50	0.88	0.94	0.56	25	20	55	(s)
40	20	0.88	0.72	0.84	25	45	35	not shown
40	30	0.88	0.84	0.72	25	35	45	not shown
45	15	0.92	0.65	0.86	15	50	30	(c), (t)
45	20	0.90	0.72	0.80	20	45	35	(u)
45	25	0.90	0.80	0.72	25	35	45	not shown
45	30	0.79	0.86	0.92	30	25	50	not shown
50	10	0.94	0.56	0.88	20	55	25	not shown
50	30	0.94	0.88	0.56	20	25	55	not shown
55	15	0.95	0.68	0.78	20	45	40	not shown
55	20	0.95	0.78	0.68	20	40	45	not shown
60	10	0.96	0.60	0.84	15	50	35	not shown
60	20	0.96	0.84	0.60	15	35	50	not shown

face secondarily, and the side view least. Examining Fig. 2.51, we see that (j) will serve our needs.

Having chosen Fig. 2.51(j) as a model, we turn to Table 2.2 to find values to use in the drawing. Angles for receding axes are given for (j) so we find this row in the table. Proceeding to the right, in columns 3, 4, and 5, we find values for axis scales. Note that scales for the x, y, and z axes correspond to x, y, and z axes in Fig. 2.51(a) and that each scale is given as percent of full size. In other words, the x-axis scale in our drawing will be 65 percent as large as full size or 0.65 in. on the drawing will equal 1 in. Similar values are given for the y- and z-axis scales. Columns 6, 7, and 8 provide us with angle ellipse values to use on faces I, II, and III. Refer to Fig. 2.51(a). Our finished trimetric drawing is shown in Fig. 2.53.

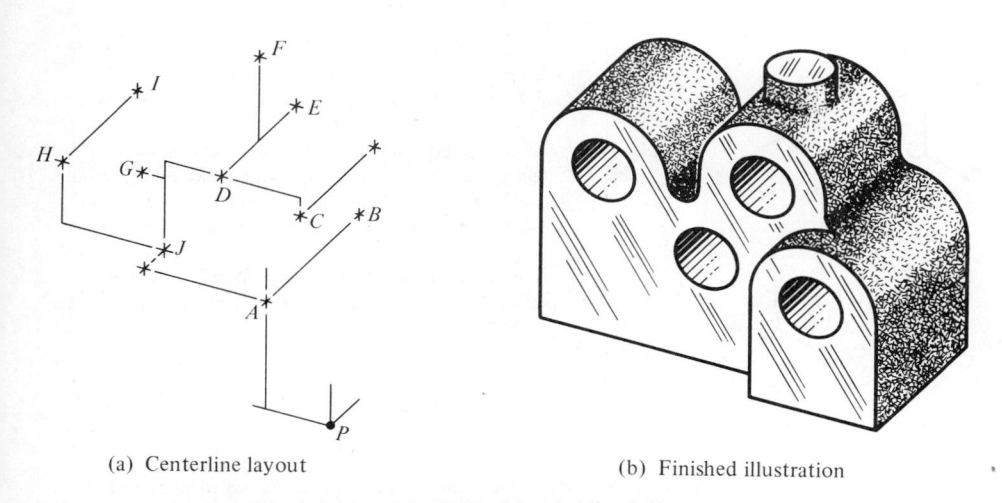

(a) Centerline layout   (b) Finished illustration

Figure 2.53 Trimetric drawing of the object in Fig. 2.52.

Table 2.2 used in conjunction with Fig. 2.51 provides a simple, accurate method to choose angle pairs, axis scales, and ellipse guides. For the interested reader, the ellipse guide values were determined using the procedure outlines on pp. 39 and 40.

Another timesaving device to use in choosing angle ellipses for specified axis angles is the ellipse wheel, shown in Fig. 2.54. One disadvantage of using the wheel, when compared with using Table 2.2 and Fig. 2.51, is that the illustrator does not see an object nor does he know axis scale values.

In the section that follows a true axonometric projection scheme that can be used to produce isometric, dimetric, *or* trimetric pictorials is presented. Before discussing true axonometric projection, we will illustrate for trimetric, as we

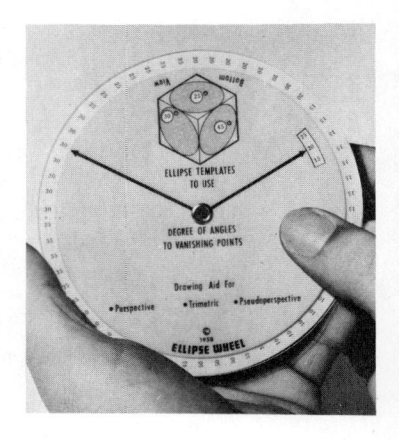

Figure 2.54
Lietz ellipse wheel. (Photo by R.T. Gladin.)

(1) (2) (3)
(4) (5) (6)
(7) (8) (9)
(10) (11) (12)

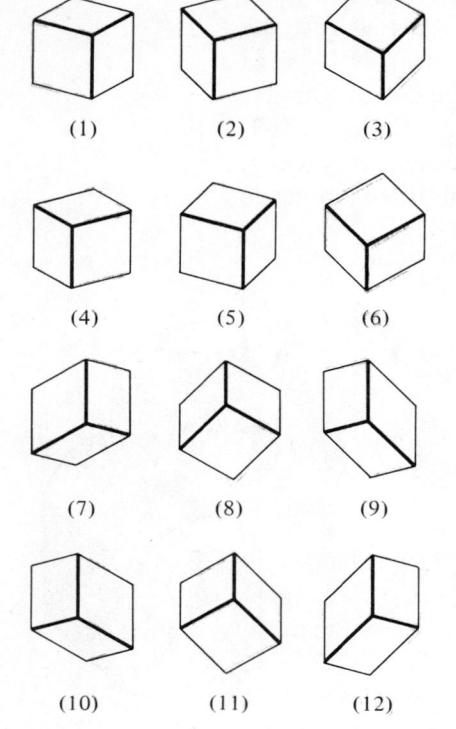

In the series of figures here we have chosen four basic axes positions: (1), (4), (7), and (10). By rotating each axes set 90° CW and CCW, we enlarge the number of basic sets to twelve. Recalling from the discussion of dimetric points of view, we see that the object can be placed on each of six faces and rotated through 90° to four positions to arrive at 12 × 6 × 4 or 288 *different* views of the same object.

We need to choose only one set of axes to complete the entire 288 views. In this case, $\theta = 15°$, $\phi = 30°$, $x = 0.65$, $y = 0.86$, and $z = 0.92$. See axes set (1).

As an exercise to be certain that rotation of axes, faces, and the object is understood, the reader should use Table 2.2 and the object below to assist him in sketching or drawing several of the 288 views.

Remember, there are an infinite number of sets of axes positions that can be chosen. The number of views is likewise infinite.

Figure 2.55 Possible views in trimetric using *one* set of axes and *one* object—there are 288 in all. Not all are shown. A good exercise would be to complete the missing parts.

did in the section on dimetric, the large number of points of view using one set of axes and one object—see Fig. 2.55.

2D True Axonometric Projection

As seen in earlier sections, in executing dimetric and trimetric drawings we were confronted with the task of determining scales, axis angles, and ellipse angles. In 1942, Theodor Schmid and L. Eckhart presented a simple method for true axonometric projection. Their method automatically eliminates using different scales on different axes.

Recall that an axonometric projection is an orthographic projection upon a plane that is oblique to the three principal axes. In earlier discussions we tipped and turned the object we viewed and left the axonometric plane fixed. In discussing true axonometric projection, we fix the object and move the axonometric plane, which is also the viewing plane. Because the viewing plane is normal to our lines of sight, triangle *ABC* shown in Fig. 2.56 is true size—lines in the plane are true length.

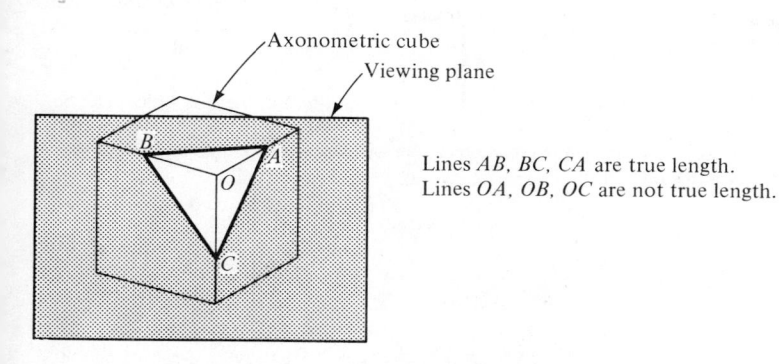

Lines *AB, BC, CA* are true length.
Lines *OA, OB, OC* are not true length.

Figure 2.56 Establishment of planes for true axonometric projection.

Now, if plane *OAB* is rotated about line *AB* into the axonometric plane (the plane of this page), the orthographic view of that principal plane is shown in true measure. Similarly, if the other two planes are rotated about lines *BC* and *CA* into the axonometric plane, the other orthographic views are shown true size.

A simple geometric principle gives us a basis for such rotations: Any two lines drawn from the end points of a diameter of a circle to a point lying on the circumference of the circle form a right angle. In our case, we used a cube so if a right angle appears in the axonometric plane after revolving the planes, we know that true length lines result. It follows then that if an angle is shown true size in a plane, the angle has been revolved into that plane. In the true axonometric projection scheme, each angle shown true size in the axonometric plane has been rotated into the axonometric plane. In addition, all features of the object that lie in the plane of the angle are shown true size and length.

To follow the procedure of true axonometric projection in a few simple steps, refer to Fig. 2.57.

1. Draw the three isometric axes *a*, *b*, and *c* [Fig. 2.57(a)].
2. Draw *AC* perpendicular to axis *b*, *AB* perpendicular to axis *c*, and *BC* perpendicular to axis *a*, establishing the axonometric plane *ABC* [Fig. 2.57(a)].

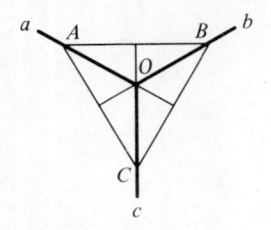

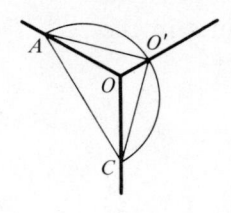

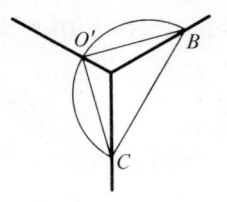

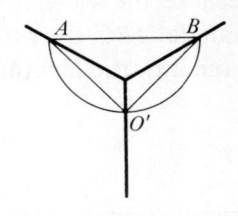

(a) Draw isometric axes *a*, *b*, and *c*. Draw perpendiculars, establishing plane *ABC*.

(b) Revolve isometric planes into plane of paper. Angles $AO'C$, $BO'C$, and $AO'B$ are each right angles.

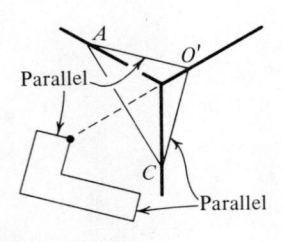

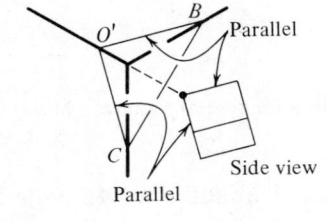

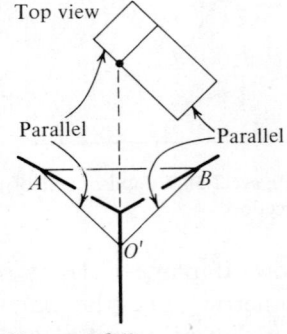

(c) Draw orthographic views, noting lines that *must* be parallel. Note carefully that point *P* on each orthographic view lies on an extended isometric axis. If this were not the case, lines projected from two views would intersect, but lines from the third view would not intersect with them.

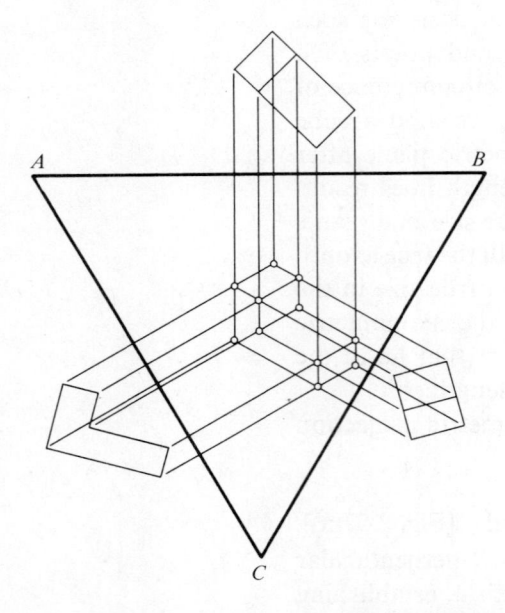

(d) Composite drawing of the three parts in (c), showing how projted lines intersect at circled points to form the object. The size of plane *ABC* has been enlarged for clarity. This fact does not alter the procedure in any way.

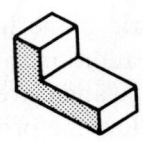

(e) Final drawing after removing construction lines.

Figure 2.57 True axonometric projection procedure for isometric.

52

3. Revolve faces OAB, OBC, and OAC into the axonometric plane, establishing axes $O'A$, $O'B$, and $O'C$ [Fig. 2.57(b)].
4. Draw orthographic views using axes $O'A$, $O'B$, and $O'C$ [Fig. 2.57(c)].
5. Project lines from the orthographic views perpendicular to AB, AC, and BC. The intersection of these common projection lines locate points on isometric principal planes from which the object may be formed [Fig. 2.57(d)].
6. Remove construction lines [Fig. 2.57(e)].

The procedure is applicable to dimetric and trimetric representation as shown in Fig. 2.58 and 2.59, respectively. Because the method is identical in all three cases, we did

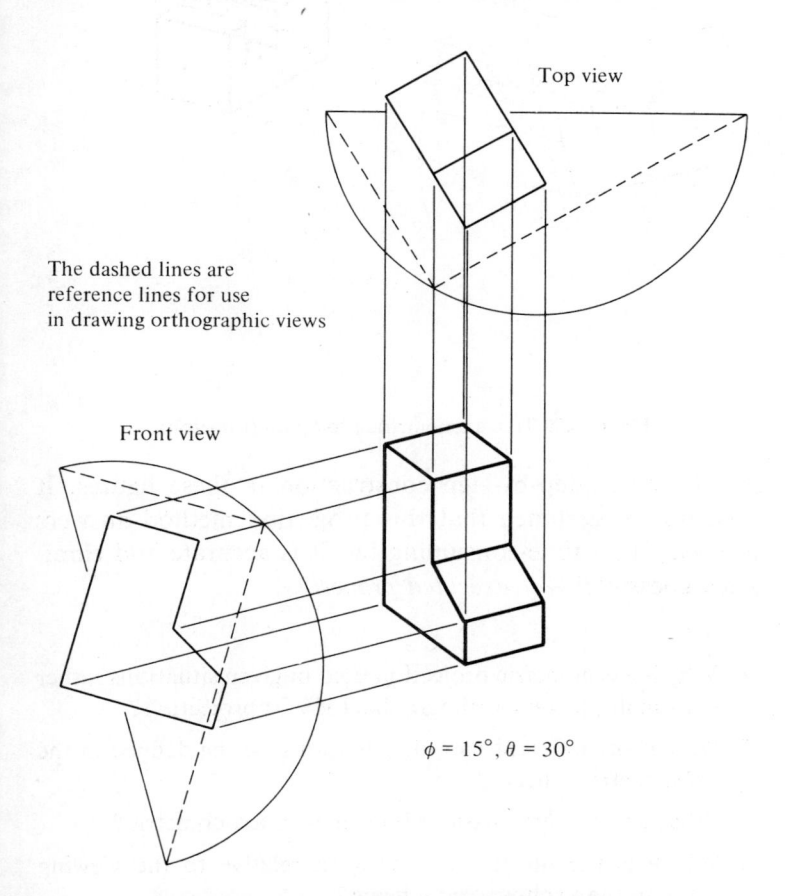

Figure 2.58 True axonometric projection (dimetric).

Dashed lines are used in drawing orthographic views—for references.

Top view

Front view

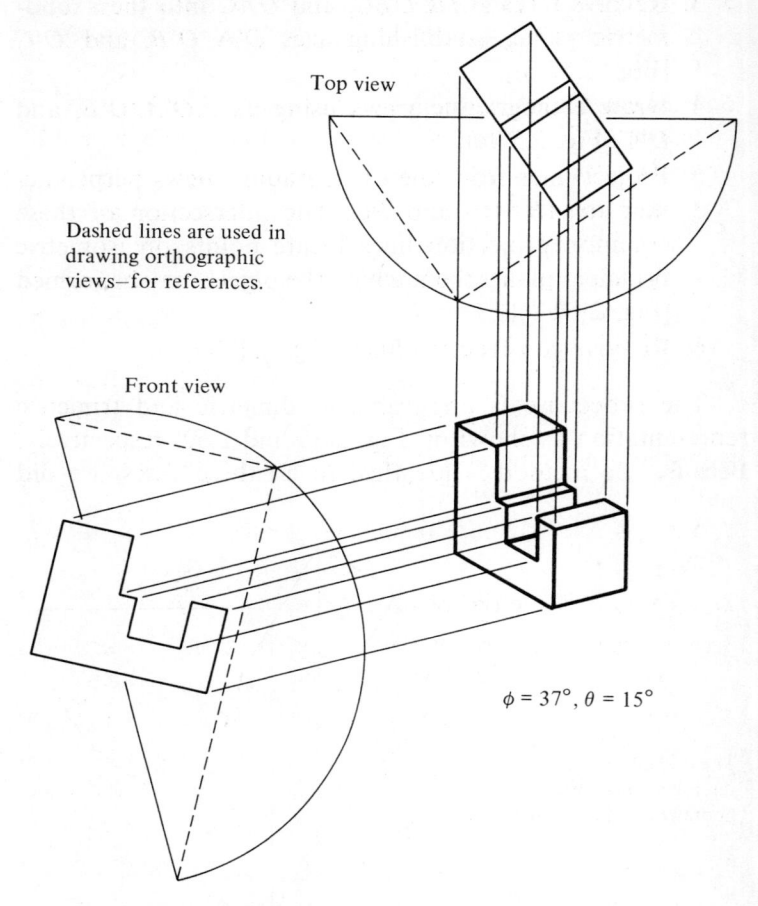

$\phi = 37°, \theta = 15°$

Figure 2.59 True axonometric projection (trimetric).

not show the step-by-step construction in these figures. It must not be assumed that this projection method answers all needs. It is time-consuming but it is accurate and eliminates guesswork—*if executed properly*.

QUESTIONS

1. Why is axonometric projection used in given situations rather than multiple view orthographic (MVO) projection?
2. How many different viewing situations can be defined in the axonometric scheme?
3. What are the three basic subschemes of axonometric?
4. Where is the illustrator positioned relative to the viewing plane in the axonometric scheme?

5. Why do the receding axes in isometric recede at a 30° angle to horizontal? Your answer involves the goemetry of isometric.

6. How much are dimensions foreshortened in isometric? Why? Is it necessary to use the foreshortened values? Why or why not?

7. What is the best viewing position for constructing an isometric drawing of an object?

8. In isometric, are the three faces of the object shown emphasized equally? If not, which face(s) is (are) emphasized most? Least?

9. Describe briefly the box method for constructing an isometric. Why is this technique so important?

10. Is the center line layout method as important as the box method? Why or why not?

11. What is the difference between an oblique and an inclined surface?

12. What is an isometric line? An isometric plane?

13. Are angles often true measure in both isometric *and* MVO projection? Why or why not?

14. Describe the four-center method for constructing an ellipse.

15. What are ellipse guides? Name two types. Why are they useful?

16. What is dimetric projection?

17. Can we emphasize faces of an object in dimetric? How is this possible?

18. What is an asymmetrical dimetric? A symmetrical dimetric?

19. Define dimetric projection.

20. In choosing axes positions for dimetric, should angles or scales be chosen first? Why? Can *either* be chosen first?

21. How many different scales are used in dimetric?

22. Describe the projection technique used to determine angle ellipse values for the three faces of a dimetric drawing.

23. Describe trimetric projection.

24. What is the advantage of using trimetric as opposed to isometric? What are some disadvantages?

25. Can you see an advantage in using true axonometric projection?

PROBLEMS

1. Draw an isometric cube with sides $2\frac{1}{8}$ in. long.

2. Draw, in isometric, a rectangular plate (3 in. × 2 in. × $\frac{1}{4}$ in. thick). Centered in the plate is a 1-in. hole.

3. The object in Fig. P2.1 is to be drawn in isometric. Do not include dimensions. Use box construction. Measurements are in inches.

4. Draw the object in Fig. P2.2 in isometric. Use box construction. Measurements are in inches.

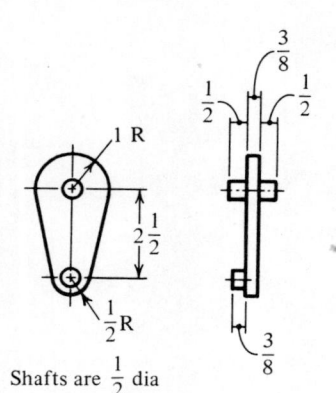

Figure P2.3

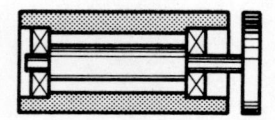

Figure P2.4

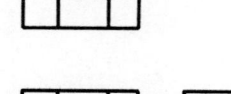

Figure P2.5

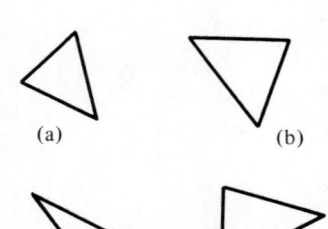

Figure P2.6

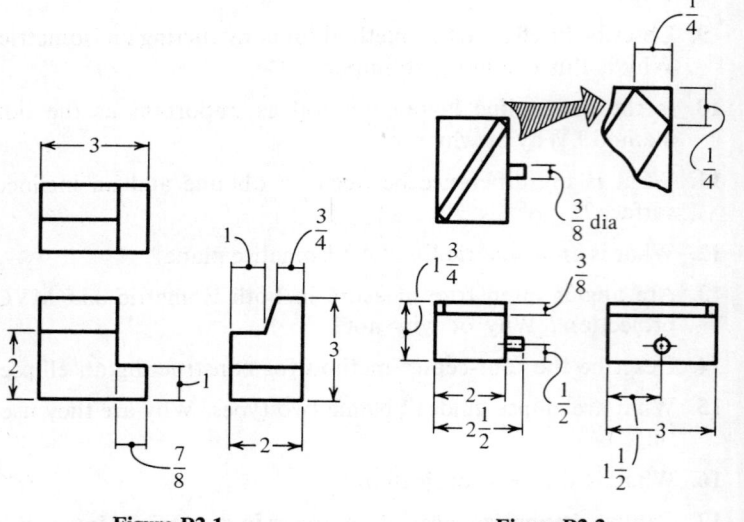

Figure P2.1

Figure P2.2

5. The object in Fig. P2.3 lends itself well to using the center line layout construction in isometric. Using that method of construction, make an isometric drawing of the object. Measurements are in inches.

6. Using the box construction method, make an isometric drawing of the object in Fig. P2.4. Choose your own scale.

7. The shaft-bearing cylinder assembly in Fig. P2.5 is to be drawn in isometric section. Choose an appropriate scale.

8. Draw the triangles in Fig. P2.6 in each of the three isometric planes. Scale should be 2:1.

9. Make an isometric drawing of the objects in Fig. P2.7. Choose any convenient scale.

10. The object in Fig. P2.8 is to be drawn in isometric. Use box construction. Measurements are in inches.

11. Make an isometric drawing of the object shown in Fig. P2.9. Use box construction. Measurements are in inches.
12. Construct an ellipse using the following methods:
    (a) Four-center
    (b) Point-by-point plot
    (c) Diagonal

The ellipse is to have a major axis 4 in. long and a minor axis $2\frac{1}{4}$ in. long.

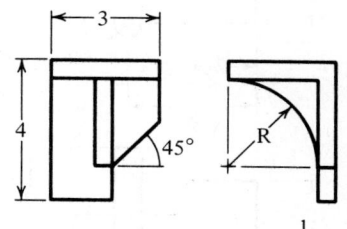

Web and angle thickness is $\frac{1}{2}$ in.

Figure P2.8

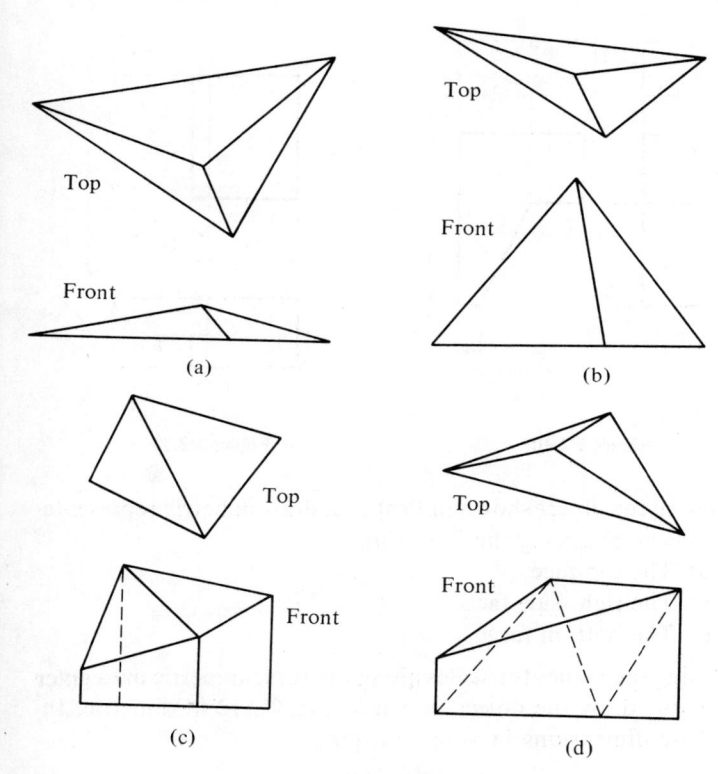

Figure P2.7

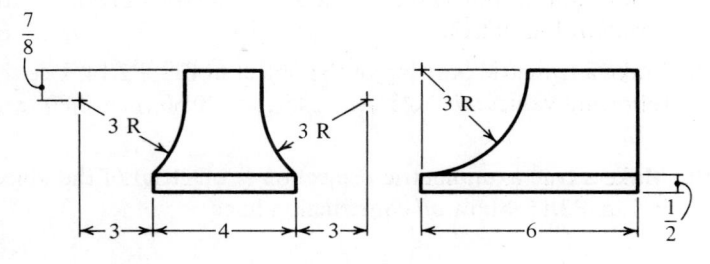

Figure P2.9

58 / Chap. 2
Axonometric Projection

13. Make an isometric drawing of the object in Fig. P2.10 and dimension the drawing using the aligned method. Trace the drawing and dimension it using the unidirectional method.

14. The simple object in Fig. P2.11 is to be drawn in dimetric.
    (a) First, draw an asymmetrical dimetric.
    (b) Next draw a symmetrical dimetric. *Note:* Do not use 30° receding axes.

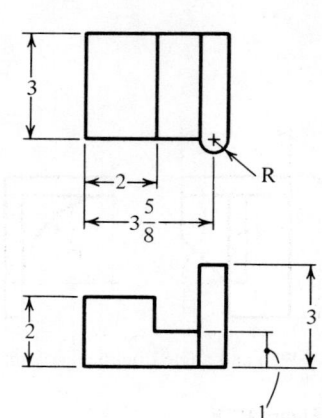

Figure P2.12

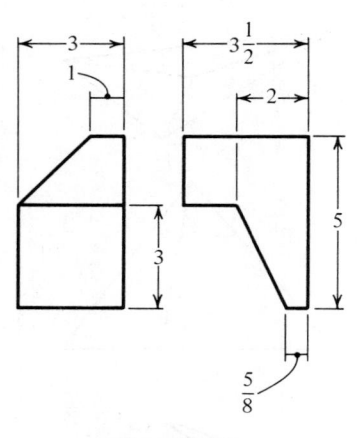

Figure P2.10

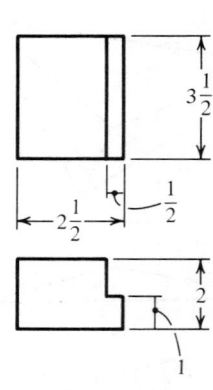

Figure P2.11

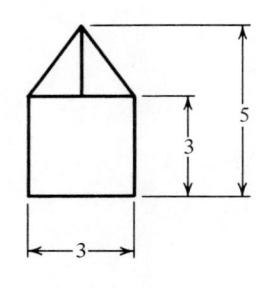

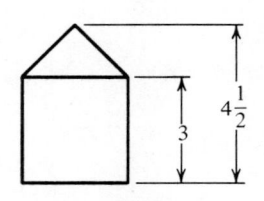

Figure P2.13

15. Using the object shown in Prob. 14, draw dimetric representations emphasizing the following:
    (a) The top face
    (b) The right-side face
    (c) The bottom face

16. Using the values for scales along the three dimetric axes given below, draw the object shown in Fig. P2.12 in dimetric. Include dimensions in your drawing.

$$L = \tfrac{3}{4}, \quad R = \tfrac{3}{4}, \quad H = 1$$

17. Using values from Table 2.2, make a trimetric drawing of the object in Fig. P2.13.

18. Make a trimetric drawing of the object in Fig. P2.14. Use the following values: $\theta = 25°$, $\phi = 45°$, $x = 0.80$, $y = 0.90$, $z = 0.72$.

19. Make a true axonometric projection (isometric) of the object in Fig. P2.15. Show *all* construction lines.

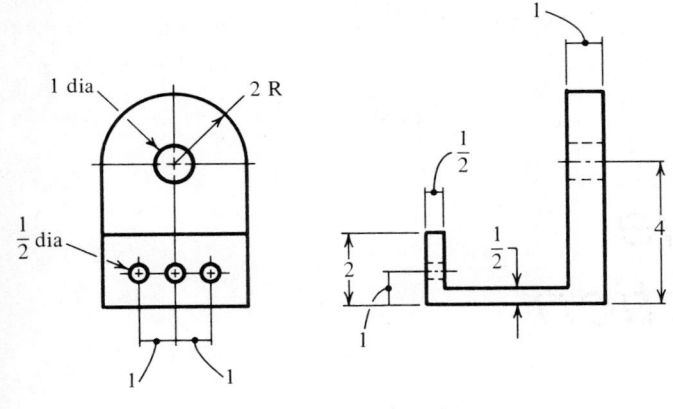

Figure P2.15

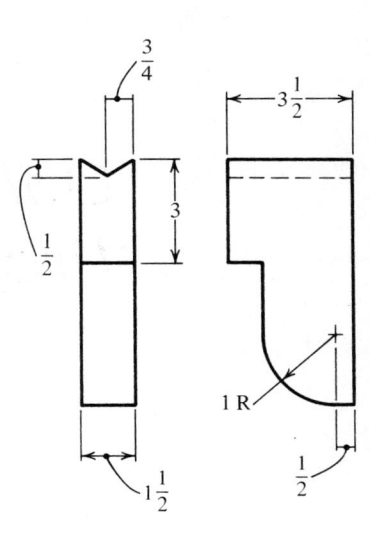

Figure P2.14

20. Make a true axonometric projection (dimetric) of the object in Prob. 19.
21. Make a true axonometric projection (trimetric) of the object in Prob. 19.
22. Problems as assigned by instructor from Appendix H.

3

Oblique Projection

In previous chapters, multiple view orthographic and axonometric projection have been discussed. We saw that orthographic projection employed multiple plane views to describe three-dimensional objects, whereas axonometric simulated three dimensions by employing a scheme that showed three faces of an object simultaneously. In the oblique projection scheme a cross between orthographic and axonometric is used. If we were to draw the front view of an object (orthographic) and project along a receding axis to show depth, an oblique projection results.

In the language of the illustrator, the oblique projection scheme is described as follows: By being positioned an infinite distance from the object (projectors are thus parallel) and directing our line of sight such that projectors are *oblique* to the viewing plane will produce an oblique projection. As a general rule, one of the principle planes of the object is parallel to the viewing plane* (see Fig. 3.1).

This one fact (one principal plane of the object being parallel to the viewing plane) is in some cases reason enough

---

*We are not, however, required to place a face parallel to the viewing plane. In Sec. 3H we see a special case (clinographic) that does not conform to the "general" rule.

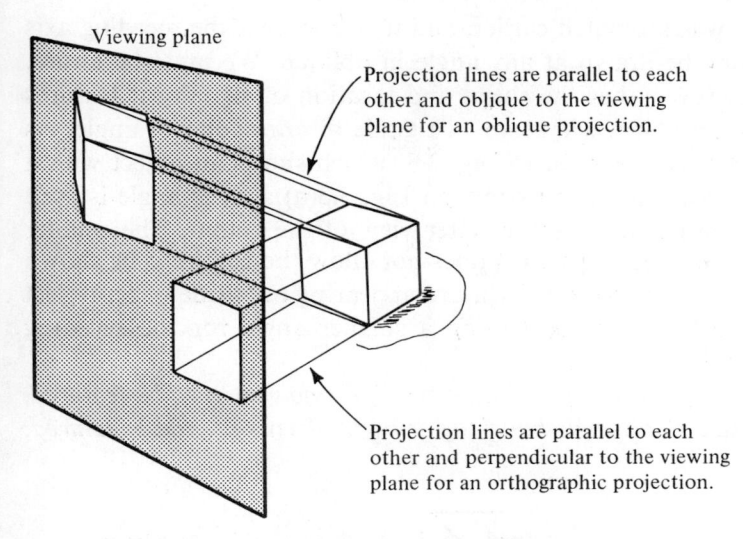

Figure 3.1 Oblique projection geometry.

to employ oblique projection to present a pictorial drawing. As an example, consider the object shown in Fig. 3.2(a). We see immediately that to represent this thin, link-like object in axonometric calls for liberal use of ellipses, as in Fig. 3.2(b), because nearly every line is circular. Because a projection scheme that places one principal object plane in the viewing plane is available, the front view of this link-like object may be drawn in orthographic projection, thus eliminating ellipses. Life is much easier under these circumstances. Figure 3.2(c) is an oblique drawing of the object shown in (a). The object is well represented and a great deal of time and effort was saved by using this scheme.

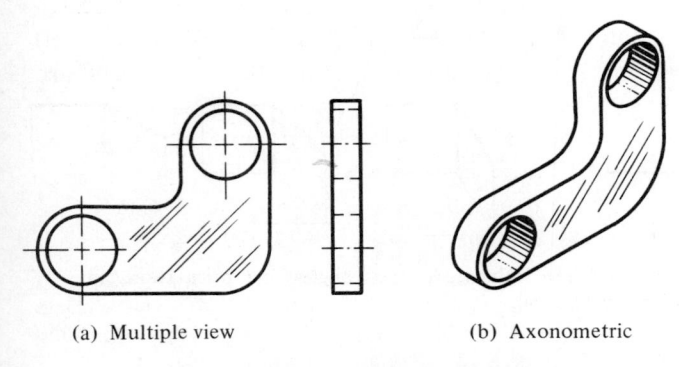

(a) Multiple view   (b) Axonometric   (c) Oblique

Figure 3.2 An object to be drawn in a pictorial scheme.

3A
Receding Axis Angle

It was intimated earlier, and it is true, that the receding axis may be drawn at any angle in oblique. We must be aware, however, that the shape and location of significant features of an object will serve as a guide to our choice of angle. As an example, refer to Fig. 3.3, which shows an object with a square cutout in its top. In Fig. 3.3(a) a large angle is used in order to obtain a better view of the cutout. The smaller angle used in part (b) does not allow the cutout to be shown as well. Similarly, a feature appearing on a side of an object will be shown best using a smaller angle for the receding axis.

A simple rule of thumb is *if a side view is to be featured, use a small angle but if top or bottom views are to be featured,*

(a) Receding axis at 45°   (b) Receding axis at 30°

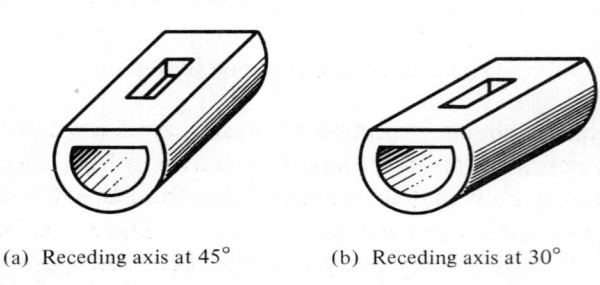

Figure 3.3 In oblique, the angle at which the receding axis lies affects emphasis on faces of the object being featured.

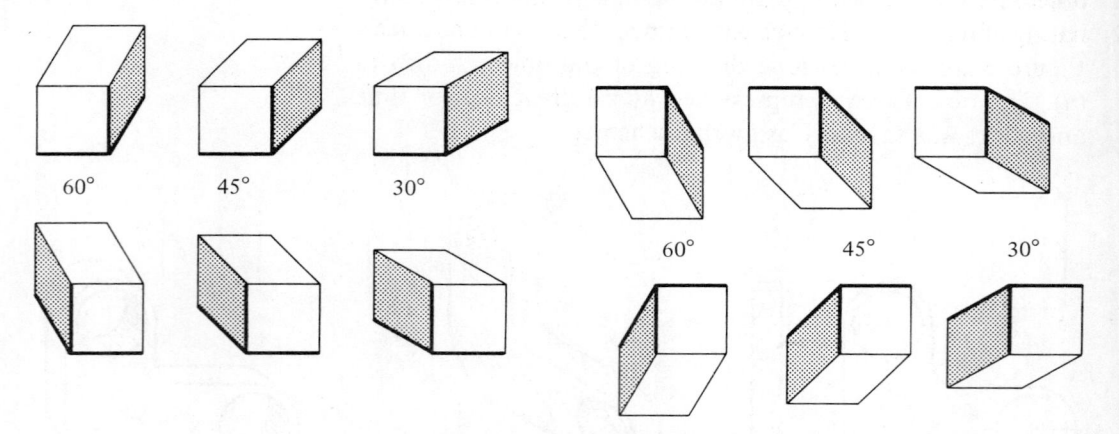

60°   45°   30°

60°   45°   30°

Figure 3.4 The influence of axis angles and orientations in oblique projection.

use a large angle. The groupings in Fig. 3.4 illustrate this rule of thumb. Notice that when a large angle (60°) is used, top or bottom surfaces are featured and when a small angle (30°) is used, side surfaces are featured. If a 45° receding axis is employed, top (or bottom) and side views are emphasized equally.

3B Length of Receding Lines

Because we see objects in perspective (receding, parallel lines converge to a point) in everyday circumstances, an oblique drawing will appear unnatural. The degree to which "built-in" distortion is unpleasant depends on several factors: The angle at which receding lines are drawn, the shape of the object, and the length of receding lines when compared with full measure lengths in the viewing plane.

In Fig. 3.5(a), receding lines are drawn full length resulting in a drawing of a cube that does not look like a cube: The receding lines appear to be too long and to *diverge* as we progress from the front to the back of the cube. Our eyes tell us that the cube is represented by a "perspective" in which the vanishing point is *between* us and the object—a seldom-used scheme.* In Fig. 3.5(b), distortion is reduced but the cube still appears too deep. By foreshortening the depth measurements to $\frac{5}{8}$ and $\frac{1}{2}$ of full size in Fig. 3.5(c) and (d), respectively, the more cube-like appearance sought is attained. In Fig. 3.5(e), foreshortening to $\frac{3}{8}$ of full size is too drastic but distortion is not evident.

In the case of true length receding lines we have what is

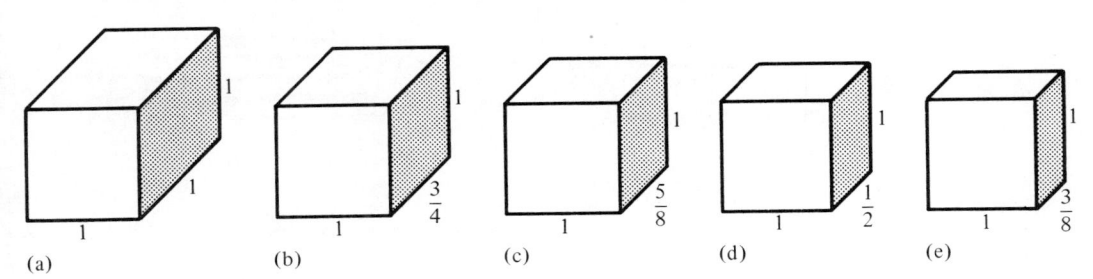

Figure 3.5 Comparison of lengths of receding axes in oblique.

*Think about this statement. Then sketch the "perspective" scene described. The statement *does not* imply that one-point perspective is seldom used.

(a) Cavalier projection (b) Cabinet projection

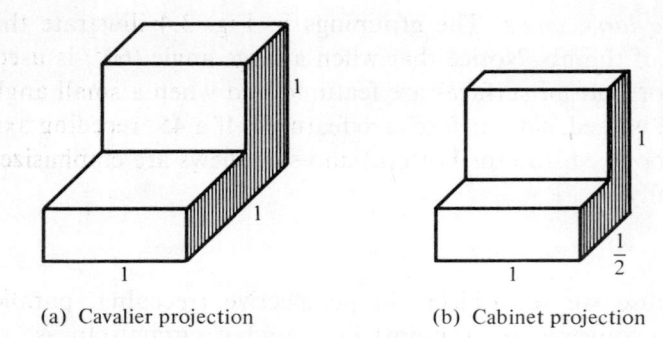

Figure 3.6 Comparison of cavalier and cabinet oblique drawings.

called a *cavalier projection*,† Fig. 3.6(a). If a one-half of true length receding scale is used, the resultant drawing is called a *cabinet projection*,† Fig. 3.6(b).

3C Positions of Objects

Each object represented in oblique is a special case, but general statements can be made concerning the position of objects relative to the viewing plane. Figure 3.7(a) is a classic example of how *not* to use an oblique drawing. In general, it may be stated that objects characterized by great length

(a) Oblique (b) Perspective

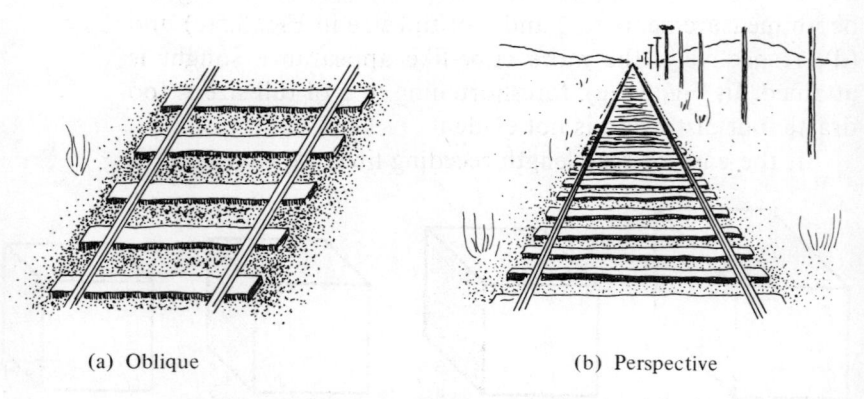

Figure 3.7 The use and misuse of oblique—a classic case.

†For those interested in history, the origin of the two oblique projections, cavalier and cabinet, are presented. During medieval times, drawings of fortifications (made on horizontal projection planes) depicted the central portion of the fortification as being highest. This central portion was dominant and was, as a result, called *cavalier*. Cabinet projections derive from the early use of such projections in the furniture industry.

should not be drawn in oblique with the long dimension along the receding axis.

Other examples will give insight as to proper positioning of objects. Recall that one principal plane usually is parallel to the viewing plane in oblique. Because of this fact, we can place features in this plane and draw them easily. If we were to place these same features in the plane of the receding axis, we increase the difficulty of executing the drawing. The three objects shown in Fig. 3.8 demonstrate proper positioning.

We should see immediately that Fig. 3.8(a) is preferable to (b), (c) is preferable to (d), and (e) is preferable to (f). In (a) and (c), circular contours are parallel to the viewing plane and the object looks natural. (An illustrator should always strive for natural appearance.) In (b) and (d) the circular contours look unnatural and are difficult to draw. In (e) circular bend corners are in the viewing plane and the long dimension of the object is *parallel to the viewing plane*, resulting in a natural appearance. In (f) the long dimension of the object is normal to the viewing plane (along the receding axis) and all radii are shown as ellipses. The object appears longer than it really is, is unnatural in appearance, and the drawing is difficult to execute.

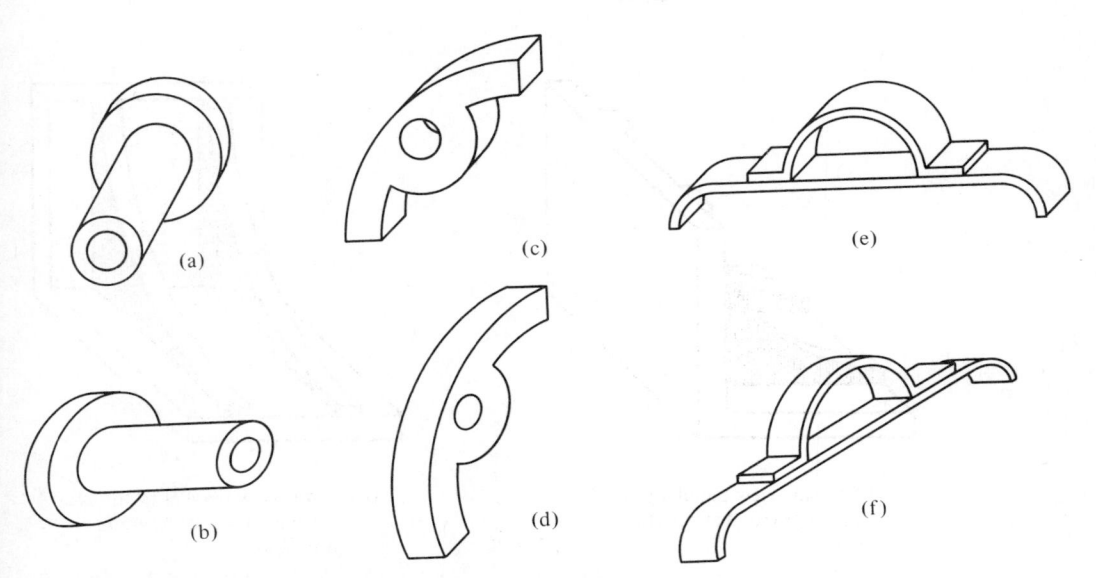

Figure 3.8 Proper and improper positioning of objects in oblique.

3D Offset Measurements

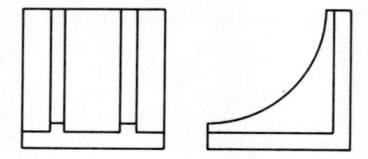

Figure 3.9
Two curved webs present a problem in oblique. How do we show them?

In many instances, we will be drawing objects composed of surfaces that are circular or curved and lying in planes parallel to either the viewing plane or oblique planes. Those parallel to the viewing plane are drawn as if a front orthographic view were being made. A different tact must be employed if an object such as the one in Fig. 3.9 is to be drawn in oblique.

First, the position from which we wish to view the object is chosen. If the right-side view is positioned parallel to the viewing plane, the curved webs are easy to draw, but the object is not shown to good advantage—Fig. 3.10(a). Rather than accept an unsuitable position, we will use Fig. 3.10(b). The two webs are now a problem. How do we draw them?

The wise reader has probably surmised that we will use a series of planes and offset measurements to construct the webs. Figure 3.11 illustrates the step-by-step procedure.

Two important facts should be kept in mind when employing offset measurement construction

1. If a receding scale of less than full measure is used (as in cabinet oblique), offset measurements *parallel* to the receding axis must be made using the reduced scale.

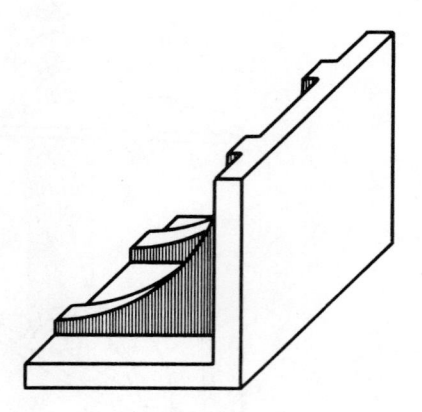

(a) Right side view parallel to the viewing plane. Webs partially hidden.

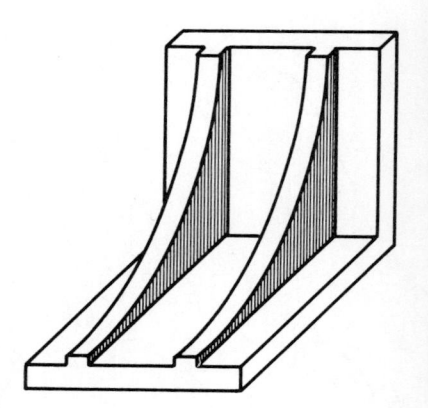

(b) Front view parallel to the viewing plane. Webs are in full view.

Figure 3.10 Two possible oblique views of the bracket.

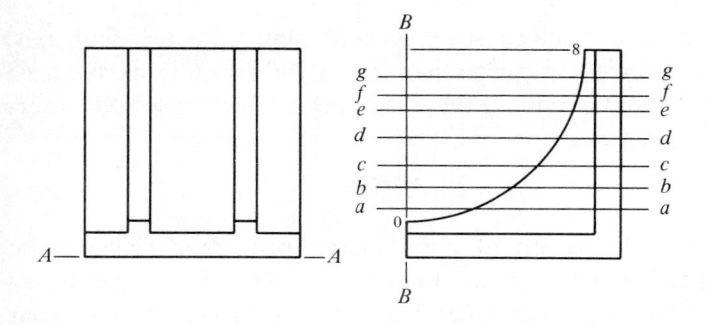

(a) Pass a series of planes through the object at various distances above base plane $A-A$. These do not need to be equally spaced planes.

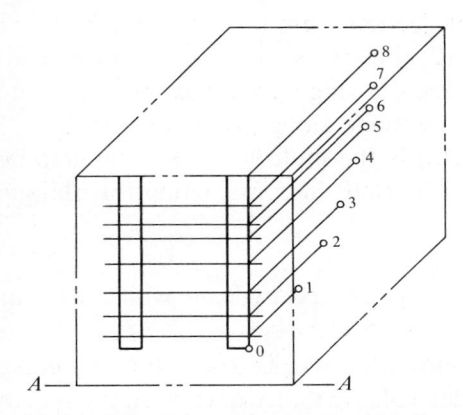

(b) Draw the minimum size box in which the object will fit. Locate planes $a-a$ through $g-g$ in the front face of the box. Draw the webs on the front face of the box. At the points of intersection of the webs and planes, draw lines parallel to the receding axis. Transfer distances from plane $B-B$, locating points 1–7. Points 0 and 8 are located automatically.

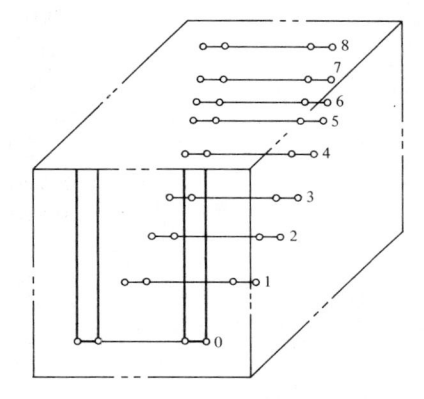

(c) Draw lines parallel to plane $A-A$, through points 0–8. Draw lines parallel to the receding axis at intersection points as was done in (b). Now points on each edge of both webs are located. Intersection lines are omitted here to avoid confusion.

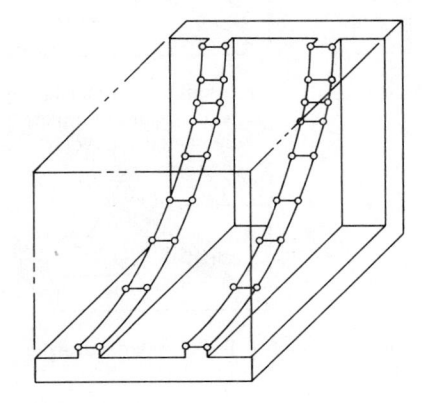

(d) Complete the outline of the object. Using an irregular curve, draw a smooth curve through points 0–8 to form the webs.

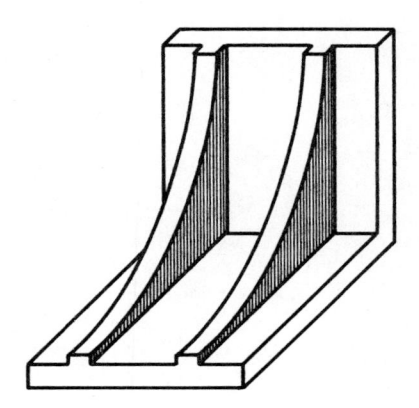

(e) The completed illustration.

Figure 3.11 Constructing curved webs using offset measurements.

68 / Chap. 3
Oblique Projection

2. If a reduced scale is used along the receding axis, circles on planes parallel to the receding axis can be drawn only by the offset measurement method—four-center ellipse construction will not work.

3E
Construction Methods

In our discussion of axonometric projection schemes we learned that two basic, interrelated methods for constructing objects are available: The box and the center line layout methods. In oblique projection these same two methods are applicable. Figure 3.12 illustrates the steps required to execute a cavalier oblique drawing by the box method. Note that all measurements are made along principal axes.

Shown in Fig. 3.12(a) is the multiple view orthographic drawing of the object. The steps in constructing the oblique drawing are

1. Draw the minimum-size rectangle in which we can inscribe the front face of the object.
2. At any angle θ, draw the receding axis lines to complete a rectangular volume that will enclose the object [Fig. 3.12(b)]. Remember that the drawing is a cavalier

(a) Multiple view drawing

(b) Inscribe front face in the rectangle and complete the rectangular volume

(c) Complete the drawing of the object by measuring depths

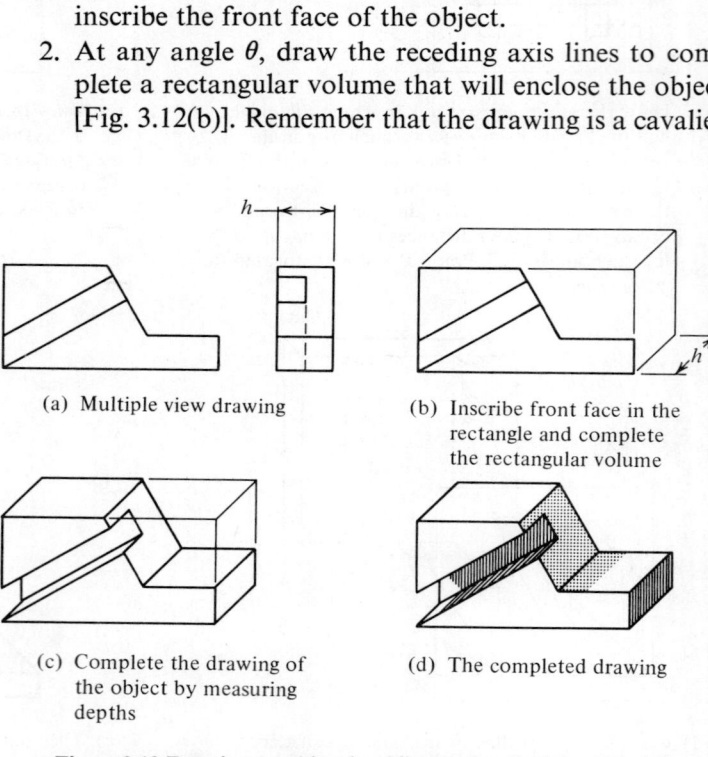

(d) The completed drawing

Figure 3.12 Drawing an object in oblique using the box method for construction.

drawing so we measure *full scale* along the receding axis—dimension h in Fig. 3.12(a) equals dimension h in Fig. 3.12(b).
3. Lay off all the dimensions [Fig. 3.12(c)].
4. Darken the object lines and remove construction lines [Fig. 3.12(d)].

The other method mentioned, center line layout, is applicable in oblique when an object such as the one shown in Fig. 3.13 is to be drawn. Note that this object has three axial center lines from which faces and features may be located. To illustrate the center line layout method for constructing an oblique pictorial drawing, we perform the construction of this object step-by-step in Fig. 3.14.

1. Starting with point A, draw a receding axis line at any angle θ. From the multiple view drawing, determine the size of and lay off the bolt circle (dia S) and locate points a, b, c, and d. Next locate points B and G along the receding axis. These distances are obtained from the multiple view drawing. Note that all faces parallel to the viewing plane are not coplanar. We must, therefore, locate points E and F by offset mea-

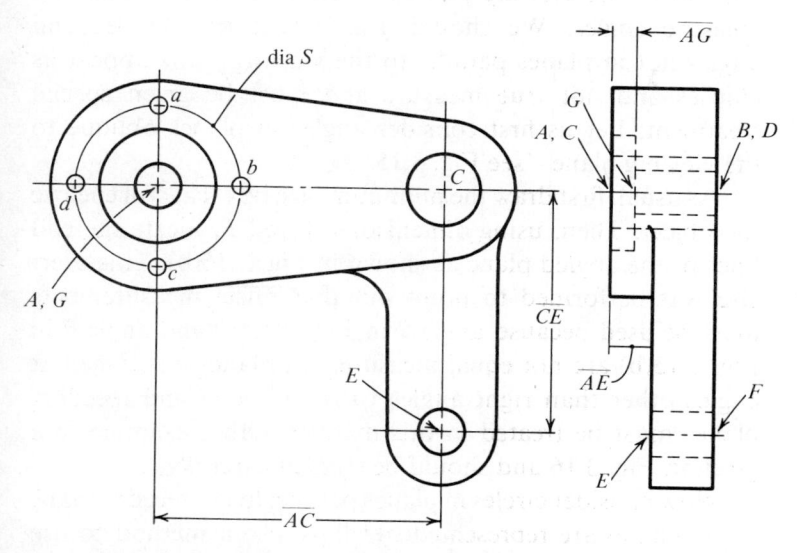

Figure 3.13 An object that can be drawn in oblique by using the center line layout method for construction.

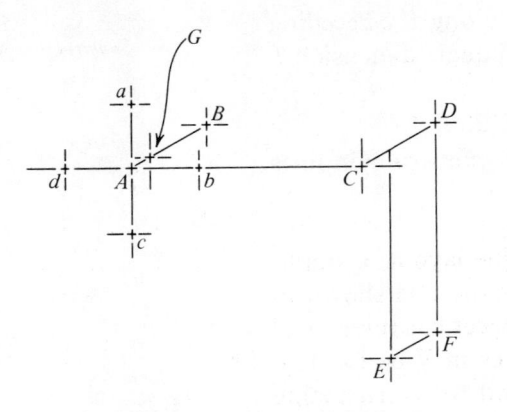

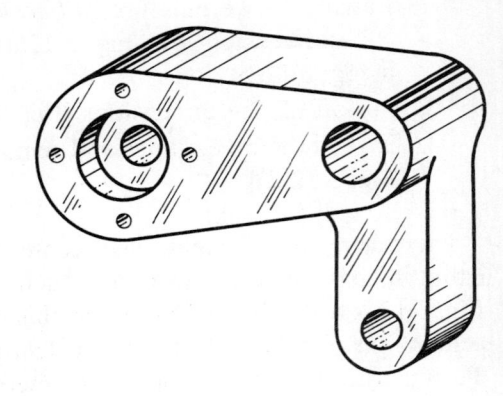

(a) Locate all centers in proper planes   (b) Draw *circles* and tangents

Figure 3.14 Center line layout method for construction applied to oblique.

surements. Lay off distances AC and DF. Then draw the other two receding axes at angle θ.

2. After locating all centers, draw the circular outlines, darken outlines, and remove construction lines [Fig. 3.14(b)].

3F Circles and Angles

We know that circles and angles in oblique that lie in planes parallel to the viewing plane are shown as circles and true measure angles. We should also expect that circles and angles not in planes parallel to the viewing plane appear as ellipses and not true measure and must be given special treatment. Let us first consider angles in planes oblique to the viewing plane—see Fig. 3.15.

As usual, first draw the minimum-size box that will enclose the object. Then, using dimensions A and B, locate the end lines of the angled plane as shown in Fig. 3.15(b). This exercise was performed to point out that offset measurements must be used because angle θ in Fig. 3.15(a) and angle θ in Fig. 3.15(b) are not equal measure. All planes positioned at angles other than right angles to the viewing and receding planes must be treated in this manner. Other examples are given in Fig. 3.16 and should be studied carefully.

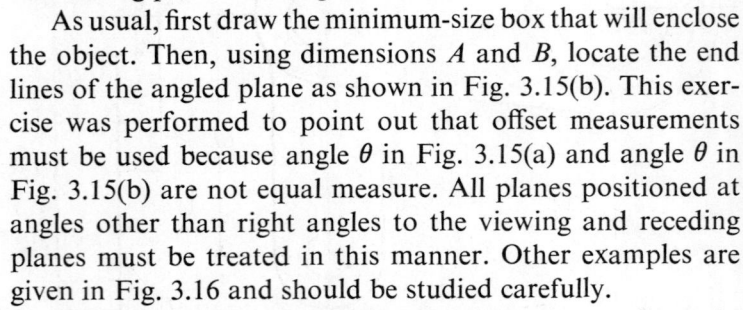

Now consider circles in planes parallel to the receding axis. These circles are represented by ellipses so a method to use in drawing ellipses must be determined. In the section on isometric drawing, three methods for constructing ellipses

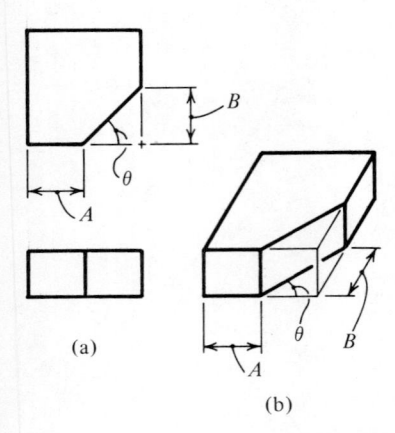

Figure 3.15 Use of offset measurements to draw an angle in oblique.

Shaded surfaces lie in principal planes

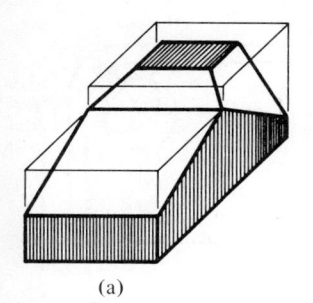

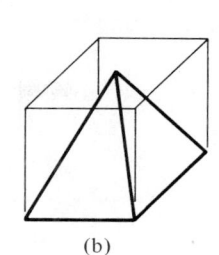

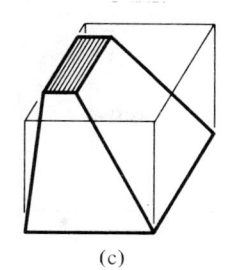

(a)   (b)   (c)

Figure 3.16 Examples of angled surfaces drawn in oblique.

were discussed: four-center, offset measurement, and diagonal. We are at liberty to use any of these three methods *if the receding scale is full size*. If the receding scale is less than full size, neither the four-center nor the diagonal method can be used—only the offset measurement method will work. We should, therefore, always be aware of the choice for receding scale values. For details on the three construction methods, refer to p. 23 in Chapter 2. Although isometric drawing is discussed there, the *method* is applicable in oblique as well.

3G
Sections and Dimensions

Occasionally we may wish to employ a section view of an object to represent interior structure of the object. Because full sections rarely show the exterior of the object well, a half-section, shown in Fig. 3.17, will most often be best. In general, we may state that the considerations given to section views in isometric can be applied to sections in oblique.

Note direction of section lines.

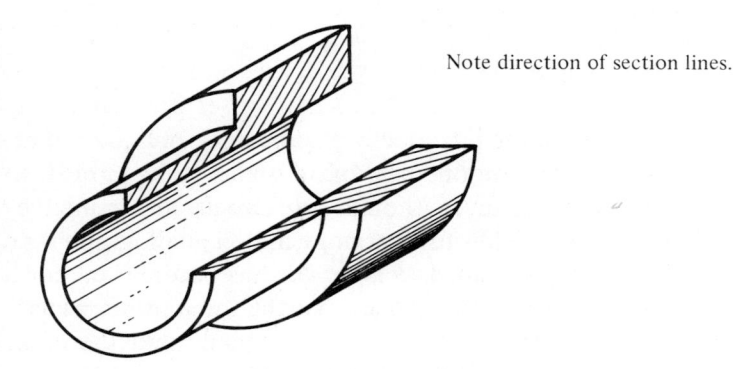

Figure 3.17 A section view in oblique.

71

(a) Aligned convention

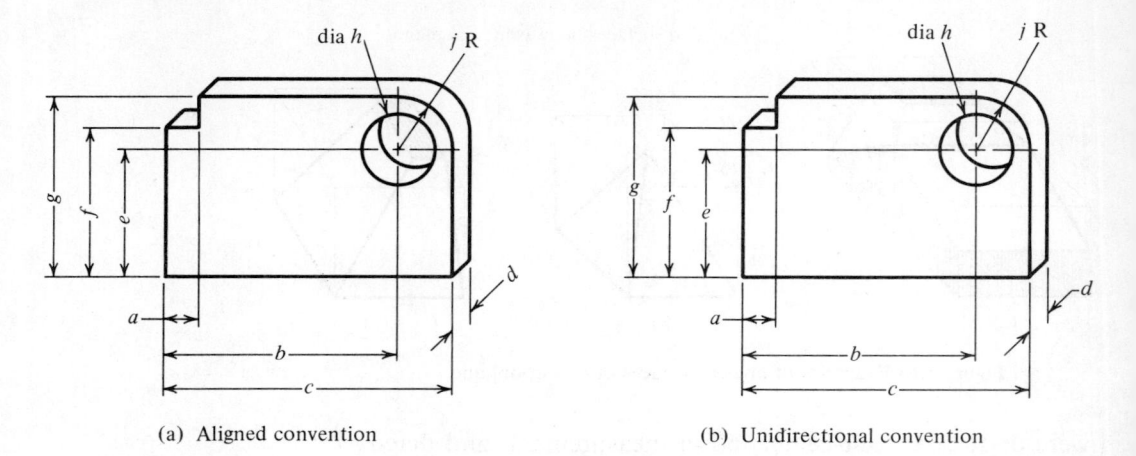

(b) Unidirectional convention

Figure 3.18 Two methods acceptable for dimensioning oblique drawings. Note dimension *d* in both methods.

When an oblique drawing must be dimensioned (Fig. 3.18), we are able to apply the same principles used in dimensioning isometric drawings

1. All dimension and extension lines must lie in or parallel to the principal planes of the object.
2. All dimensions must either lie in the planes of the object to which applied, Fig. 3.18(a), or be set so as to read from the bottom of the drawing, Fig. 3.18(b). We suggest that the unidirectional method is more practical, in that time (which equals money) is saved with no noticeable effect on quality.
3. Place no dimensions on the object, unless clarity is gained by doing so.

3H
Clinographic—A Special Case

As mentioned in the introductory comments, oblique projection does not require one face of an object to be parallel to the viewing plane, even though advantages are gained by doing so. In the field of mineralogy and crystallography, an oblique subscheme called *clinographic* has become standardized. In this scheme, the angles that the three principal axes of the crystal make with the viewing plane and the angle projectors (lines of sight) make with the viewing plane are

18°26'
Position for projection
Projectors
9°28'

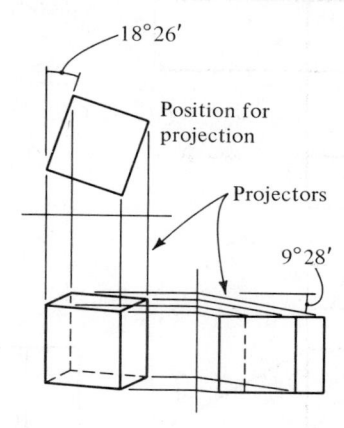

Figure 3.19 Clinographic projection—a special case of oblique.

fixed. In other words they are always the same. The angles are shown in Fig. 3.19.

QUESTIONS

1. Define (or describe) oblique projection.
2. Give two reasons for using oblique rather than trimetric, assuming either projection scheme will show the object suitably.
3. At what angle is the receding axis drawn for oblique?
4. If we wish to feature the bottom of an object, should the receding axis angle be large or small? Explain your answer.
5. What optical illusion is manifested in oblique? *Hint*: What happens to receding lines in a perspective drawing?
6. What is a cavalier projection? A cabinet projection?
7. If an object of great length is to be drawn in oblique, what general statement concerning axis–object relationship may be made?
8. Why is oblique projection advantageous to use when an object is made up of many circles and curves?
9. What is clinographic projection?

PROBLEMS

1. Make an oblique drawing of the object shown in Fig. P3.1. Use a receding axis angle of 30° and box construction. Use a receding axis scale of $\frac{1}{2}$ full size. Dimensions are given in inches.
2. The object in Fig. P3.2 is to be drawn in oblique, using a 45°

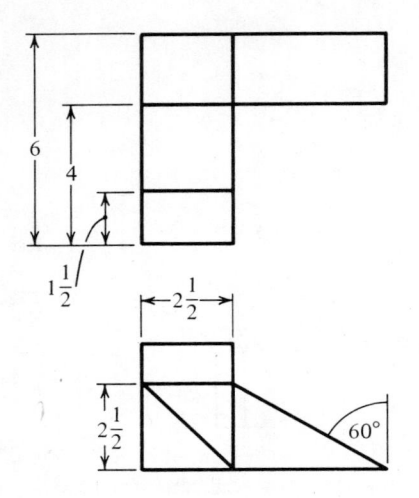

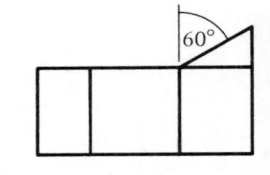

Figure P3.1

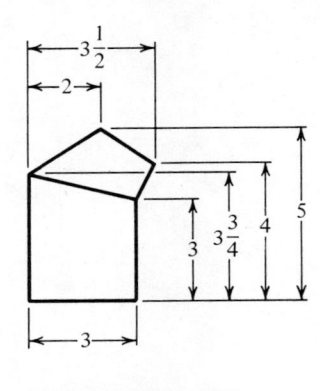

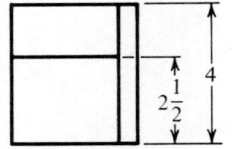

Figure P3.2

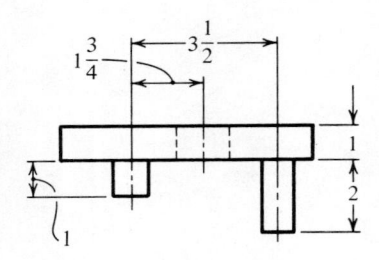

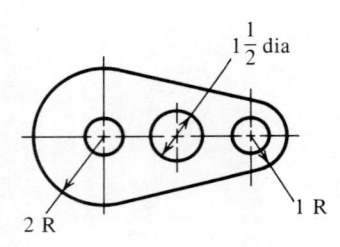

Figure P3.3

Shafts are 1 dia

receding axis angle. Use box construction. Choose your own receding axis scale. Dimensions are given in cm.

3. Make an oblique drawing of the object in Fig. P3.3. Be sure to specify your choice for receding axis angle *and* scale.
4. Make an oblique drawing of the object shown in Fig. P2.14.
5. Make a cabinet oblique for the object shown in Fig. P2.10.
6. Make a cavalier oblique for the object shown in Fig. P2.10.
7. Make an oblique drawing of the object shown in Fig. P2.8. Compare the oblique and isometric drawings. Which is a better representation (in your opinion)? Why is one better?
8. Problems as assigned by instructor from Appendix H.

4

Perspective

Most of us have heard, read, or uttered phrases in which the word *perspective* was used. More often than not we grasped immediately what was meant. For example, consider the meaning of perspective in each of the sentences that follow.

1. He is not seeing things in proper perspective.
2. My perspective of the problem is different from his.
3. A perspective drawing is more realistic than an oblique.

In sentence 1, the viewer does not see things as they really are. Perhaps he is not giving enough emphasis to an important aspect of whatever it is he is viewing.

It has long been said that no two people see the same thing in the same way. Sentence 2 reiterates this saying: He and I are looking at the problem differently. Perhaps he is examining the problem on the basis of cost, whereas I look at the problem strictly from an engineering vantage point.

The last of the three sentences is extremely important to an illustrator—it is a true statement. If we were to alter the sentence and state that a perspective drawing is more realistic than *any other* pictorial drawing scheme, the statement would still be correct. In perspective, we see things (objects or scenes) as they are, but from one particular vantage point at a time.

We have no projection scheme that can surpass perspective in ability to show a three-dimensional object in a natural condition. Each of the other schemes has a distinctive drawback: Multiple view orthographic projection requires the reader to assemble the object in his mind; axonometric projection schemes distort features of an object because convenient (as opposed to correct) scales are used on receding axes; oblique projection distorts for the same reason as axonometric. Although each of these projection schemes is useful and has a place in pictorial representation, perspective provides the most realistic representation.

When we think or speak of architecture and architectural drawing, we immediately think of perspective drawing. The architect wants his client to see a design (often a complex, beautiful structure) as it is going to be, with no distortions *inherent to the drawing scheme.* The client will usually be someone not trained in the graphic arts, so the drawings must be "real" and not an exercise in imagination. We can apply these same criteria to pictorial drawings in scientific disciplines.

4A
Use of Perspective Drawings

As we stated, architecture and perspective drawing are synonymous. As illustrators we seldom will be called upon to make an architectural rendering or drawing and because architectural drawing is a study in itself, we will not discuss perspective drawings relative to architecture. Several references are listed at the end of this chapter and although the references emphasize architecture, much practical knowledge (which can be applied to *any* perspective drawing) is contained in the texts.

Because a perspective drawing of an object represents the object as we would see it from a *particular* viewing point and gives us the most realistic drawing, we might think that perspective is the saving grace of all illustrators. Unfortunately, executing a perspective drawing of a complex object is a tedious and exacting chore. If the object has many curvilinear surfaces or planes, the disadvantage of distortion inherent to the other schemes (axonometric, oblique) is more than offset by the disadvantage of time spent projecting points in perspective. Certain simple objects can be drawn easily in perspective and will be effective. No unbreakable rule can be (or has been) made concerning when to use or not to use a particular projection scheme: The illustrator must make this decision. In general, we may say that the more complex the object, the less likely it is that we should consider using a perspective drawing to represent the object.

One point should be made clear: Good perspective drawings (or, as a matter of fact, any other pictorial drawings) do not come from reading a book. Practice, patience, and attention to the principles of the scheme yield results. To execute good perspective drawings requires *devotion* to the three attributes mentioned above. We will not be overnight successes.

4B Terminology and Concepts

Because the perspective technique is unique*, terminology and concepts associated with the projection scheme are also unique. In the short descriptions and figures that follow, we will define and discuss the more common characteristics of perspective drawings and variations from drawings made using other projection schemes.

PROJECTORS

Figure 4.1 illustrates a basic difference between perspective and orthographic projection schemes. In orthographic schemes the projectors are drawn *parallel* to each other and *perpendicular* to the picture plane (*PP*) as if the viewer were stationed at an infinite distance from that plane.

In the perspective scheme neither the object nor the picture plane changes from its counterparts in the other schemes. The only change is that we (the observer) are not stationed at infinity: We are located at the station point (*SP*). As a result, projectors drawn from points on the object to our eye *converge* and *are not perpendicular* to *PP*.

---

*Isometric, dimetric, trimetric oblique and multiple view orthographic schemes have common features.

Picture plane (*PP*)

Projectors

Station point (*SP*)

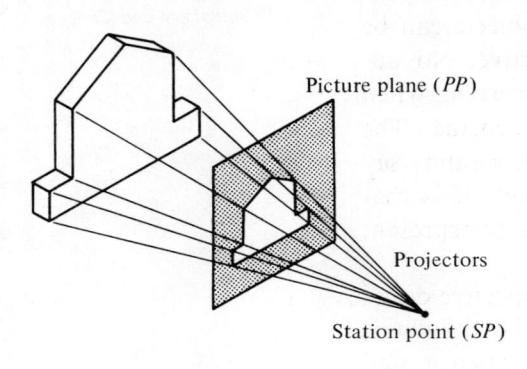

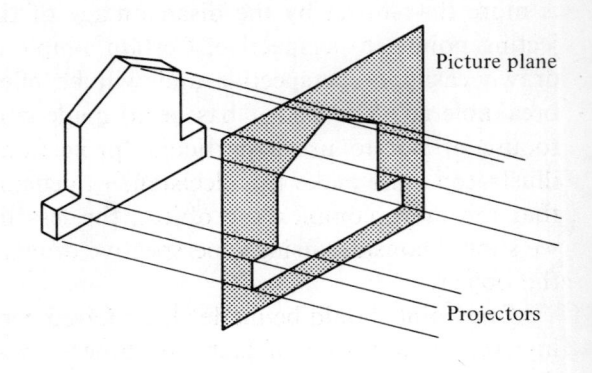

(a) Perspective: projectors converge

Picture plane

Projectors

(b) Orthographic and oblique: projectors are parallel

Figure 4.1 Comparison between perspective and orthographic and oblique projection schemes.

Shapes in perspective

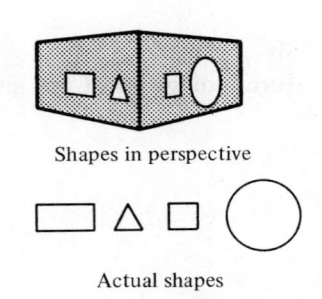

Actual shapes

Figure 4.2
Geometric shapes are as we *see* them in perspective—not as we define them.

SHAPES

If we draw the side view of an object using the multiple view scheme, squares, rectangles, circles, and other geometric shapes appear as they are defined. In other words, a square appears as an equal-sided quadrilateral with all internal angles being 90°. In perspective, these same geometric shapes are represented as we *see* them. The distinction is subtle but real. Neither angles nor areas represented in perspective usually* appear as true measure. Squares become quadrilaterals with *unequal* sides and angles that can be less than or greater than 90°. Circles are drawn as ellipses, as illustrated in Fig. 4.2.

SIZES

We saw that shapes in perspective are as we see them from *SP*. The same may be said for sizes. If we look down a row of telephone poles at the side of a road, the poles farthest from us appear to be shorter than those nearer to us. In Fig. 4.3, the pole in back of *PP* appears shorter (height = h_1) than the pole in front (height = h_2) when projected into *PP*. The pole located *in* the viewing plane is true height, *h*.

As the distance a point is located from *SP* increases, we see from Fig. 4.4 that equal widths and areas appear

---

*In some *rare* instances, when everything meets the necessary criteria, areas or angles will be true measure.

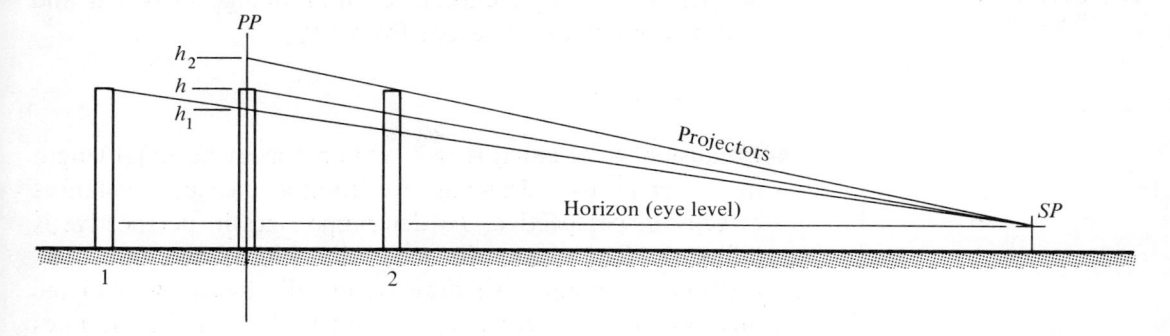

Figure 4.3 Objects in back of the picture plane (*PP*) appear to be shorter than objects in or in front of *PP*.

smaller. Area *A* is the same as area *B* (heights and widths are identical) in a multiple view drawing, but the perspective indicates that area *A* is larger. This seemingly untrue picture can be changed by changing the viewing angle. For example, two different top views of the same object are shown in Fig. 4.5. In Fig. 4.5(a) the viewing angle is small, resulting in a perspective drawing shown below the plan view, while in (b) the viewing angle is larger. The resulting per-

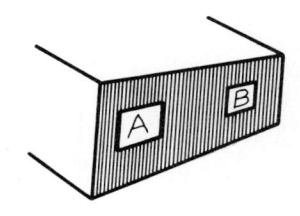

Figure 4.4 Features appear to become smaller as we recede from *SP*. This concept is referred to as *dimunition*.

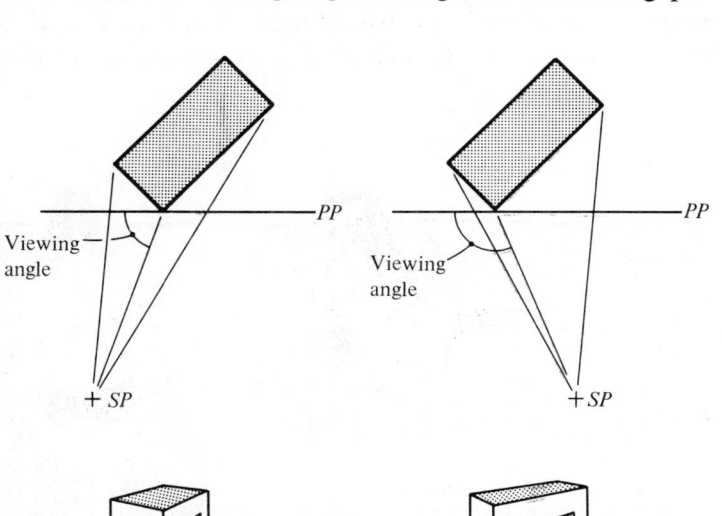

Figure 4.5 The size of the viewing angle affects a perspective drawing.

spective does not accentuate a rapid change in height and width so much as we recede from *SP*.

MEASUREMENTS

Because lines of equal length seldom appear as equal length in a perspective drawing, we cannot measure distances directly in perspective. To determine sizes in perspective is difficult. Heights are the most difficult to determine. As methods of perspective drawing are discussed, we will see methods of measurement. Remember that only those lines that lie in *PP* are true measure: All other lines are either less than or greater than true scale.

HORIZONS

Every perspective drawing has a horizon, just as every scene we view in real life has a horizon: eye level. An airline passenger flying at 10,000 feet sees a different horizon than the passenger seated in an aircraft that is awaiting take off. Further, we must always keep in mind the relationship between station point (*SP*) and the horizon. *SP* is the point at which the observer is located. Horizon is the level at which the observer's eyes are located. Figure 4.6 (a) to (c) illus-

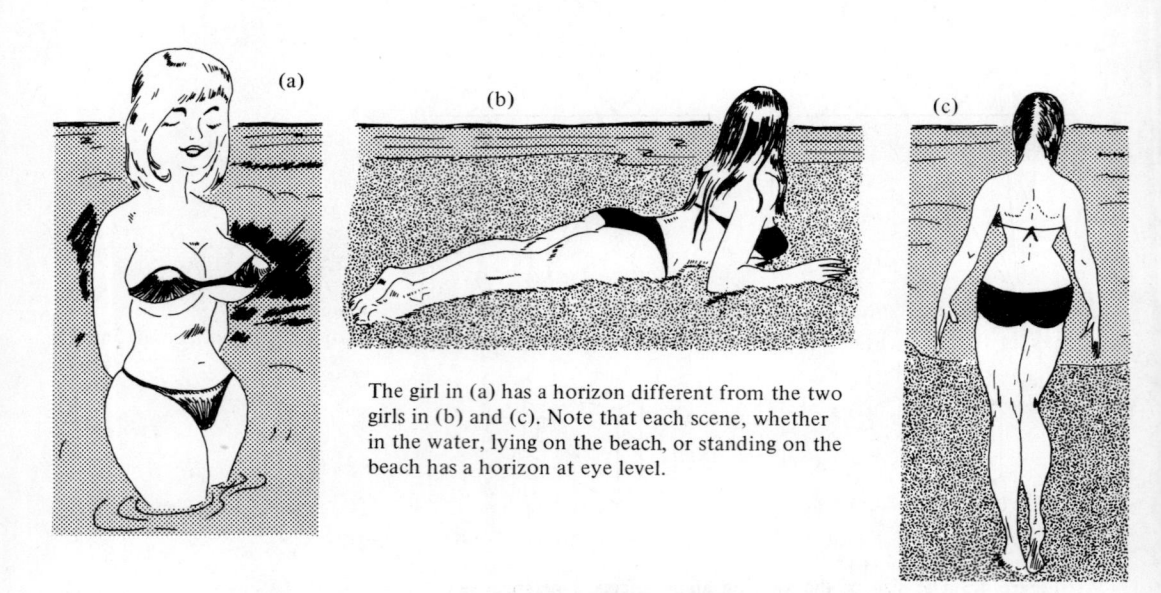

The girl in (a) has a horizon different from the two girls in (b) and (c). Note that each scene, whether in the water, lying on the beach, or standing on the beach has a horizon at eye level.

Figure 4.6 The horizon is *always* at eye level.

trates how one scene can have several horizons, depending on our position in relationship to the scene.

We look up at features above the horizon and look down at those features below the horizon. We are able to see both a ceiling and a floor in a perspective drawing if our horizon is located between the two features. *No other projection scheme can make this statement.*

Another interesting feature of perspective drawing is that by using it the illustrator can vary area sizes by merely placing the horizon different distances above or below the area. In Fig. 4.7 the same area above (or below) the horizon changes appearance, from a line at the horizon to a large area at the greatest height above the horizon.

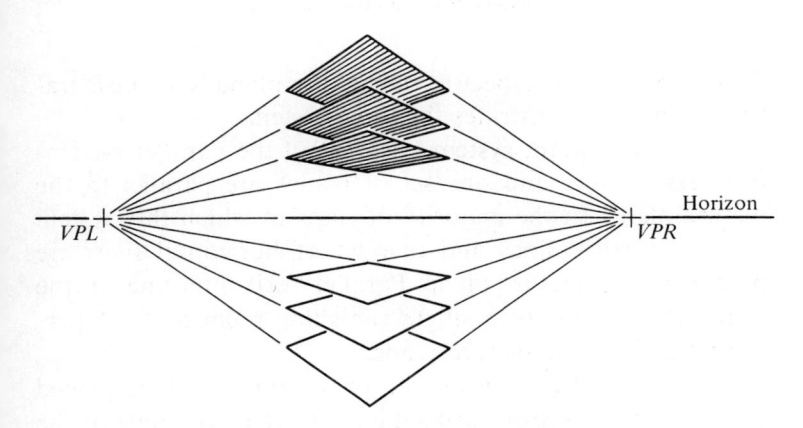

Figure 4.7 Horizontal areas change in appearance as the distance above and below the horizon changes. At the horizon, a horizontal area is a line.

VANISHING POINTS

Every set of parallel lines *not in the picture plane* converges to a point called a *vanishing point* (*VP*). If the set of converging lines is horizontal, as in Fig. 4.8, the vanishing point is located on the horizon line. In later discussions we will see how to determine the location of vanishing points.

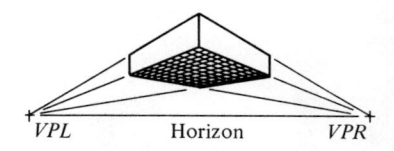

Figure 4.8 Two sets of horizontal lines converge to vanishing points, which are (in this case) located on the horizon.

Perspective systems are classified in a logical manner: The number of vanishing points used to make a drawing determines the name of the system being used, i.e., one-point, two-point, or three-point system. In addition, the position

4C
Perspective Systems

Morris Fig. 4.9
P width

(a) One-point   (b) Two-point   (c) Three-point

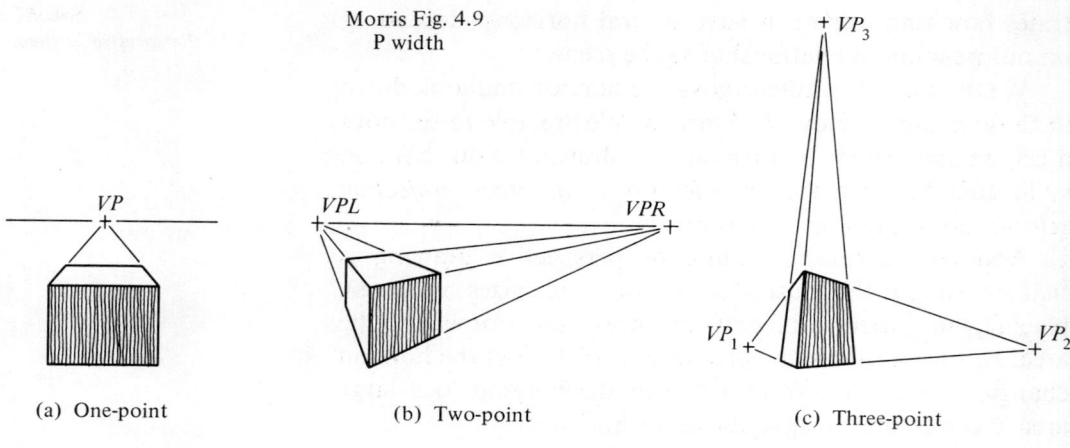

Figure 4.9 Perspective systems.

of the object with respect to the picture plane is a consideration. Figure 4.9 illustrates the three systems.

In the one-point system (also called the parallel system) two sets of lines and one set of planes are parallel to the picture plane. In the majority of cases in which this system is used, vertical lines and one set of horizontal lines are parallel to the picture plane. Parallel horizontal lines in the third set converge to a single vanishing point and are perpendicular* to the picture plane.

An object drawn using the two-point system is placed such that both sets of horizontal lines are at an angle to the picture plane. Vertical lines are parallel to the picture plane. Horizontal lines converge to their respective vanishing points.

Going one step further in three-point perspective, the object is tilted with respect to the viewing plane such that all three sets of lines converge to their respective vanishing points.

Before we proceed to discuss these methods, the important points below should be examined carefully.

1. Before attempting to execute a perspective drawing, an illustrator should be *thoroughly familiar* with the principles of multiple view orthographic projection. To learn perspective techniques without knowing these principles is extremely difficult.

*The lines may not *look* parallel but by definition they are.

2. Practice makes perfect—or nearly so. No one can learn how to make a perspective drawing unless he practices. Books can tell *how* but cannot *do*.
3. Executing perspective drawings is the most tedious and demanding (both in time and accuracy) of all pictorial schemes. We must never be in a hurry to complete a perspective drawing and hope to produce an accurate drawing that is well done.

ONE-POINT PERSPECTIVE

Because only *one* set of lines converges to a vanishing point, a logical name for one system is *one-point perspective*. A box-type building (shown in Fig. 4.10) will be used to illustrate the simple steps involved in executing a one-point perspective drawing using the *common method*.

First, we make a plan* view that includes the position of the station point. Note that the front face of the building lies in the picture plane and, therefore, is shown full scale in the perspective drawing. We are at liberty to place *SP* where we like, but the following general rule should be adhered to: *The minimum distance from the object to SP should be measured such that all parts of the object lie within a 60° cone of rays drawn from SP*. A minimum cone of 45° is permissible but the 60° cone is preferable. Note that by

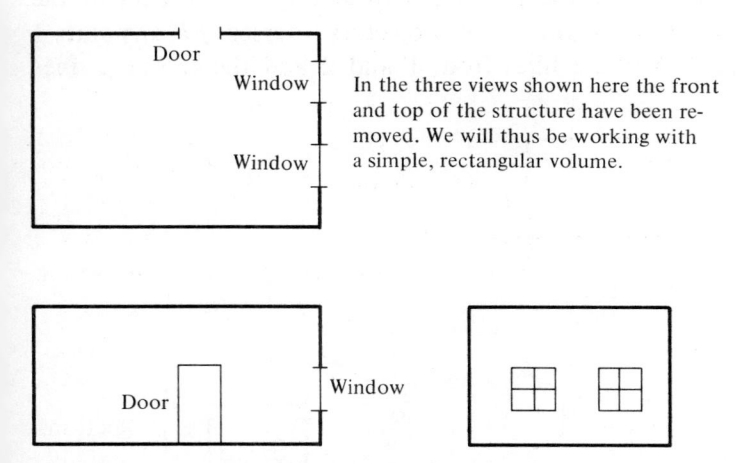

In the three views shown here the front and top of the structure have been removed. We will thus be working with a simple, rectangular volume.

Figure 4.10 A building to be drawn in one-point perspective.

*Plan means top or view from the top.

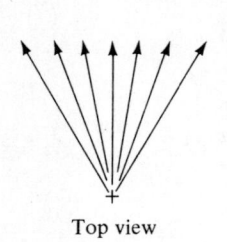

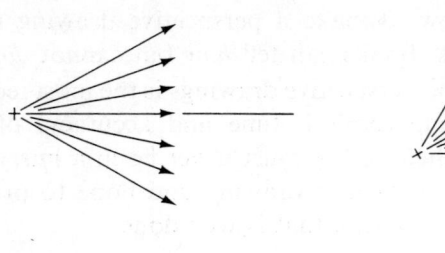

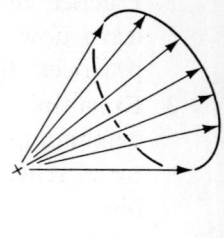

Top view   Side view   The cone of rays

Figure 4.11 Because we speak of a *60° cone of rays*, we imply three dimensions. Thus, a plan *and* an elevation view are needed to draw in perspective.

saying *cone of rays* we imply three dimensions, as shown in Fig. 4.11.

After we draw the plan view and place *PP*, the horizon is located with respect to an elevation of the object as shown in Fig. 4.12.

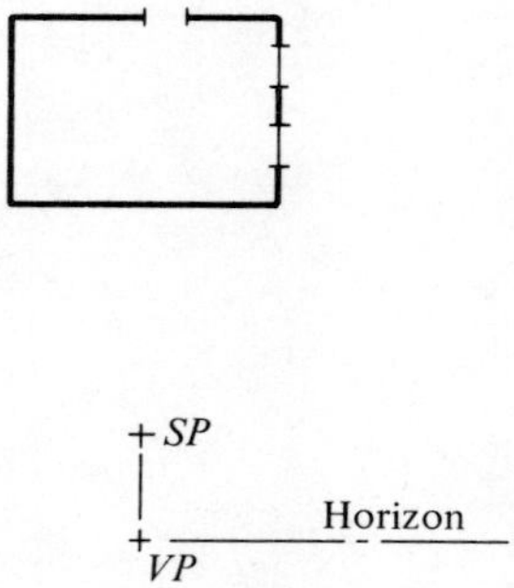

As a third step in making a one-point perspective, we must draw vertical lines downward from the plan view and horizontal lines to the left from the elevation view. The intersection of these sets of lines locate points on the object that lie in the picture plane. To locate the vanishing point (*VP*), we draw a vertical line from *SP* until the line intersects the horizon line. See Fig. 4.13.

Next we draw projectors from the rear corners of the object toward *SP*. These projectors intersect *PP* at points 1 and 2. Vertical lines from 1 and 2 and the receding lines

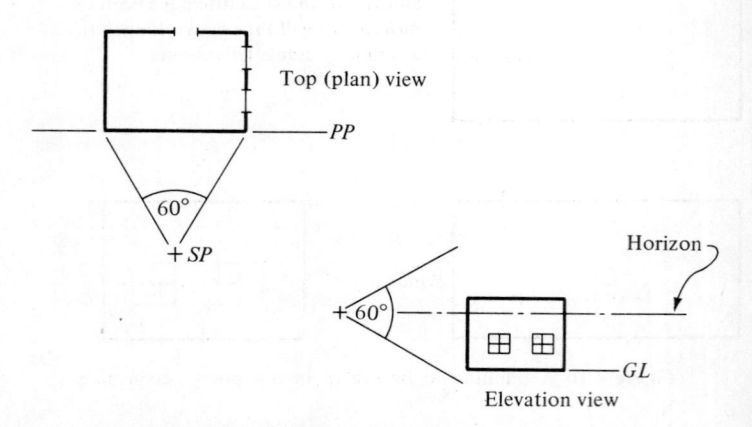

Figure 4.13 Locating the vanishing point in a one-point perspective.

Top (plan) view
— *PP*
60°
+ *SP*

Horizon
+60°
— *GL*
Elevation view

Figure 4.12 As always, the horizon is at *eye level*.

84

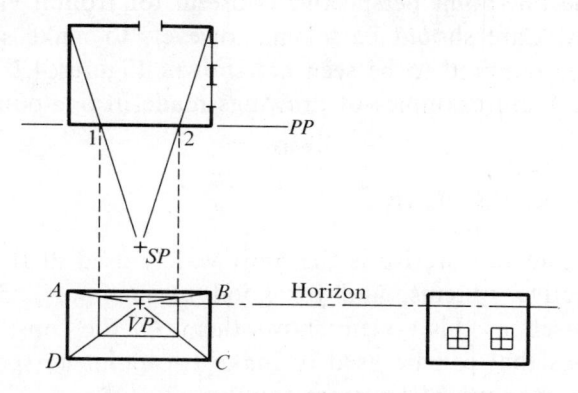

Figure 4.14 Project points from the plan and elevation views into the perspective view.

from *A, B, C,* and *D* to *VP* intersect to locate the rear surface of the object—Fig. 4.14.

The last step is to draw in details—windows and doors—as shown in Fig. 4.15. Note the construction lines used to determine heights of doors and windows.

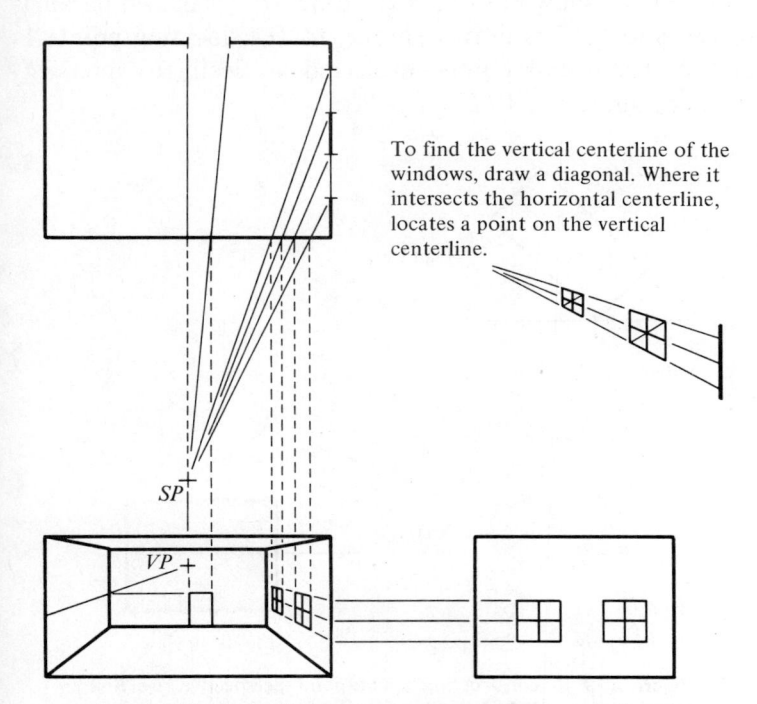

To find the vertical centerline of the windows, draw a diagonal. Where it intersects the horizontal centerline, locates a point on the vertical centerline.

Figure 4.15 Put details into the perspective view to complete the drawing.

86 / Chap. 4
Perspective

Figure 4.16
An example of the one-point perspective system representing a table. The vanishing point is located at eye level—the horizon.

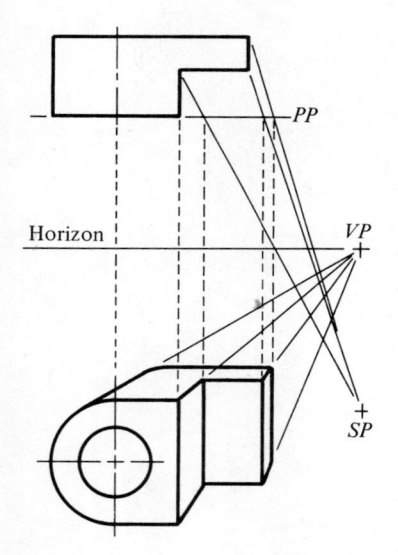

Figure 4.17
A one-point perspective drawing that resembles an oblique drawing. The circular shapes of the object are circular because the planes in which they lie are parallel to *PP*. Follow the construction in detail.

The one-point perspective is useful for frontal views of objects. Care should be taken, however, to make sure all features required to be seen are shown. Figures 4.16, 4.17, and 4.18 are examples of drawings made in one-point perspective.

TWO-POINT PERSPECTIVE

Two-point perspective is the most widely used of the three perspective systems, and for good reason—we ordinarily see objects as this system shows them. Of the construction methods that can be used to make two-point perspectives, the common method is most popular.

As in the case of a one-point perspective, we will outline a step-by-step procedure to follow in making a two-point perspective, again using the common method.

First of all, we construct a plan view and an elevation as shown in Fig. 4.19, locating a vertical edge of the object in or parallel to *PP*.

Then we locate the right and left vanishing points (*VPR* and *VPL*) as shown in Fig. 4.20: Line *SP*-1 is drawn parallel to *OB* and *SP*-2 is drawn parallel to *OA*, locating points 1 and 2. These two points, projected vertically to intersect the horizon, locate *VPL* and *VPR*.

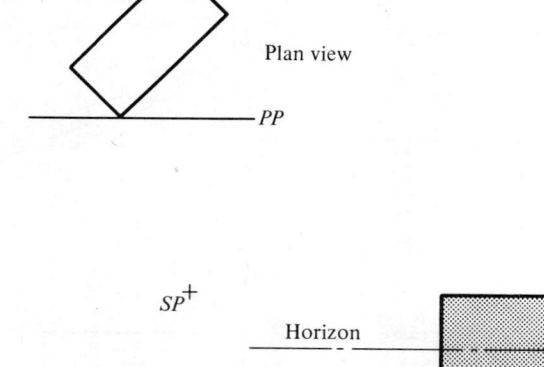

Figure 4.19 In constructing a two-point perspective, we first locate and establish all pertinent points and planes.

Sec. 4C / 87
Perspective Systems

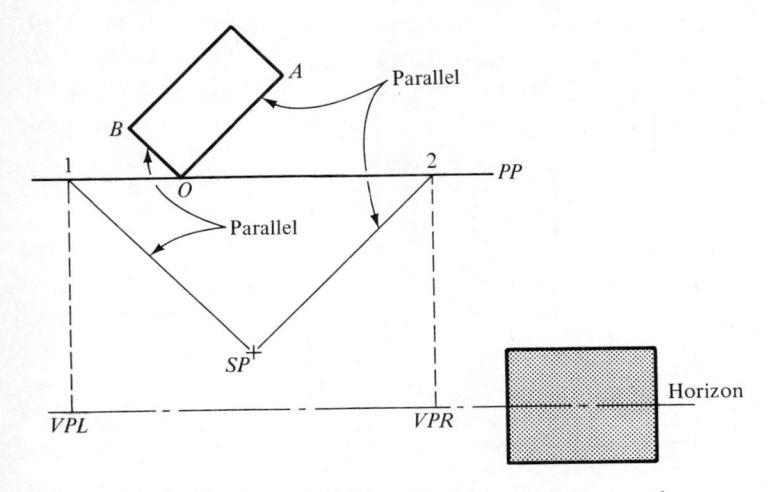

Figure 4.20 Finding vanishing points in two-point perspective, common method.

We then proceed to make the perspective as shown in Fig. 4.21, using the elevation view to locate heights in the perspective. Figures 4.22, 4.23, and 4.24 are examples of two-point perspective drawings made using the common method.

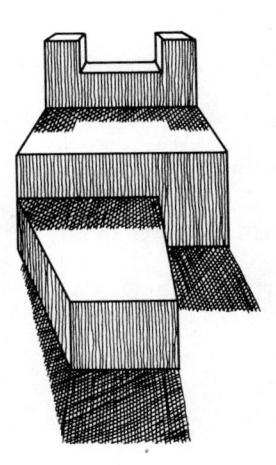

Figure 4.18
A one-point perspective.

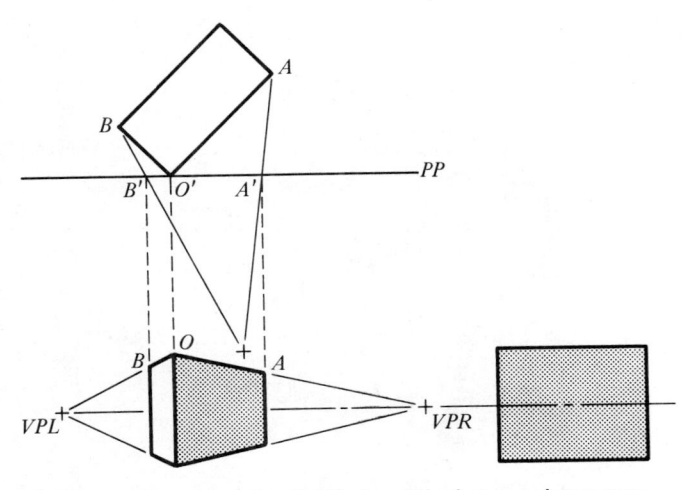

Figure 4.21 Construction details for a simple two-point perspective. Note that because one edge of the object is in the picture plane, that edge is true length in the perspective drawing.

88 / Chap. 4
Perspective

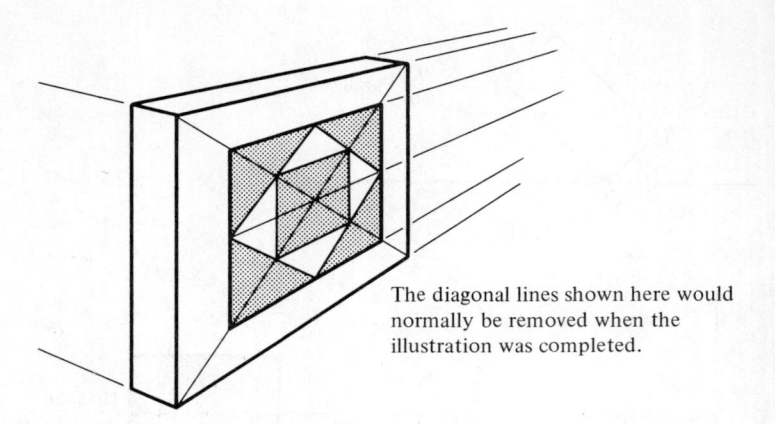

The diagonal lines shown here would normally be removed when the illustration was completed.

Figure 4.22 A two-point perspective drawing that demonstrates the use of diagonals to locate the centers of rectangles.

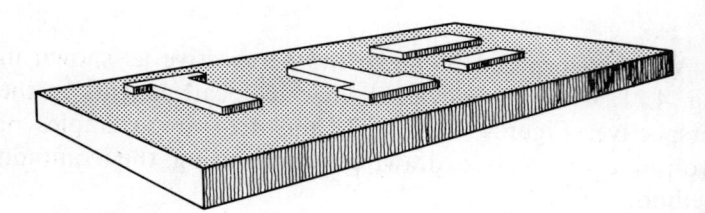

Figure 4.23 A two-point perspective of an electronic semiconductor chip.

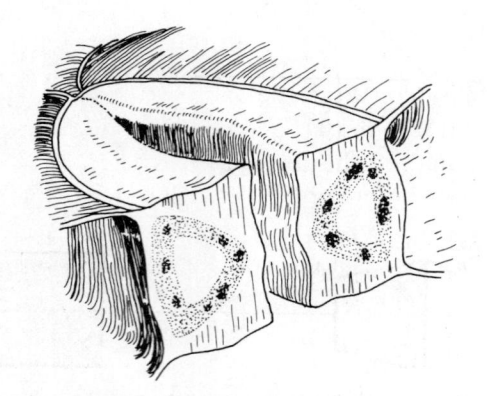

Figure 4.24 A two-point perspective drawing of a biological specimen—a plant guard cell.

THREE-POINT PERSPECTIVE

Three-point perspective drawing is used less often than the other two types—one-point and two-point. The reasons for this lack of use are few but compelling and convincing. First of all, a three-point perspective demands *thorough* knowledge of theory. Second, the illustrator will find the three-point difficult to construct. The third and last reason is one not usually considered, but it is valid—the space required to make a three-point is large. Thus, most of us will rationalize and say the one- or two-point perspective will suffice.

In most cases one- or two-point perspectives *will* suffice. After all, nearly all of us are used to seeing vertical lines *not* converge to a point. In photographic illustrations, wherein the photographer intends to dramatize height, the concept of a third vanishing point is important. With these thoughts in mind, we leave the reader with the idea that if he wishes to dramatize height, he should consider three-point perspective. Otherwise, he should stick to the simpler methods.

Fig. 4.25 is shown as a five-part construction process. Follow the steps carefully. Then imagine the work necessary to make a three-point perspective of a *complex* object. This one is *simple*.

Step 1. Construct a plan view of the object.
Step 2. Using the plan view, construct an elevation view. Locate *SP* and draw *CV* from *SP* to the center of the elevation. Draw *PP* perpendicular to *CV*.
Step 3. Rotate *PP*, *SP*, and the elevation view so that *PP* is vertical.
Step 4. Using the plan view and the rotated elevation view, construct the axonometric plan view. Note that *SP* must be directly below the geometric center of the axonometric plan. Otherwise the three-point perspective will lean to one side or the other.
Step 5. Project lines in both the axonometric plan and elevation to the *SP* for that view, locating intersection points with *PP*. Project these intersections vertically and horizontally, locating points on the three-point perspective. Connect the points to complete the object.

Step 1
Plan

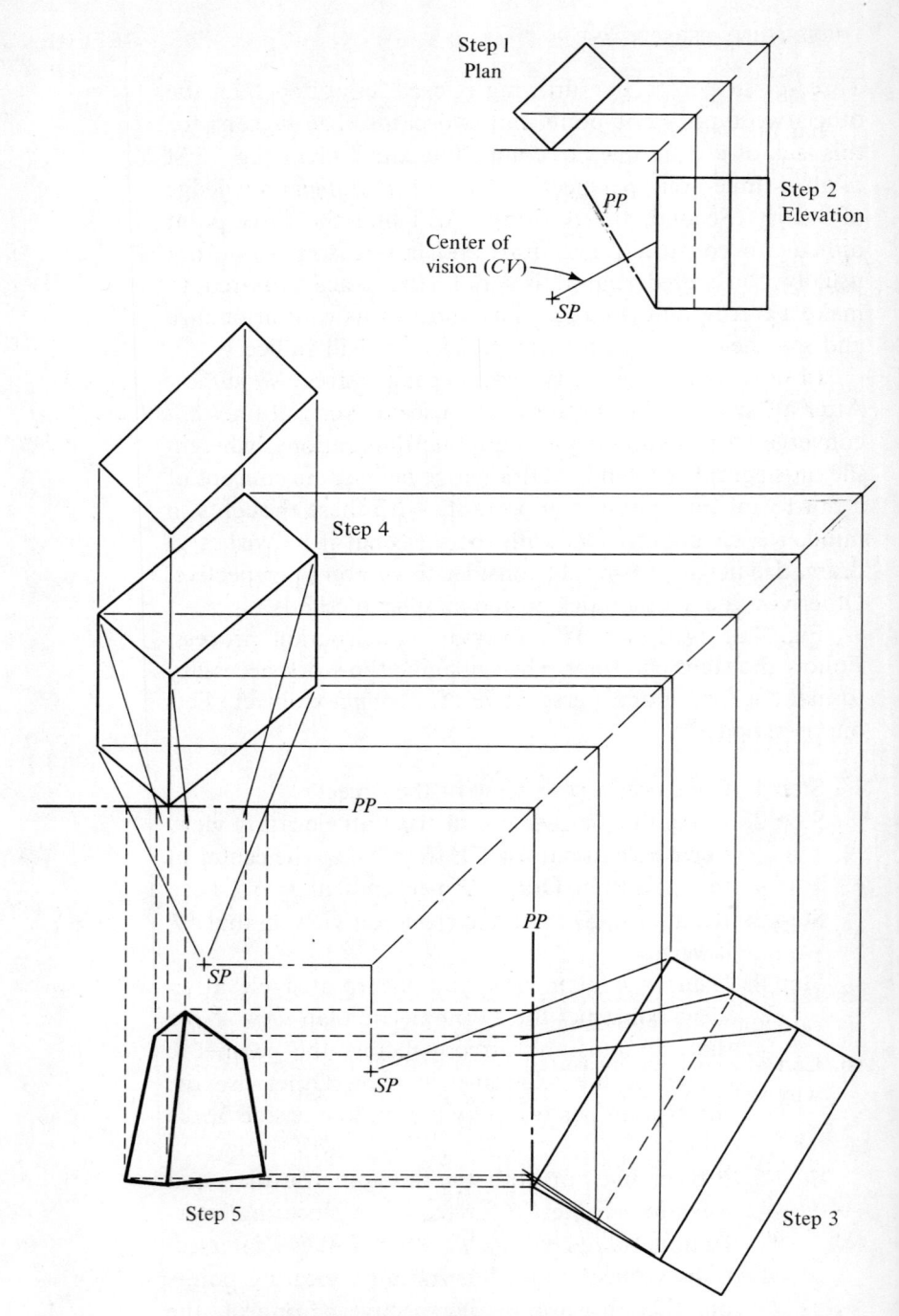

Step 2
Elevation

PP

Center of
vision (CV)

SP

Step 4

PP

PP

SP

SP

Step 5

Step 3

Figure 4.25 A three-point perspective drawing—a complex undertaking.

REFERENCES

1. E. R. Norling, *Perspective Made Easy*. New York: The MacMillan Company, 1939.
   This is an extremely simple-to-understand book. The author has literally employed a building block (brick) approach to demonstrate fundamentals.

2. A. Loomis, *Three-Dimensional Drawing*. New York: The Viking Press, 1960.
   An excellent source to use as a guide to perspective. A good share of the illustrations are of the human form (in stipple board), but the perspective section is good.

3. C. L. Martin, *Architectural Graphics* (2nd ed.). London: The MacMillan Company/Collier-MacMillan Limited, 1970.
   An easy-to-understand text, although quite detailed. The illustrations are coordinated well with the text and are well labeled.

4. J. D'Amelio, *Perspective Drawing Handbook*. New York: Tudor Publishing Company, 1964.
   An inexpensive paperback with many good examples, hints, and procedures. Mostly sketches.

QUESTIONS

1. Define perspective projection.
2. Why is perspective projection so widely used in architectural endeavors?
3. Can perspective be put to good use in technical illustrating? Explain your answer.
4. What is a station point? Where is it located in relation to the picture plane?
5. If a portion of an object is in the picture plane, what may be said about the measurements in *PP*?
6. Can distances be measured directly in perspective? Why or why not?
7. What is a horizon? Where is it located? Does it serve a function? What function?
8. What is a vanishing point? How do you locate a vanishing point on a two-point perspective drawing?
9. What are the three perspective systems?
10. Describe how to determine the distance between *SP* and the object being drawn.

PROBLEMS

1. Suppose you have two circular cylinders, each of the same length that is eight times its diameter. (*Hint*: Make diameter equal $\frac{1}{4}$ in.) Draw a top view (orthographic) of the following arrangement:
   (a) Station point (*SP*)
   (b) Picture plane (*PP*)
   (c) Place the cylinders parallel to both *PP* and the horizon. In other words, you will see the cylinders in full length. Place one cylinder a distance equal to 4 diameters behind *PP* and the other cylinder a distance 12 diameters behind *PP*.
   (d) Now draw a front view of the scene, indicating what is seen from *SP*. Choose *SP* so you can see all cylinders.

2. Repeat Prob. 1(a) and (b). Then place the cylinders parallel to *PP* but perpendicular to the horizon. Use the same distances as in Prob. 1(c). Repeat Prob. 1(d).

3. Repeat Prob. 1(a) and (b). Then place the cylinders such that they are parallel to the ground but perpendicular to *PP*. The axes of the two cylinders lie along the same line. The cylinders are laid end-to-end. Repeat Prob. 1(d).

4. Repeat Prob. 1(a) and (b). Then place the cylinders 8 diameters apart such that they are parallel to the ground but perpendicular to *PP*. Repeat Prob. 1(d).

5. Study the side view in Fig. P4.1. Then draw the view as you would see it from *SP*. *Note*: Three positions (*A*, *B*, and *C*) are required.

6. The elevation and plan views in Fig. P4.2 show rectangular solids drawn at various positions. Illustrate, by means of a front view, how this scene appears from *SP*. Why are two orthographic views necessary in this problem?

7. Sketch (or draw with instruments) a definition of the perspective technique. Include such things as the picture plane, sta-

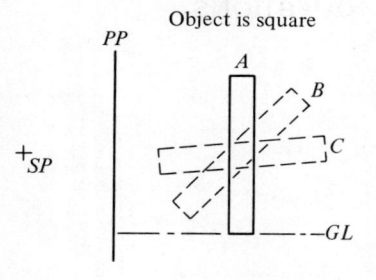

Figure P4.1

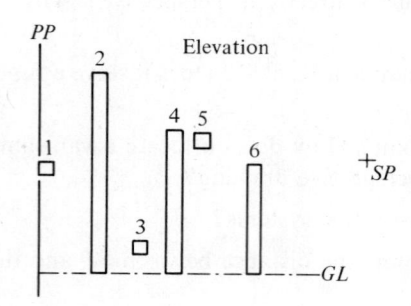

Figure P4.2

tion point, horizon, and notes explaining relationships that exist among parts of the technique.

8. Make a one-point perspective drawing of the object shown in Fig. P4.3. Leave all construction lines in the drawing. Use a 60° cone of sight.
9. For each of the orientations of the *cube* in Fig. P4.4, make a two-point perspective drawing. Choose an appropriate size for the cube. Position *SP* such that the horizon is at the middle of the cube in elevation.
10. Establish a horizon that will allow you to look *down* upon the cubes in Prob. 9. Now make two-point perspective drawings of each part.
11. Repeat Prob. 10 but look *up* this time.
12. The set of cubes in Fig. P4.5 are oriented in different positions with respect to *PP*. Note that *each* has a different pair of vanishing points. Make a two-point perspective. One cube is smaller than the other three.
13. Make a two-point perspective drawing of the object shown in Fig. P4.3. Indicate where all points of interest (*SP*, *VP*, etc.) lie.
14. Make a two-point perspective of the object in Fig. P4.6. Establish a horizon such that you are looking *down* on the object. (The object is a bird house.) Choose suitable dimensions. Place *PP* in front of the house.
15. Repeat Prob. 14, but establish the horizon such that you are now looking *up* at the bird house.
16. Repeat Prob. 14, placing *PP* in the following positions:
    a) In the plane in which the front of the house lies.
    b) In a plane in the middle of the house.
    c) In the plane in which the back of the house lies.
    Now compare the three parts. Describe what has happened.

Figure P4.3

For each drawing place *SP* in elevation such that you will look down on the cubes. Use two-point perspective.

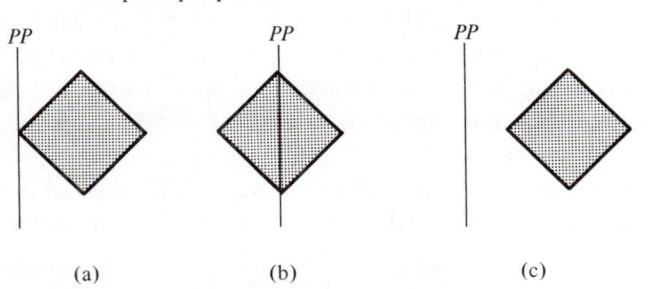

(a)   (b)   (c)

Figure P4.4

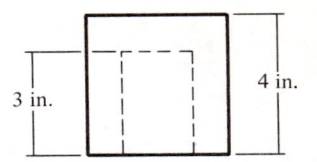

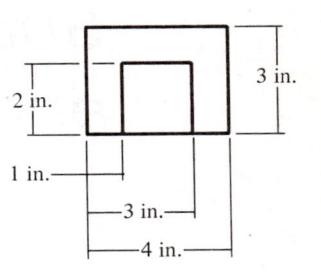

Plan

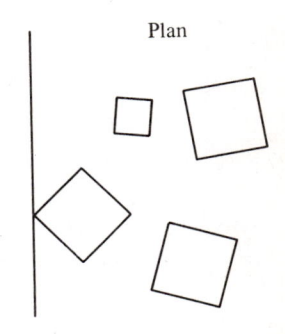

The base of each cube rests on *GL* in elevation. Your drawing should be made so that you are looking over the top of the cubes.

Figure P4.5

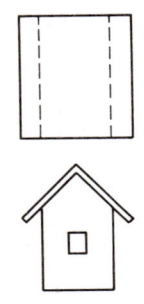

Figure P4.6

5

Shades and Shadows

When a scene before us is (as the poets say) bathed in sunshine, most of us are subconsciously aware of shade and shadow resulting from the sunlight. We are consciously aware, however, of the fact that if we are in direct sunlight, we are warmer than if we were standing in shadow. We are able to stand in shadow (not shade) because an object (tree, building) blocks rays of sunlight.

It is also relatively safe to say that although we are conscious of the cooling effect of shadows, most of us give little thought as to how a shadow fits into the scenery. Every object that extends above the ground will cast a shadow when the sun is shining. Because shadows are a part of *every* overall scene, we should be aware of the importance of shadows and use them to make pictorial drawings more realistic and definitive. A much more natural and expressive drawing will result if shadows are used properly. As an example, observe the shadow cast by the insect shown in Fig. 5.1—a fire ant.*

The shadow informs us (if we observe closely) of a little-known fact about the locomotion of ants: Only three legs

---

*This illustration is reproduced here in black and white. The original is a water color owned by Mr. Dennis Curtin, who allowed the reproduction to be used in this book.

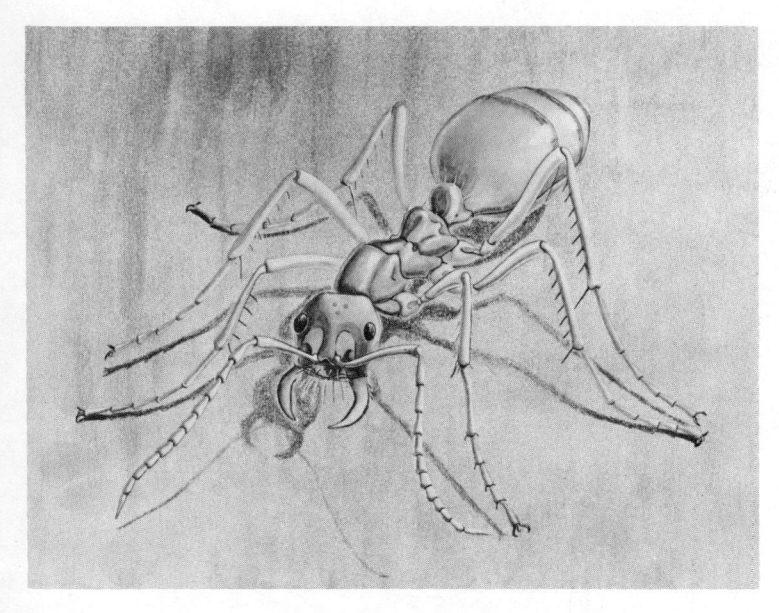

Figure 5.1 A dramatic example of using shadow in a technical illustration. Artist: Mrs. Alice Prickett.

are in contact at one time with the surface on which the ant is walking: The ant is supported on a tripod. The artist added shadows of the legs to show this important fact. Use of shadow like this adds expression and realism.

Although we may not be able to illustrate a fact so dramatically by using shadows (as in the case of the fire ant), we must be aware that shadows are important to pictorial drawing schemes. In some cases, we can even make use of shadows on multiple view orthographic drawings.

5A Definitions

Because shadow and shade are integral parts of a scene added *after* the object is drawn, we treat them separately from the drawing schemes. Certain definitions and principles that apply to shadows (and shade) do not apply to the projection scheme.

SHADOW

Suppose that sunlight strikes a picnic table illuminating the tabletop scene. If we place our picnic articles (basket, thermos, glass, and other opaque objects) on the table, rays of light from the sun will strike these objects. Because sunlight does not pass *through* opaque objects, certain well-defined areas of the tabletop will be in shadow, as shown in Fig. 5.2.

Figure 5.2 Rays of sunlight are parallel. Objects that sunlight does not pass through cast shadows.

A shadow is thus defined as the area on a surface that is not lighted because an object blocks out light rays.

Example 1   In Fig. 5.3, we are required to draw the shadow of a circular-shaped plane on a surface parallel to the shape. By *definition* the shapes are identical. In Fig. 5.3(a) we make the pictorial drawing but no shadows. Then, in Fig. 5.3(b), we construct a right-side view of the scene and draw in light rays (we chose here a 45° direction of light), locating points *A*, *B*, *C*, and *D*.

Point *A* is the point at which shade separates from light on the stem supporting the plane.
Point *B* is on the diameter of the shadow.
Point *C* is the geometric center of the plane shape.
Point *D* is another point on the diameter of the shadow.

After locating the points, we transfer each to the pictorial drawing along the principal axes, Fig. 5.3(c).

Sec. 5A / 97
Definitions

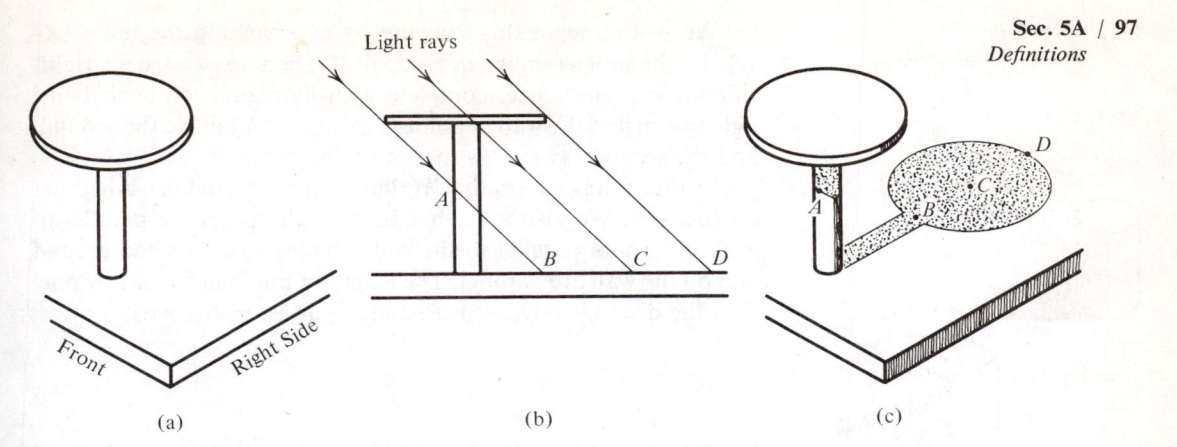

Figure 5.3 Tracing rays of light to find points in a pictorial drawing.

Assume that several rectangular-shaped posts are situated near a plane wall and that the posts cast shadows that fall upon the wall. See Fig. 5.4. The pictorial scheme used is isometric.

Example 2

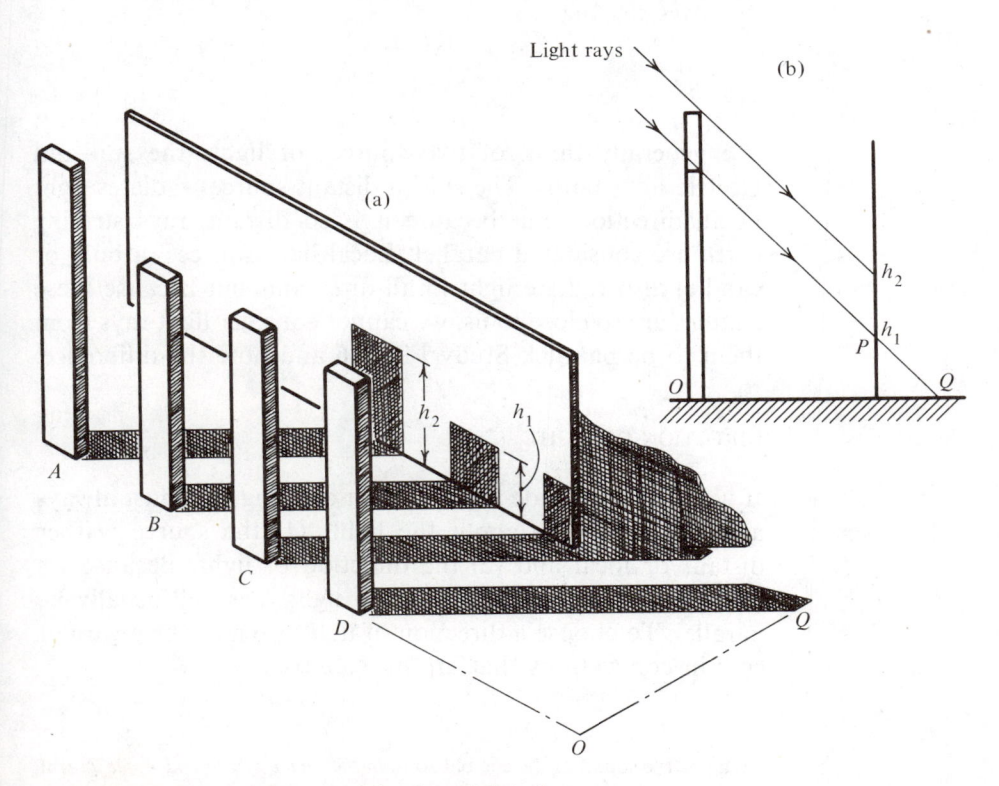

Figure 5.4 An example of parallel shadows.

We would begin this drawing by constructing the poles (A–D) and the wall as shown in Fig. 5.4(a). Then we construct a right-side view of the scene, complete with light rays. Note that one light ray strikes the wall at point P, a distance h_1 above the ground, and the second ray strikes the wall at height h_2.

In Fig. 5.4(a) we see that h_1 and h_2 are the heights of shadows on the wall. We also note that because the poles are parallel to each other and parallel to the wall, shadows cast on the ground and on the wall are parallel. The length of the shadow cast by pole D is the distance OQ, measured along an isometric axis.

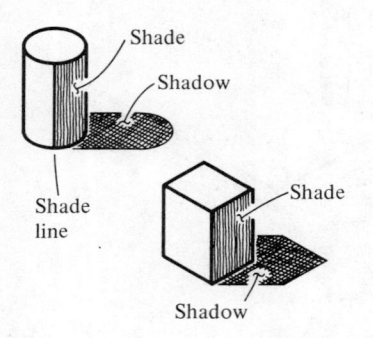

Figure 5.5 The difference between shade and shadow.

SHADE

We often speak of standing in *shade*, e.g., the shade of tree.* Actually we mean *shadow* because shade is that part of an object not in light. Figure 5.5 illustrates the difference between shade and shadow. Note that on each object, a shade line exists—a line defining the separation of lighted area from shaded area. Remember that *only objects in light can cast shadows*.

LIGHT

We generally think of two sources of light: the sun and electric light bulbs. The sun (a distant source) radiates light in all directions but because it is so distant, rays striking earth are considered parallel. Local light sources (a bulb or candle) also radiate light in all directions but because these sources are so close to us, we cannot consider light rays from them to be parallel. Study Fig. 5.6 and note the difference.

DIRECTION OF LIGHT

If we wish to include shadows in a drawing, we must always assume two things about the light: (1) the source—either distant or local and (2) the direction of light. Because we usually choose the sun as source, light rays will usually be parallel. To choose a direction of light, we must be aware of certain conventions that are in wide use.

---

*Imagine the sound of the age old song *In the Shade of the Old Apple Tree* if we were to use the proper word—shadow.

(a) Distant source

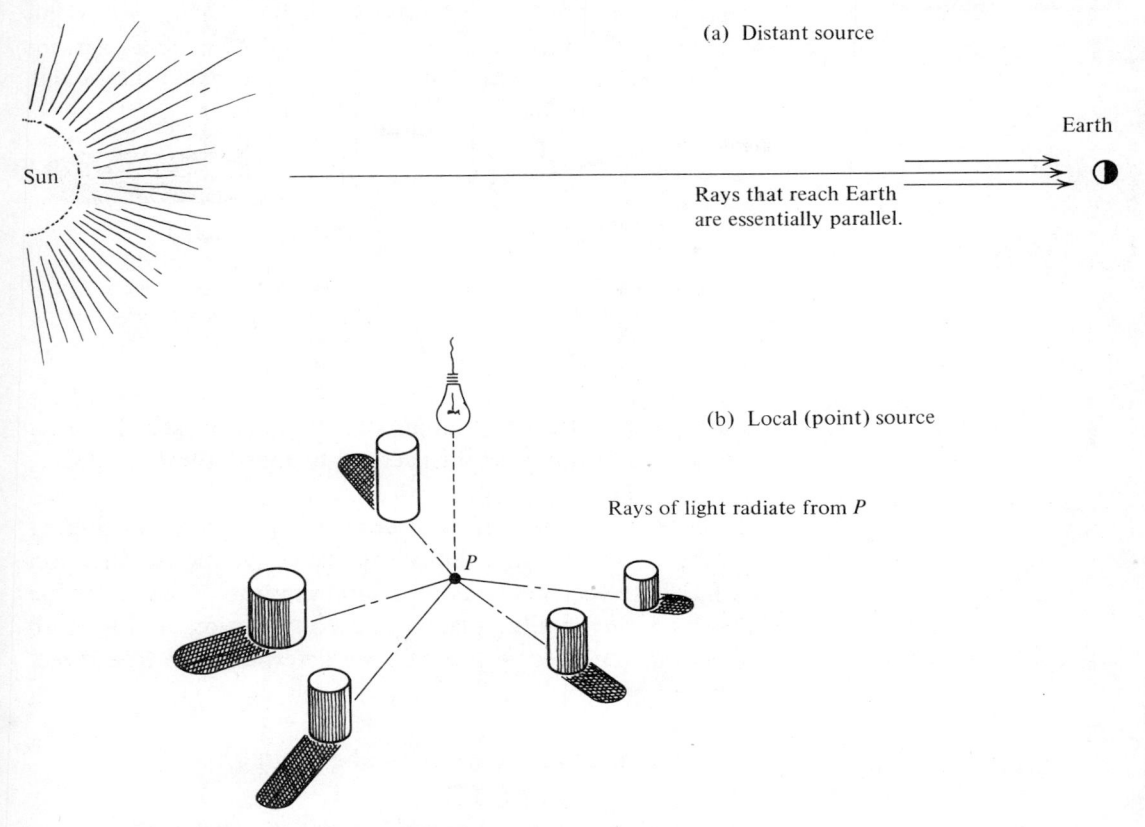

Sun

Rays that reach Earth are essentially parallel.

Earth

(b) Local (point) source

Rays of light radiate from P

P

Figure 5.6 The difference between distant and local light sources.

CONVENTIONAL DIRECTION. If we make a pictorial drawing of a cube, as in Fig. 5.7, the conventional direction of light is defined as the direction in which diagonal AB points.

45° DIRECTION. If we project diagonal AB into the front, right-side, and top planes of the cube, in each of these views AB is the diagonal of a square. This fact should give an insight as to why the 45° direction is so named: The diagonal of a square is at a 45° angle to the sides of the square. See Fig. 5.8.

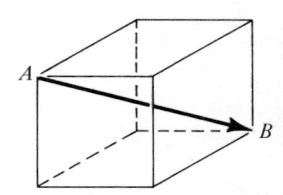

Figure 5.7 Diagram of conventional direction of light.

Each convention has advantages. By using the 45° direction, we simplify measurements involving shadow lengths. For example, if we wish to measure the length of the shadow in Fig. 5.9 using the 45° direction, we recall from geometry

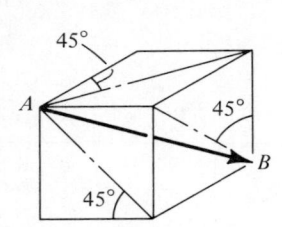

Figure 5.8 Diagram of the 45° direction of light.

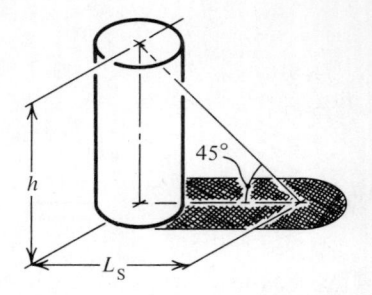

Figure 5.9 Shadow length L_s is equal to cylinder height h if the 45° direction of light is used.

that the legs of a 45° triangle are of equal length. In other words, the cylinder height is equal to the shadow length.

TRUE DIRECTION. If we examine a pictorial drawing of a cube as we did in establishing the conventional direction of light, we see that a plane containing the diagonal of the cube is a rectangular plane. The construction in Fig. 5.10 illustrates the ease with which we determine the true direction of light.

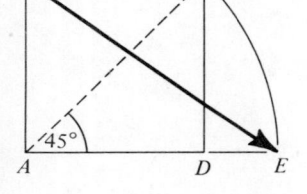

Figure 5.10 Determining the true direction of light.

1. Construct one side of a cube—*ABCD*.
2. Draw diagonal *AC*.
3. Using a compass, draw arc *CE* of radius *AC*.
4. Line *BE* indicates the true direction of light.

5B Principles

As stated earlier in this chapter, certain definitions and principles concerning shadows do not apply to projection schemes in general. Having seen a few of the basic definitions of terms relating to the study of shades and shadow we now state a few basic principles.

PARALLEL LINES

If parallel lines on an object cast shadows on the same surface or on a parallel surface, the shadows are parallel. In addition, the line on the object making the shadow is parallel to the shadow if the line is parallel to the plane in which the shadow lies. See Fig. 5.11.

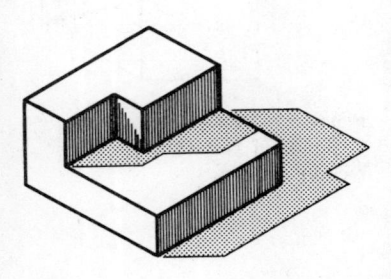

Figure 5.11 Note the lines that are parallel on the object and in shadow.

LINES THAT CAST SHADOWS

If a line on an object lies in shade *or* shadow, that line cannot cast a shadow. Why? Because no light strikes it. See Fig. 5.12.

PLANES THAT CAST SHADOWS

The shadow of a *plane* figure cast on a plane parallel to the figure is the identical shape of the figure, as shown in Fig. 5.13.

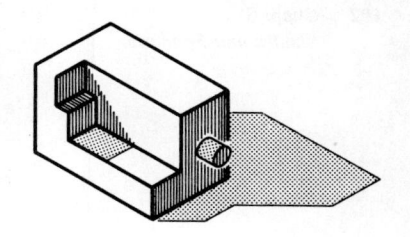

Figure 5.12 No light strikes the small ledge so it can cast no shadow. The cylinder cannot cast a shadow either.

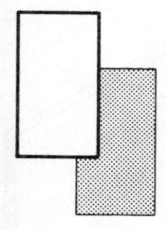

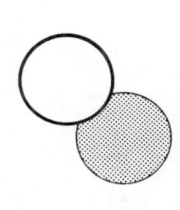

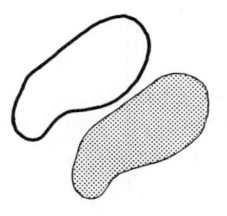

Figure 5.13 Planes cast the same-shape shadows on parallel planes.

5C Multiple View Drawings

In very few cases will we use shadow on multiple view drawings to clarify the drawing. Most often, shadows used here will give an idea of which lines cast shadows on what surfaces. For example, assume that we wish to include shadows in the drawing in Fig. 5.14(a). By constructing the front view of the object [see Fig. 5.14(b)] and drawing the light rays, we can "see," in a more familiar setting called a *plane* view, where shade begins and ends—points *A* and *B*. We also get a

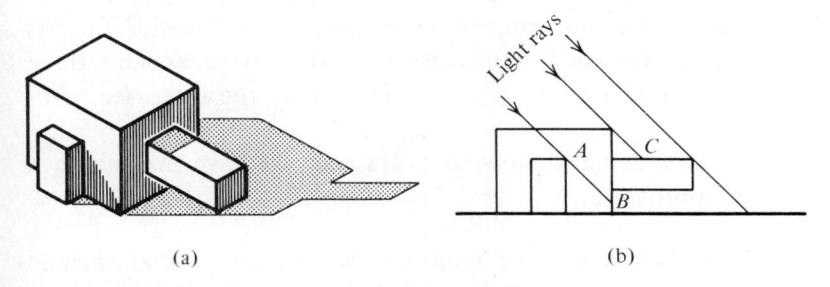

(a)   (b)

Figure 5.14 Using a multiple view drawing to locate shadow points.

101

qualitative feel for where shadows begin and end and the relationship of these end points to the object itself.

Assume that we have two objects set out different distances from a wall. The side view in Fig. 5.15 illustrates that one object casts a shadow *on* the wall, whereas the object farthest from the wall does not. The taller of the two objects casts a shadow on the shorter, as seen in the top view. We can thus use multiple view drawings to assist in constructing the shadows. In fact, for beginners, this method is recommended strongly.

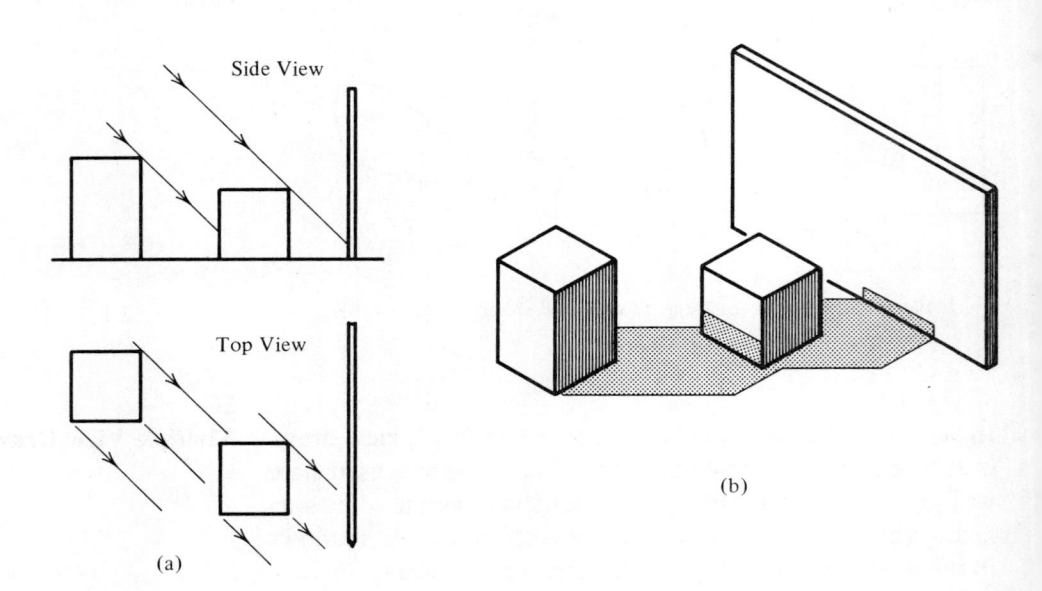

Figure 5.15

5D Pictorial Drawings

Although including shadows in a pictorial drawing is sometimes a complex problem, we produce a much better illustration if shadows are present. In every pictorial scheme three faces of an object are shown explaining the increased complexity.

To include shadows in a drawing, we have two methods of approach:

1. We can make multiple view drawings that include shadow beginning and end points and transfer these points (using the proper scale factors) to a pictorial drawing.

2. We can locate shadow on the pictorial drawing by intersecting light ray paths with shadow lines.

Method 1 is simpler, less demanding in terms of theoretical knowledge of projection techniques, but requires more time and effort in terms of detail-type drawing. Method 2 is a much faster technique but, as mentioned above, the illustrator must know the theory.

We suggest that the beginner take the extra time to make multiple view aids and as he becomes more adept, use the direct projection method.

DIRECTION OF LIGHT

Before adding shadows to a pictorial drawing, we must first choose a lighting scheme, i.e., choose the position of shadows —front, sides, or rear. Then we must establish a direction of light. In each pictorial scheme, we must be aware of subtle differences.

ISOMETRIC. The isometric scheme incorporates the use of equal measure along receding axes that are symmetrical about the vertical axis. To find the conventional direction of light for isometric we perform the construction listed below and illustrated in Fig. 5.16.

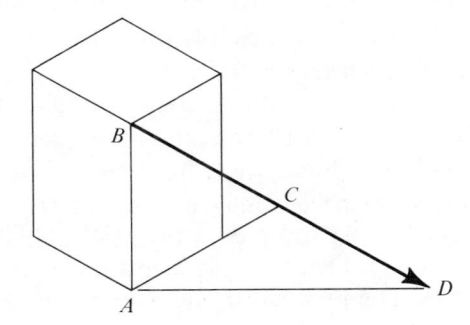

Figure 5.16 Constructing the direction of light angle for an isometric drawing.

1. Construct an isometric rectangular volume taller than it is wide or deep.
2. Measure distance $AC = AB$ along the right receding isometric axis.
3. Measure distance $CD = AB$ along a line parallel to the left receding isometric axis.

104 / Chap. 5
Shades and Shadows

Figure 5.17
The shadow of *AB* is *AB'*; the shadow of *CD* is *CD'*.

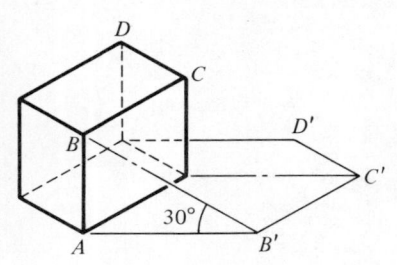

Horizontal line that is the shadow of *AB*

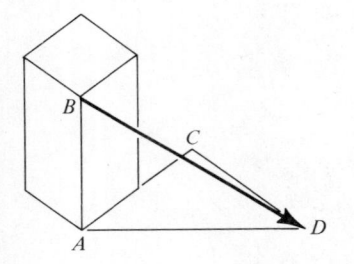

Figure 5.18
Construction for direction of light for a symmetrical dimetric: $\theta = \phi$.

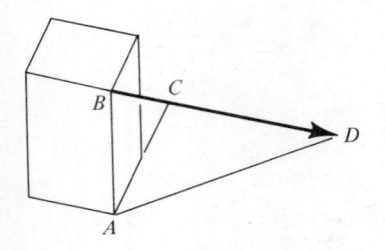

Figure 5.19
Construction for direction of light for an asymmetrical dimetric: $\theta \neq \phi$.

4. Connect *B* to *D*. The line *BD* is the direction of light. Note that line *BD* is at 30°.
5. Connect *A* to *D*. The line *AD* is the shadow of line *AB*.

From this one figure we may draw a conclusion that will make life simpler. In *any* pictorial drawing scheme that uses symmetrical receding axes, for the conventional direction of light the shadow of a vertical line is cast along a *horizontal* line. Figure 5-17 illustrates this statement.

Other directions of light may be our choosing and will be correct. The conventional direction is shown here because it is simple to work with and is, in most cases, effective.

DIMETRIC. To construct the conventional direction of light for the dimetric scheme, we must bear in mind that *two* different scales are used and that we can use *two* types of dimetric drawings—symmetrical and asymmetrical. The construction procedure is identical to that used in isometric.

Note in Fig. 5.18 that the two axis angles are equal; i.e., $\theta = \phi$. As we saw in Chapter 2, it is more convenient to choose scales for dimetric drawings and have the angles θ and ϕ determined as a result of the chosen scales. In Fig. 5.18, $L = 1$, $R = 1$, and $H = \frac{3}{4}$. As a result,* $\theta = \phi = 37°$. Because $\theta = \phi$, the two lines *CD* and *AC* are made equal in length and are the equal legs of an isosceles triangle *ACD*. Thus, *AD* (the shadow of *AB*) is a horizontal line—perpendicular to *AB*. As in the case of isometric, the rectangular volume is taller than it is wide or deep.

If we are constructing the direction of light for an asymmetrical dimetric, Fig. 5.19, the same construction procedure is used. The shadow line is not, however, a horizontal line.

For the asymmetrical dimetric case, let $H = R = \frac{3}{4}$ and $L = 1$. Then $\theta = 60°$ and $\phi = 15°$ See Table 2.1.

TRIMETRIC. The procedure used above (for isometric and dimetric) to construct the conventional direction of light is also used for the trimetric scheme. The problem of measurement scales remains: We must contend with three scales— one scale for the vertical axis and one scale for each receding axis. Figure 5.20 is an example illustrating the construction of the direction of light for a trimetric drawing. In this

---
*Refer to Chapter 2, p. 37 for an example of how to determine angles.

figure $\theta = 15°$, $\phi = 20°$, x scale = 0.68, y scale = 0.78, and z scale = 0.95. (Refer to Table 2.2, p. 48 for θ, ϕ, and the scale values.) Remember, in trimetric the scale values are based on percent of unity.

OBLIQUE. For this pictorial scheme we use the same construction method as before to determine the conventional direction of light. Depending upon our choice of receding axis scale, we must be aware that more than one scale is being used. A comparison between construction for a cavalier and a cabinet projection is made in Fig. 5.21.

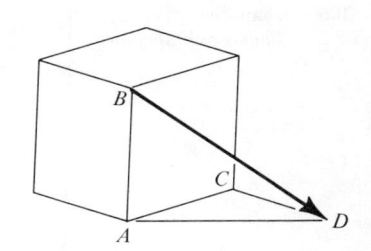

Figure 5.20 Construction for direction of light for a trimetric drawing.

(a) Cavalier

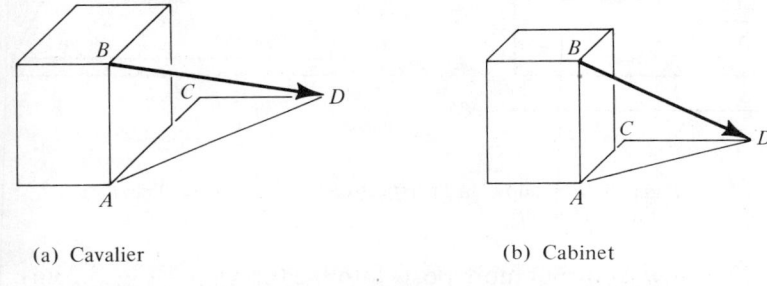

(b) Cabinet

Figure 5.21 Construction for direction of light for oblique projection.

Before we pass on to consider shade and shadow in perspective, let's make two general comments.

1. The construction of the conventional direction of light for axonometric and oblique schemes is not difficult. We must, however, be sure to measure distance AB in back of and to the right of the vertical line *to the correct scale*.
2. To use the conventional direction of light after we construct it, we merely project light rays at *that* angle. Where these lines intersect axes and shadow lines, points of *change in direction* of lines are found.

PERSPECTIVE. Shadows in perspective are an integral part of the scheme but can be (depending on the system used) a complex proposition. We will be concerned here with elementary considerations. The interested student is referred to the books listed at the end of Chapter 4 for more detail.

Two schemes for shadow presentation are possible in perspective: (1) light rays parallel to the picture plane and (2) light rays oblique to the picture plane.

106 / Chap. 5
Shades and Shadows

Light rays parallel to the picture plane. If we sketch the picture plane and a post as shown in Fig. 5.22(a) and assume that the direction of light is 45°, the resulting shadow is as shown in Fig. 5.22(b).

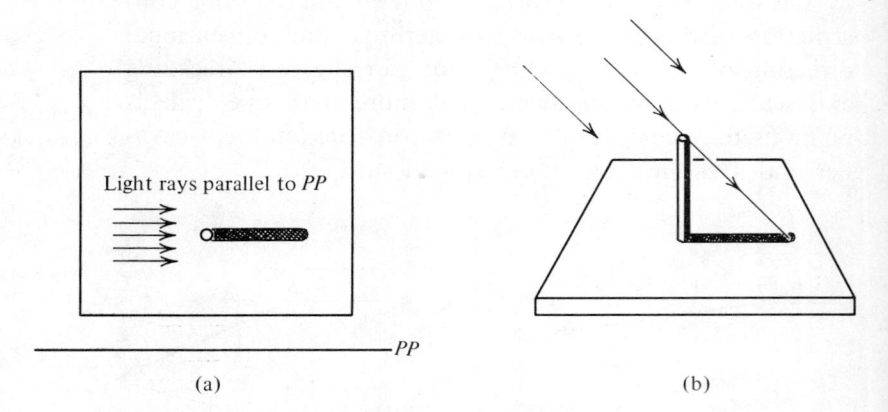

Figure 5.22 Shadows in a perspective drawing in which light rays are parallel to *PP*.

Now let us put more posts into the top view—Fig. 5.23(a). Because a 45° direction for light rays is used, the length of each shadow is equal to the height of the post casting the shadow—Fig. 5.23(b).

If posts are replaced with a rectangular solid placed such that we must use the two-point perspective scheme, our problem of constructing shadows is more complex: Vanishing points must now be used to illustrate convergence.

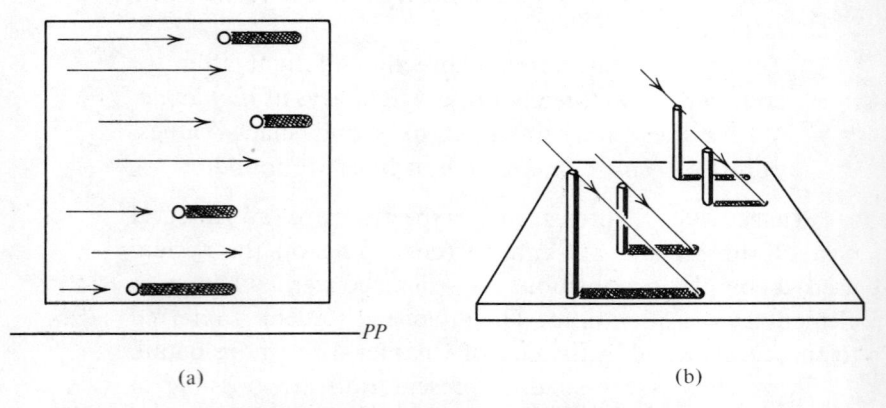

Figure 5.23 An example of how to determine length of shadow in perspective when light rays are parallel to *PP*.

In Fig. 5.24(a), note that $A'B'$ and $B'C'$ are parallel to AB and BC. In Fig. 5.24(b) the line A_1A' is parallel to the picture plane. $A'B'$ is a line radiating from A' to VPR. Note also that point A' is located by the intersection of A_1A and a light ray drawn at 45° through point A.

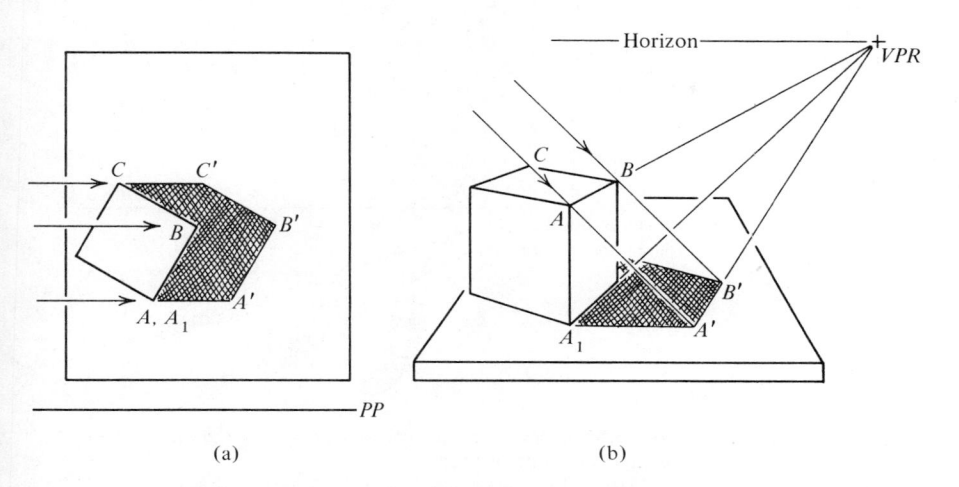

Figure 5.24 Determining a vanishing point for shadows.

Light rays oblique to the picture plane. If light rays are not parallel to the picture plane, then the rays must converge to a vanishing point. Although the rays arrive parallel to one another (Fig. 5.25), in perspective they must appear to converge or, in other words, meet at a vanishing point.

In viewing the illustration in Fig. 5.26, we may have the feeling that an impossible task confronts us. How do we determine the angle for light rays and shadows? Actually, it

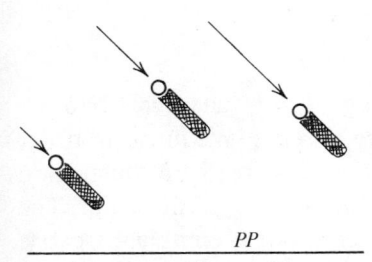

Figure 5.25 Light rays (viewed from top) as they arrive oblique to the picture plane.

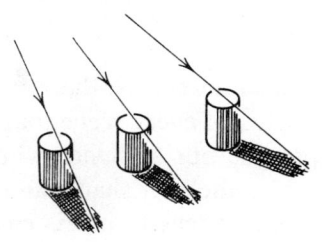

Figure 5.26 The light rays appear to converge.

is a simple matter. Examine Fig. 5.27. The *shadows* converge to *VPL*, the vanishing point for the *entire* scene. Thus we have merely to draw a line from *VPL* through posts to determine *direction* of shadows.

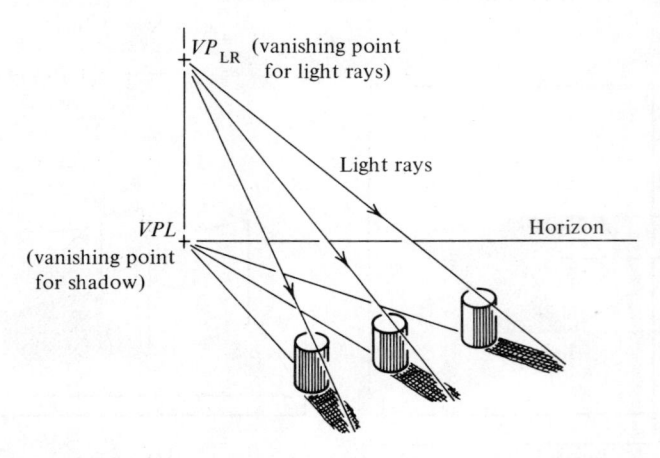

Figure 5.27 Determining the vanishing point for light rays when the rays are oblique to *PP*.

Because light rays also converge and because light rays are in the *same* plane as the shadows, the vanishing point for light rays is in the same plane as the vanishing point for shadows. In other words, by projecting a line vertically upward from *VPL*, we pick VP_{LR}, the vanishing point for light rays.

To give the reader food for thought, we mention the fact that in all cases mentioned previously the sun was behind the picture plane. In other words, we could see the sun. Consider the fact that the sun is, at times, in *front* of the picture plane—behind us. What happens to shadows now?

5E Closure

As we indicated at the opening of this chapter, shadows are a part of every scene that we observe. We must, in order to provide our audience with the most realistic illustration possible, include shade and shadows in a drawing. The material presented in this chapter is not a complete treatise by any stretch of the imagination. What is intended is to provide a beginner with basic tools with which he may pursue a more rigorous treatment.

REFERENCES

1. A. Loomis, *Three-Dimensional Drawing*. New York: The Viking Press, 1968.
2. J. D. D'Amelio, *Perspective Drawing Handbook*. New York: Tudor Publishing Company, 1964.
3. C. L. Martin, *Architectural Graphics* (2nd ed.). London: The MacMillan Co./Collier-Macmillan Limited, 1970.
4. C. L. Stong, *The Scientific American Book of Projects for the Amateur Scientist*. New York: Simon and Schuster, Inc., 1960.

QUESTIONS

1. What is shade? Shadow?
2. What objects can cast shadows?
3. Describe the two sources of light—distant and local.
4. Name the three directions of light and give a brief description of each.
5. How can you characterize shadows cast by parallel lines on parallel surfaces?
6. How would you characterize the shape of the shadow of a plane figure cast on a surface parallel to the plane figure?
7. Why are shadows (and shade) important to an illustrator?

PROBLEMS

1. Figure H.6 (Appendix H) is illuminated by a local light source from the 45° direction. Show all shade and shadow in a *sketch*. What axonometric scheme was used to make this drawing?
2. Using a second axonometric scheme that is different from the one used to execute Fig. H.4, *sketch* the figure. Include shade and shadow in your sketch. Use a distant light source and the conventional direction.
3. Using a distant light source and true direction of light, sketch in the shade and shadows for Fig. H.29.
4. Make a dimetric drawing of Fig. H.41. Assume a distant light source. Next, using the 45° direction for light, include shade and shadow.
5. Repeat Prob. 4, but change the direction of light to conventional.
6. Repeat Prob. 4, but change the direction of light to true. Which of the drawings is best: that done in Prob. 4, 5, or 6? Give a basis for your choice.

Shades and Shadows

7. Make an oblique drawing of Fig. H.57. Use any receding scale and angle you wish. Include shade and shadow. Use any direction of light that you wish.

8. Use Fig. H.1, H.4, and H.7 as the elements of one scene. Place them in any position you please. Now, make a perspective drawing of the three objects. Using a local light source, include shade and shadow.

9. Repeat Prob. 8, but use a distant light source.

10. Repeat Prob. 8, but use isometric as the projection scheme.

11. Do the first four problems at the end of Chapter 4 and include shade and shadow.

12. Make a trimetric drawing of Fig. H.24. Include shade and shadow. Choices of direction of light and source is yours.

13. Problems as assigned by your instructor from Appendix H.

Part II

Tools of the Trade

For every profession that comes to mind, certain equipment is used by members of that profession. An auto mechanic, for example, would be hard pressed to perform his duties without the aid of wrenches, screwdrivers, and related tools. A surgeon uses scalpels, hemostatic clamps, X-ray equipment, and suchlike. Photographers are identified by their cameras, electronic flash light sources, enlargers, and other paraphernalia. An illustrator is no different. He can be identified by equipment in his possession: Triangles, T squares, pens, and pencils.

If we examine the role of equipment in the execution of a profession, we find in each case certain basic equipment and other specialized equipment used to ease the burden of executing the work. If an auto mechanic had in his tool chest only a pair of pliers with which to loosen and tighten bolts, he could do the job. His job would be simpler and, if he charged by the hour, his customers would be happier if he owned a set of socket wrenches. An appendectomy could conceivably be performed using a razor blade with no anesthesia in unsterilized surroundings, although we certainly would not be happy or confident to have the surgery performed in such a manner. A box camera is suitable for some snapshots but, clearly, any attempt to use a box camera to photograph an amoeba would result in failure. A 2H pencil, a triangle, and a T square will be equipment enough for an illustrator to do simple orthographic and axonometric drawings consisting of straight lines. Add to his equipment list a bow compass, a few irregular curves, and a set of inking pens and his capabilities are expanded.

The point to be made is simple Although equipment alone does not make an illustrator, anyone who professes to be (or to become) an illustrator must possess certain *basic* equipment and as he becomes more expert and wealthier, he may buy specialized equipment. In the pages that follow, we will describe briefly equipment relating to the technical illustrator.

Keep in mind that price is an important consideration when purchasing equipment, but we must never be quick to pay less for an item that is not accurate or that gives us less versatility. The old adage that says "You get what you pay for" is true. Good equipment will last a lifetime. Junk will last a short time. Be selective.

6

Essential Equipment

6A Pens

The word *pen* is synonomous with the word *ink*. To execute a drawing in ink, we must use an inking device, referred to as a pen. Because so many different pens are sold, knowledge about them will assist in choosing an inking instrument for a particular job.

TECHNICAL FOUNTAIN PENS

A technical fountain pen is an inking instrument designed to allow ink to flow from a reservoir through a hollow point and onto the drawing surface to produce a line of *constant thickness* (*weight*). Pens are available that will produce many different line weights. The constant thickness line is, by far, the most important feature of technical fountain pens. A disassembled technical fountain pen is shown in Fig. 6.1(a); in Fig. 6.1(b) the principle of operation is shown schematically.

Many different companies manufacture technical fountain pens and each manufacturer will claim that his product performs best for reasons stated in the advertisement. The *fact* is that subtle differences such as line weights, jewel tips, and

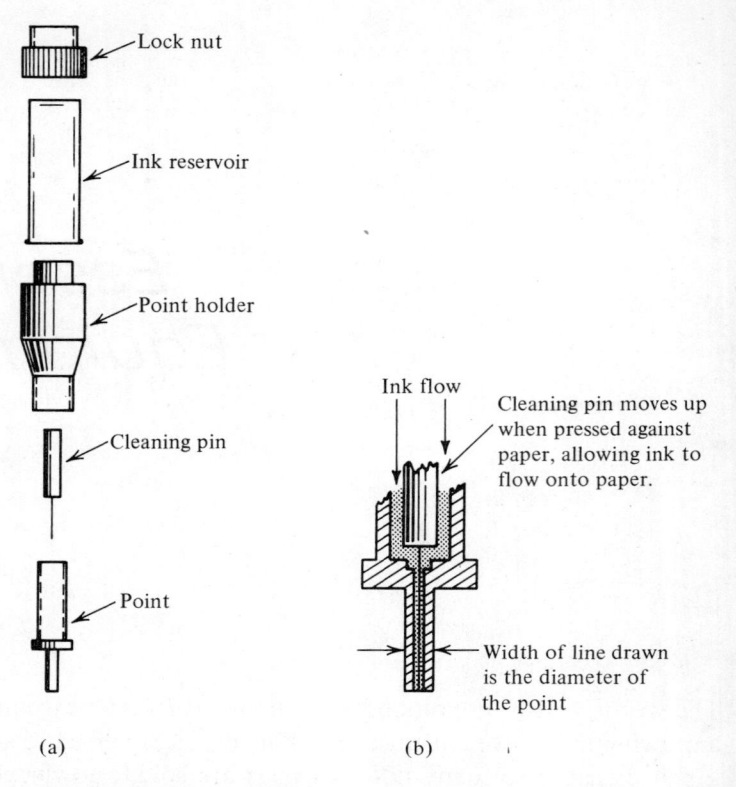

Figure 6.1 The technical fountain pen used in technical illustrating.

plastic points exist but the overall concept in each case is the same.

Technical fountain pens can be used for drawing straight or curved lines, for lettering in either scriber-aided or cutout template styles or for freehand lettering. It must be kept in mind that when a technical fountain pen is used, best results will be obtained if (1) the pen point is positioned perpendicular to the drawing surface (see Fig. 6.2); (2) the pen point is at all times free from dirt (a tissue to wipe the point works fine); and (3) the pen mechanism is clean (residual carbon in the ink will slowly become hardened in the point, stopping the ink flow).

KEUFFEL AND ESSER (K.&E.) LEROY RESERVOIR PENS. These instruments are well made, durable, dependable, and expensive. Figure 6.3(a) shows a seven-pen set of Leroy pens that is suitable for a beginner. The accompanying chart

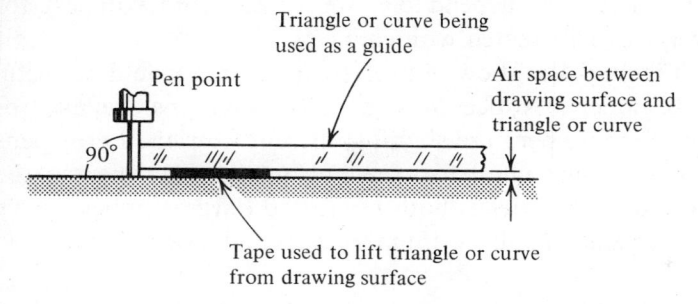

Figure 6.2 Proper position in which to place technical fountain pen. Note that the instrument is held against the triangle or curve, that is lifted from the drawing surface by tape attached to the triangle or curve.

(a) Set of seven pens.   (b) Line weights available.

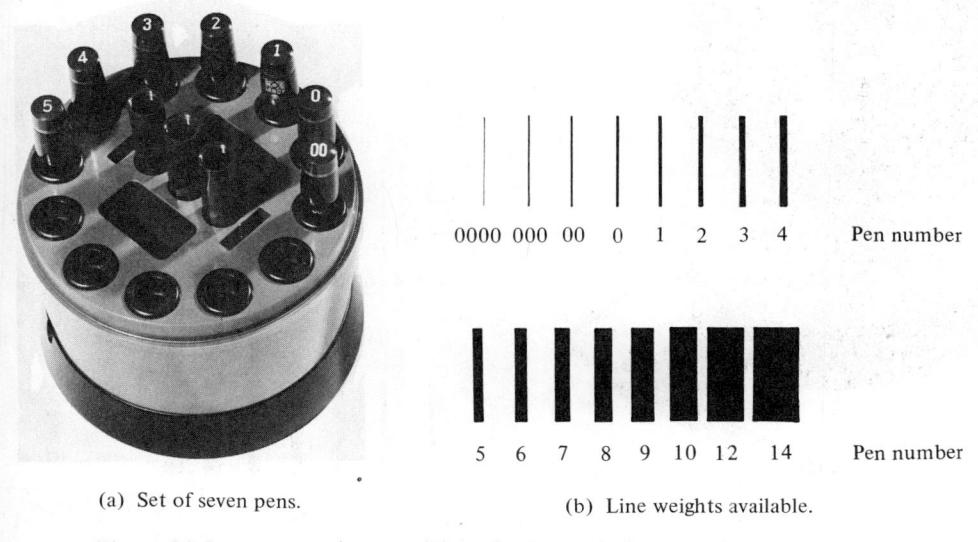

Figure 6.3 Leroy reservoir pens. (Photo by R.T. Gladin.)

in Fig. 6.3(b) shows the variety of line weights available. Note that the line weights vary from light to heavy as the pen numbers vary from small to large. The pens are also color coded to indicate line weights.

Leroy pens may be used as lettering pens (in conjunction with the Leroy lettering templates) and as ruling pens. In either use, they are superb instruments and with proper care, use, and cleaning will last indefinitely.

KOH-I-NOOR RAPIDOGRAPH PENS. Although these pens cannot be used with Leroy lettering templates (the standard lettering templates of the industry), they are excellent ruling

116 / Chap. 6
Essential Equipment

pens. They are dependable, well made, and will last for many years if treated with care.

Figure 6.4(a) shows a twelve-pen set that would be useful to beginners. Notice in Fig. 6.4(b) that line weights for Rapidograph pens are slightly different from the Leroy pens with the same numbers—see Fig. 6.3(b). Each pen in the Rapidograph series is both numbered (large number, heavy line; smaller numbers, thinner lines) and color coded.

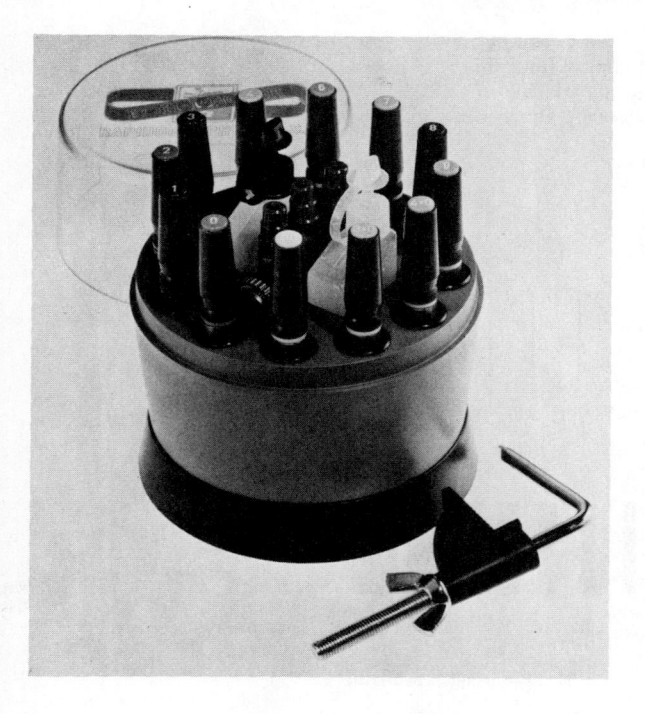

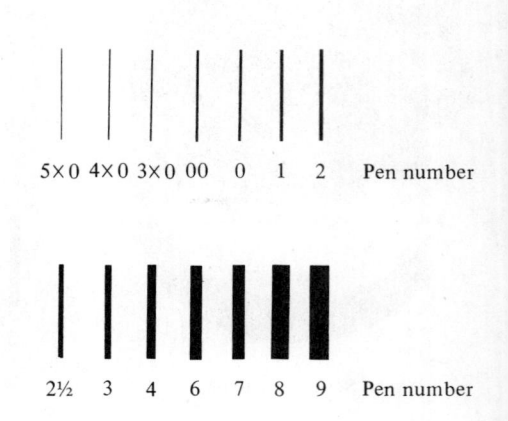

(a) Set of twelve pens.
(Courtesy KOH-I-NOOR Rapidograph, Inc.)

5×0 4×0 3×0 00 0 1 2   Pen number

2½ 3 4 6 7 8 9   Pen number

(b) Line weights available.

Figure 6.4 Rapidograph pens (*courtesy KOH-I-NOOR, INC.*).

A. W. FABER-CASTELL 990 PENS. These pens are compatible with the Leroy lettering sets and are excellent ruling pens. As mentioned earlier, all technical fountain pens are similar. The 990 pens are different from Leroy and Rapidograph pens in that a cartridge of ink is used, rather than detachable reservoirs, and line thicknesses are given in millimeters (mm) rather than inches (in.). The instruments are

(a) Filling TG pen

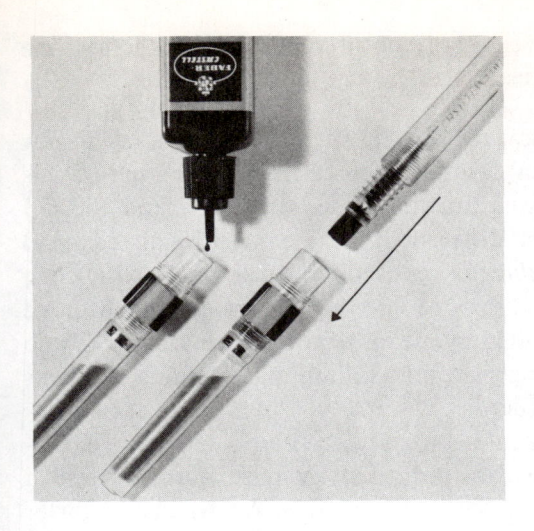

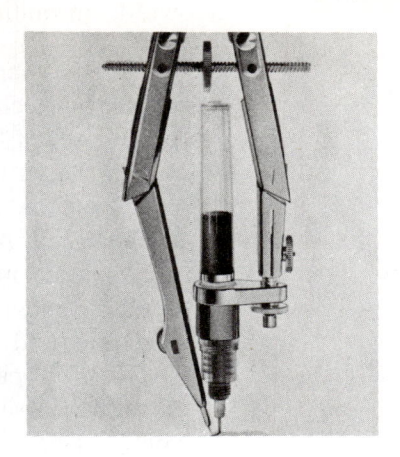

(b) A starter set

(c) Compass attachment

Figure 6.5 TG pens (*courtesy A. W. Faber-Castell Pencil Co., Inc.*).

coded as to line weights by both colors and the actual line widths in millimeters.

A. W. FABER–CASTELL TG PENS. The TG pen is a new concept in technical fountain pens. The main feature of this pen is the self-locking drawing cone.* In Fig. 6.5(a), the TG pen is shown to be different from a conventional technical pen. Note that *no threads* are used to attach the drawing cone to the barrel. Attaching or removing the cone from the cone socket is accomplished by means of the cone extractor. By so doing no messy fingers result. Filling and cleaning the pens is simpler and cleaner.

The TG pen can be used with Leroy lettering equipment. Line weights are indicated by both numbers and a color code and are given in millimeters. An adequate starter set would be the one shown in Fig. 6.5(b). The compass attachment shown in part (c) is a worthwhile accessory.

OTHER INKING PENS

Although the technical fountain pen is a versatile instrument, it will not be satisfactory for every job the illustrator must do. For this reason, many other types of pens are made and sold.

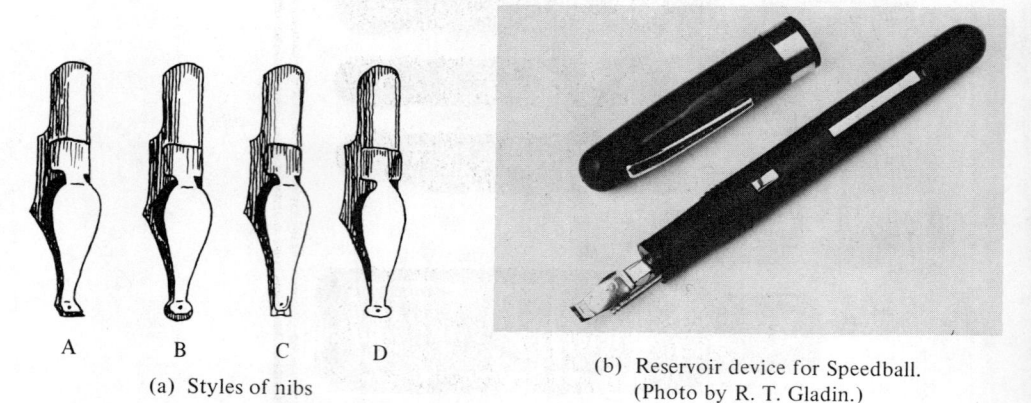

A   B   C   D
(a) Styles of nibs

(b) Reservoir device for Speedball.
(Photo by R. T. Gladin.)

Figure 6.6 Speedball nibs styles. Style A (square tip) is used for square Gothic and block letters; style B (round tip) is used for round Gothic letters and uniform lines; style C (oblong tip) is used for Roman lettering and shaded italics; and style D (oval tip) is used for bold Roman lettering, including italics. (Photo in (b) by R.T. Gladin.)

*The terminology here is that used by the manufacturer.

Listed below are several of the more often used pens and a short description of the use of each.

SPEEDBALL. This inexpensive pen is designed primarily for single-stroke lettering, freehand drawings, signs and cartooning. Four different nibs configurations shown in Fig. 6.6(a) with six different sizes for each configuration are available, along with suggested uses of each configuration. A reservoir device to use with Speedball nibs is shown in (b).

PELIKAN GRAPHOS. This pen set is a "cross" between a technical fountain pen and a nibs-type pen such as a Speedball. Ink is fed from a reservoir to interchangeable

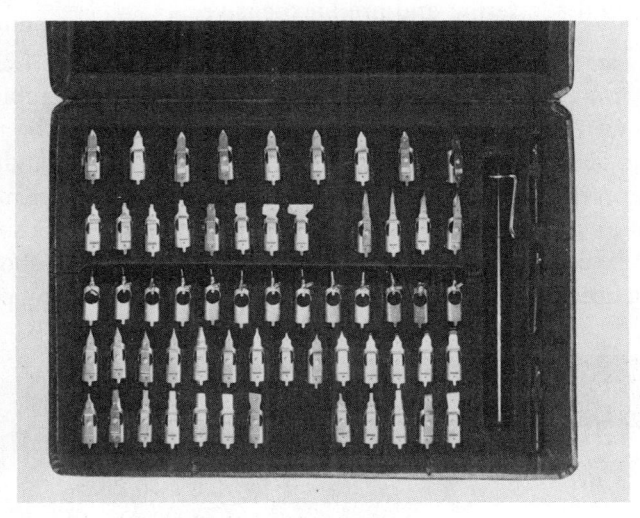

(a) Nibs in the set

RULING NIBS FOR FINE LINES

RULING NIBS for broad lines and for poster work

Drawing Nibs for fine freehand drawing sketching cartography and touch-up work

TUBULAR NIBS FOR STENCILLING WITH LETTERING GUIDES AND FOR CONTOUR LINES

ROUND NIBS for freehand lettering and sketching

Right hand slant nibs for oblique lines

Left hand slant nibs for oblique lines

(b) Uses of types of nibs

Figure 6.7 Pelikan Graphos pens (*courtesy PELIKAN Co.*).

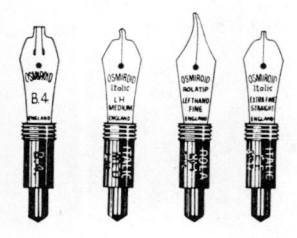

Figure 6.8 Osmiroid pen nibs.

nibs. Several nibs styles allow the pen to be used as a ruling pen (tubular nibs), single-stroke lettering pen (flat, square nibs), and a sketching pen (straight nibs). The set shown in Fig. 6.7(a) contains all nibs available. In Fig. 6.7(b) the different uses of types of nibs are shown.

OSMIROID PENS. The Osmiroid pen is similar to the Speedball pen. It is used primarily as a single-stroke lettering pen but, unlike the Speedball, the Osmiroid (shown in Fig. 6.8) is a reservoir-type that does not require repeated filling with ink. Although the manufacturer warns *not* to use water-soluble ink (most India inks are water-soluble), we have never been able to determine why. These instruments are fine for lettering and are inexpensive.

LEROY STANDARD PEN. For many years, until the Leroy reservoir-type pens came into wide use, these small, tubular pens were used with Leroy lettering sets. Although the reservoir pens are much easier to use as a ruling pen, standard pens produce the same line weights as the reservoir counterparts and cost much less. For a beginner, the cost aspect must be considered. In Fig. 6.9(a), the standard pen is shown being used as ruling pen and in Fig. 6.9(b) as a lettering pen.

(a) Ruling pen

(b) Lettering pen

Figure 6.9 Standard Leroy pens. (Photos by **R.T. Gladin**.)

CROW QUILL PENS. Crow quill pens and other inexpensive nibs are indispensible aids for sketching, freehand lettering, and fill-in pens. The drawing in Fig. 6.10(a) was made using a Gillott No. 303 pen point shown in Fig. 6.10(b). Note that line weights can be varied by pressing harder on the pen. Every illustrator should have a selection of these pens on hand. The points shown in Fig. 6.10(c) are few of the many available.

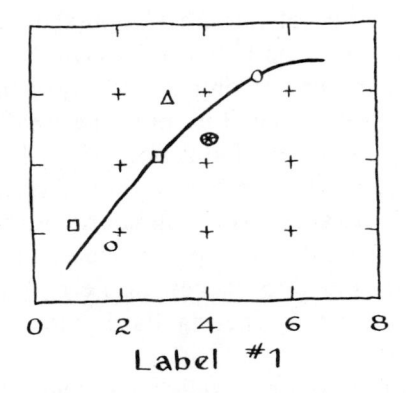

(a) Drawing made with crow quill

(b) Gillott #303 used in (a)

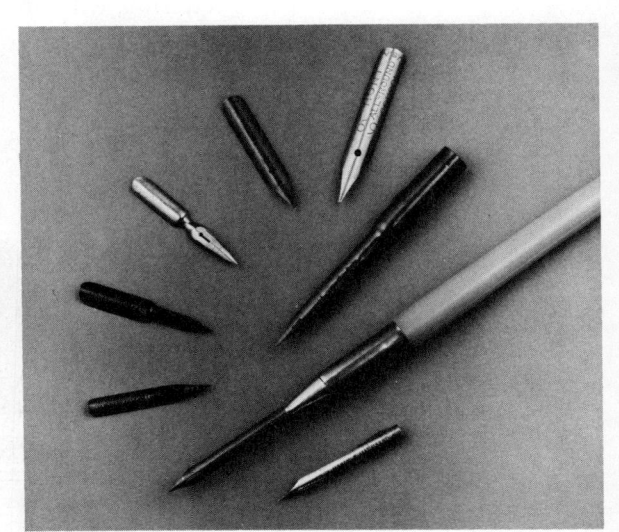

(c) Possible choices of nibs

Figure 6.10 The use and description of crow quill pens. (Photos by R.T. Gladin.)

We have discussed and illustrated 7 categories or types of pens. We could easily have discussed 20 other pens, slightly different from these. Because each is a variation of another, however, redundant descriptions are omitted, except in the case of technical fountain pens. Here the cost factor is so dominant that the purchaser must be aware of what his dollar will yield.

6B Lettering Devices

Without a doubt one of the most popular lettering devices used by illustrators is the LEROY lettering guide manufactured by Kueffel and Esser Company. Many scientific journals and style manuals distributed by publishers call this type of lettering simply *Leroy* (capitalization of all letters signifies a company trademark), an indication of how universally the equipment is accepted as *the* standard. Although several other drafting supplies companies manufacture similar lettering guides, none approaches the Leroy guide in popularity. Because Leroy is the standard, others will not be discussed.

Another popular but less well-suited device for attractive artwork is the stencil-type, cutout lettering guide. These guides are used primarily for preliminary layout where rapid lettering, with no call for technique, is required.

LEROY SETS

Shown in Fig. 6.11 is a beginner set of Leroy lettering equipment. This set contains one scriber, lettering guides

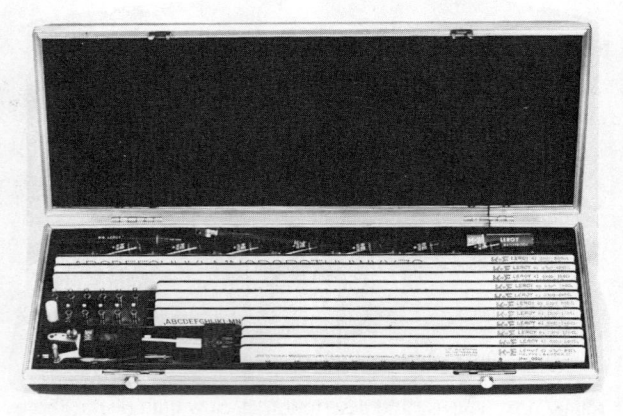

Figure 6.11 A Leroy lettering set (*courtesy K.&E. Company*).

with the standard Leroy alphabet templates ranging in size from 0.1 to 0.5 in.,* a set of Leroy standard pens, and seven reservoir pens. In the event that the reader is not familiar with this set, the following short description of its use is provided.

Referring to Fig. 6.12, the template is placed against a straightedge. Then the guide pin on the scriber is placed in the groove at the bottom of the template, while the tracer pin is inserted in the grooved letter we wish to reproduce with the pen. With *light* pressure, the grooved letter is traced. The template is then moved into position to trace the next letter or number in the string of characters to be reproduced.

Figure 6.12 Tracing a character from a Leroy lettering template. (Photo by R.T. Gladin.)

In addition to the standard alphabet templates shown in Fig. 6.12, Leroy templates of different sizes are available in Greek alphabet, mathematical symbols, electron tube and transistor symbols, electronic circuit symbols, welding symbols, Old English alphabet, and other assorted special purpose symbols and alphabets (see Fig. 6.13). In addition, custom-made templates can be obtained.† The one with arrowheads is custom made.

Leroy equipment is expensive but with proper use (it requires *no* maintenance) it will last a lifetime. Considering

---
*Minimum and maximum sizes of letters range from 0.05 to 2.00 in.
†You will pay dearly for them, however.

124 / Chap. 6
Essential Equipment

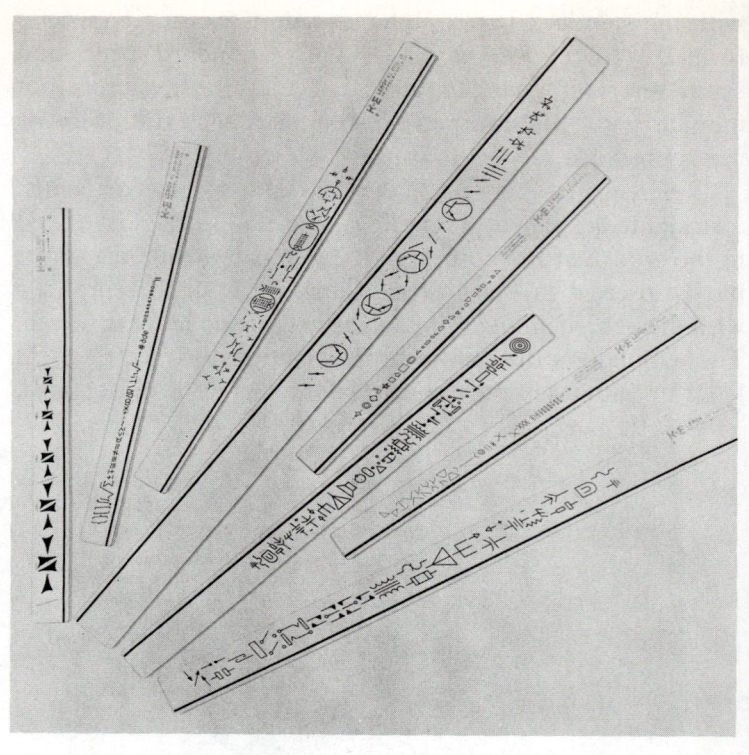

Figure 6.13 Special-purpose Leroy templates. (Photo by R.T. Gladin.)

the length of time this equipment can be used, it is one of the best investments an illustrator will ever make. Note that either of the two Leroy pen systems (reservoir or standard) will work with the lettering set discussed above.

The scriber shown in Fig. 6.14 is available in two styles—adjustable and fixed. The adjustable scriber may be used in the configuration shown in Fig. 6.14(a) to make italic letters from standard alphabet templates. If the fixed position is used, as in Fig. 6.14(b), the letters formed are vertical (called *Roman*).

Once the beginner has learned how to use the basic Leroy lettering set expertly, he may wish to expand the size of his set and include other special-purpose pieces of Leroy equipment.

SLANT–HEIGHT CONTROL SCRIBER. To increase the height of letters or numbers we normally will use a larger template and a standard scriber. To slant letters at a *specific* angle

Sec. 6B / 125
Lettering Devices

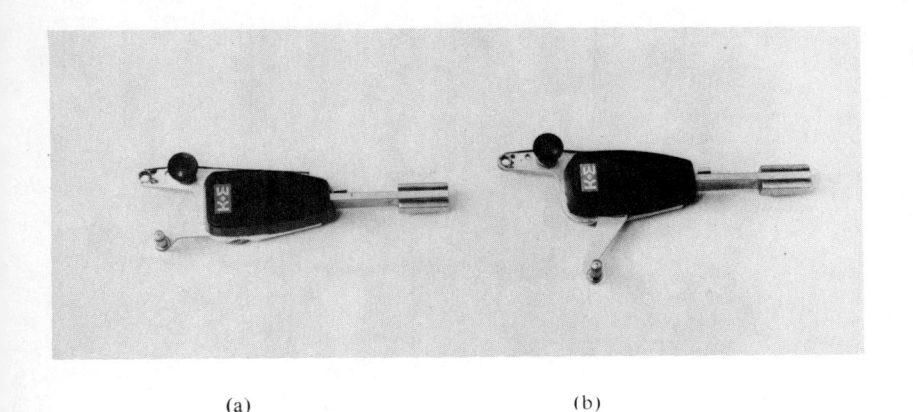

(a)   (b)

Figure 6.14 Leroy adjustable scribers provide for italic letters (right) and Roman letters (left). (Photos by R.T. Gladin.)

using the standard scriber, however, is a difficult proposition, with no assurance of repeating the angle if the setting is disturbed. The slant–height scriber shown in Fig. 6.15 solves the problem of slanting letters to a specific angle and *partially* solves the problem of increasing the letter size. We say *partially* because although the character height is increased, the width is not increased proportionally. In fact, the width is not increased at all. Thus, the characters are extended versions of the normal character.

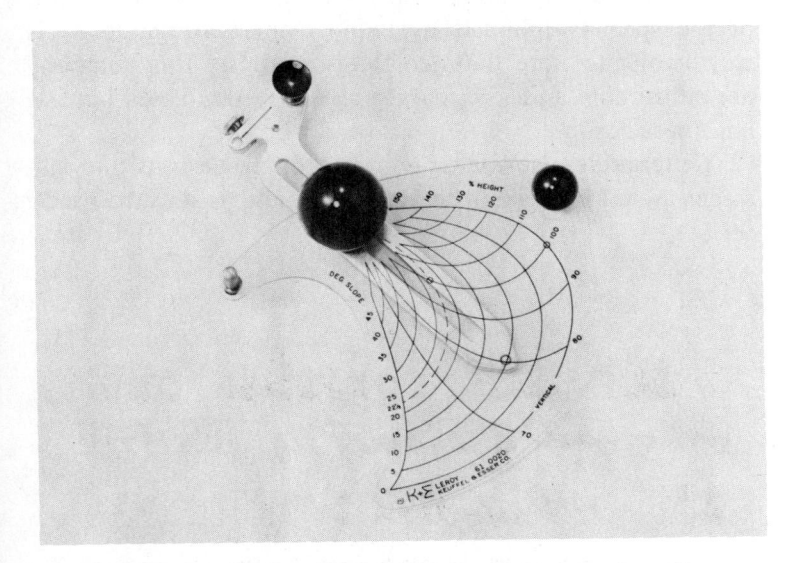

Figure 6.15 Leroy slant-height control scriber. (Photo by R.T. Gladin.)

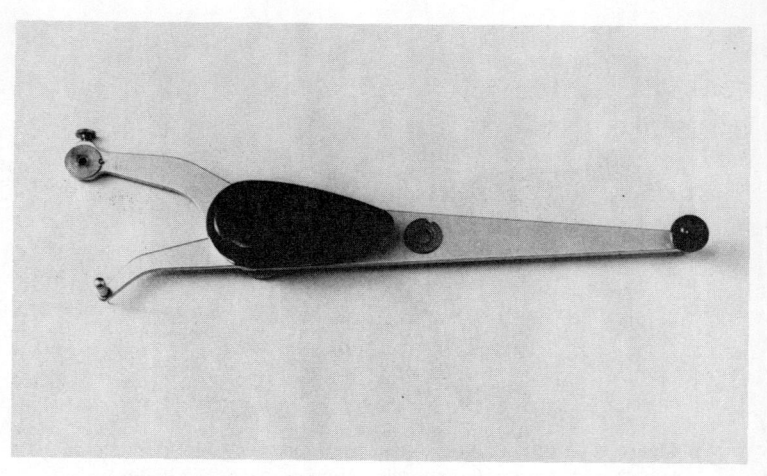

Figure 6.16 Leroy scriber use for templates larger than 0.50 in. (Photo by R.T. Gladin.)

LARGE SCRIBERS. The large scriber shown in Fig. 6.16 is used with templates larger than 0.50 in., sizes that are seldom used.

LETTERGUIDE TEMPLATES. Although the standard alphabet Leroy templates are the standard of the industry, other manufacturers, including Letterguide Co., make special alphabet templates and other helpful devices that are compatible with Leroy equipment. Figure 6.17 illustrates several of the special alphabets available from Letterguide. It is worthwhile to note that templates made by this company are as durable and as accurate as Leroy templates but are *much* less costly.

Letterguide also manufacturers ball-point pens and silk screen swivel knife instruments that can be used in the Leroy scriber.

Figure 6.17 Examples of alphabet styles available from Letterguide.

STENCIL LETTERING

KOH-I-NOOR Rapidoguides are cutout, stencil-like lettering aids. The user traces the character outline with a pen as shown in Fig. 6.18. The guides are manufactured on metal rails to raise the template off the paper surface to prevent smearing of ink while lettering. Several other companies manufacture similar lettering devices. Several different typefaces are available.

Although these devices are not quality lettering instruments, they are useful in making presentations in a hurry or for preliminary layout drawings.

Figure 6.18 Rapidoguide lettering instrument (*courtesy KOH-I-NOOR Co.*).

6C Compasses

Not all lines required to establish shapes and contours are straight lines. For this reason, no illustrator must be without a compass of some sort. A myriad of different compasses are available but the best one for an individual is that instrument with which he can obtain consistent results. The following six categories of compasses will give an indication of a *complete* set.

LEAD COMPASS

This type of compass, shown in Fig. 6.19, is available in either friction or bow styles. We recommend the bow style because settings are not disturbed by movement or accidental bumps. In addition to being available in friction or bow styles, several different sizes are available. It is recommended that $1\frac{1}{2}$ and 6 in. compasses be included in the list of equipment. Dimensions given are diameters of the largest circles that can be drawn with the instrument. Because so much of the illustrating work will be done in ink, it is fair to ask why have lead compasses. The reasoning is simple. Although an inked drawing is the final product, light blue or black pencil lines are used for rough layout work.

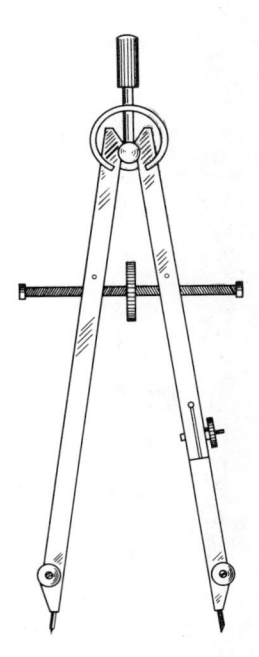

Figure 6.19
A bow-type lead compass.

NIBS-TYPE INKING COMPASS

As in the case of lead compasses, these instruments are available in either friction or bow styles. It is possible and preferable to have both the lead and nibs-type inking compass in one instrument; see Fig. 6.20.

DROP-BOW COMPASS

In order to draw small circles accurately, a drop-bow compass is an indispensable aid. Although circle templates (the cutout variety) can be used to draw circles, the small circles drawn will not be as accurate as those drawn with a drop bow. As in the case with larger compasses, the drop bow can be a combination pencil–ink instrument as shown in Fig. 6.21.

BEAM COMPASS

If it is necessary to draw very large circles, a beam compass is a must. This instrument derives its name from the fact that the stationary point (at the center of the circle) and the drawing point (at the diameter of the circle) are positioned on or fixed to a long beam—see Fig. 6.22.

KOH-I-NOOR COMPASSES

Most inking compasses require the use of nibs-type inking pens. This is not the case with the KOH-I-NOOR instru-

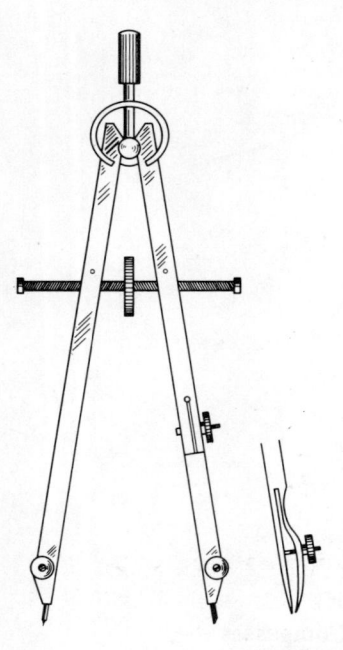

Figure 6.20 A combination ink–pencil compass.

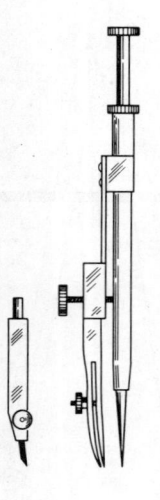

Figure 6.21 A drop-bow compass.

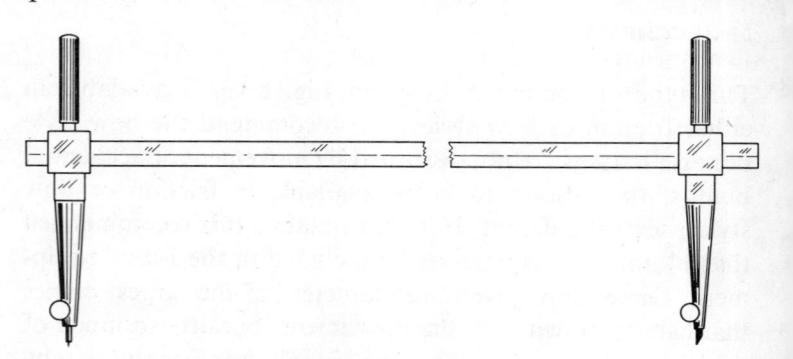

Figure 6.22 A beam compass.

(a)   (b)

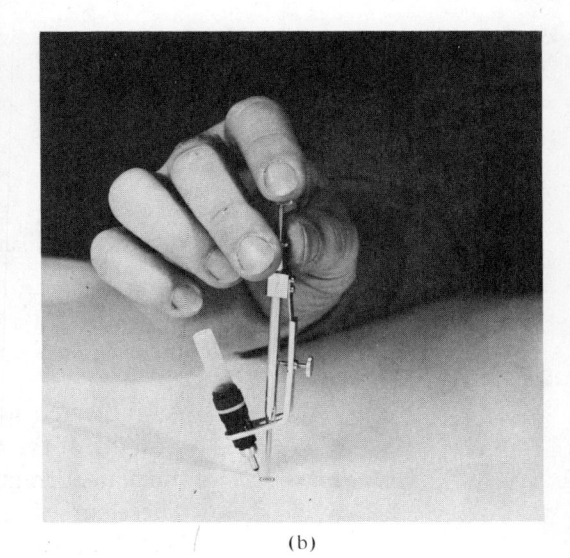

Figure 6.23 KOH-I-NOOR compasses that allow the use of Rapidograph *or* Leroy pens as nibs (Photo by R.T. Gladin.)

ments shown in Fig. 6.23. Here the illustrator is able to select a line width corresponding to either the K.&E. or Rapidograph reservoir pens and then use these pens to draw the circle. Each compass, the bow and drop bow, can be equipped with lead attachments. These compasses are recommended highly. The ease with which consistent line weights can be obtained with these instruments is worth their price.

6D Miscellaneous

TRIANGLES

Most beginning draftsmen or illustrators consider the triangle to be an unimportant part of the equipment they must use. These plastic instruments are, however, an extremely important part of their equipment. Nearly all vertical lines on a drawing will be drawn using triangles. For this reason, the triangles that become a part of an equipment inventory must be accurate; i.e., the angles must be near their specified values.

To be *well* equipped, an illustrator should have the following triangles. It is unhandy to draw 1-in. lines with a 10-in. triangle.

Type (Degrees)	Size* (Inches)
30–60	4
30–60	6
30–60	10
45	4
45	6
45	10

*The size of a triangle is indicated by the measured length along the longest vertical edge.

IRREGULAR AND SHIP CURVES

As indicated previously, not all lines on all illustrations are straight. If the curves drawn are not circular or elliptical, we must use irregular curves, commonly called *French curves*. These curves can be purchased individually or in sets. A set is useful but the curves in Fig. 6.24(a) will suffice for 90 percent of work requiring the use of irregular curves.

In some cases, long curves (called *ship* curves) will be more useful than the small curves. The ones shown in Fig. 6.24(b) can be used in most cases. The complete set is expensive and, for the most part, so much excess baggage.

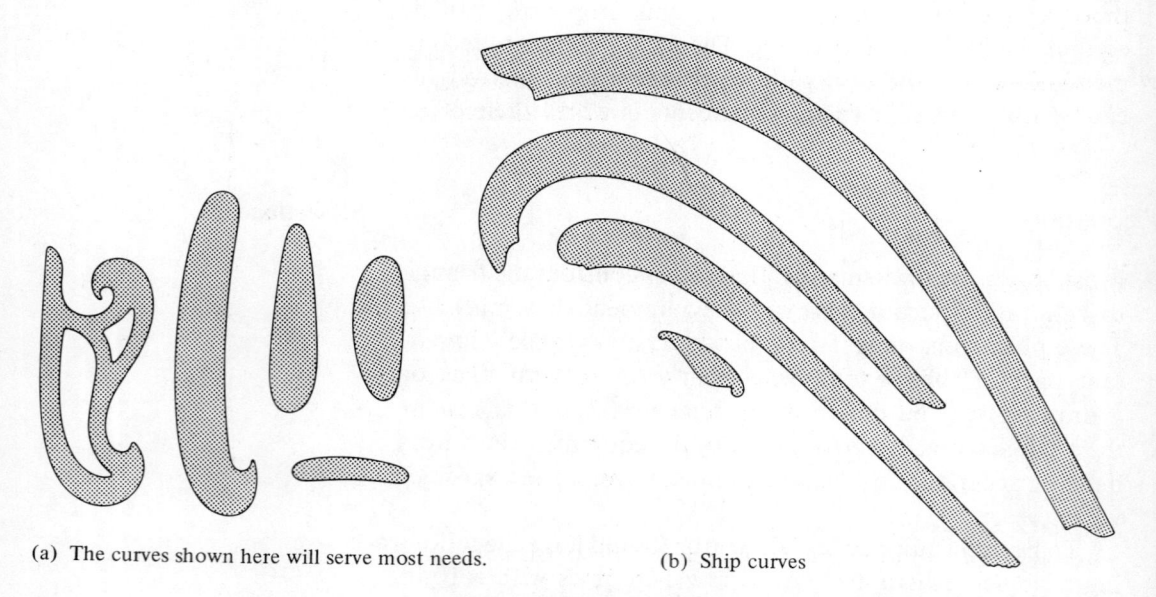

(a) The curves shown here will serve most needs.   (b) Ship curves

Figure 6.24 Irregular and ship curves used in illustrating.

PENCILS

Drawing pencils can be divided into two general groups: wooden and mechanical. Nearly everyone who has learned to write has used a wooden pencil but not so many have had occasion to see or use a mechanical drafting pencil (also called a *lead holder*) such as those shown in Fig. 6.25.

The wooden drafting pencil offers an inexpensive way to have a wide selection of lead hardnesses (see hardness scale in Fig. 6.26) on hand for such chores as pencil sketching. Shades and shadows may be added using soft lead, whereas initial outlines may be done with a harder lead. Lead holders do not offer the same low-cost versatility.

If we used one holder for many lead hardnesses, we would be forced to change leads often; using one holder for each of several hardnesses, we would spend too much money for holders. To reach a happy medium, an illustrator should have a selection of wooden drafting pencils (one or two of each hardness) and one or two lead holders. He would then be set up for jobs requiring several hardnesses (wooden pencils) and those jobs requiring primarily one hardness lead (lead holders).

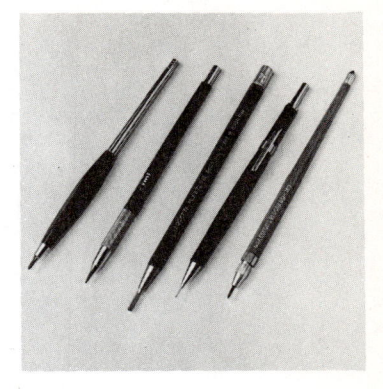

Figure 6.25
Mechanical drafting pencils.
(Photo by R.T. Gladin.)

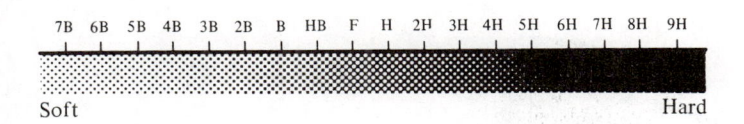

7B 6B 5B 4B 3B 2B B HB F H 2H 3H 4H 5H 6H 7H 8H 9H

Soft   Hard

Figure 6.26 Pencil lead hardness scale.

In addition to these black lead pencils, an illustrator must have several light blue pencils (wooden) for use in layout before inking: Light blue* does not reproduce during high contrast photography.

PENCIL POINTERS

Wooden pencils may be pointed by using a knife, small blade-type pointers, conventional pencil sharpeners, or electric pencil sharpeners. More exact points may be made

*Use Eagle Verithin, Sky Blue 740$\frac{1}{2}$.

with fine sandpaper pads. Whatever method works best for the individual should be used.

Mechanical drafting pencils can be pointed by using sandpaper pads, metal files, electric pointers, or small blade-type pointers.

Erasers

Although most of us do not make misteaks, we must sometimes alter our thinking to agree with someone so that his wishes are met or to exercise flexibility in our work. If we are an illustrator, we must do this quite often—at least until we are recognized experts. To allow us to alter our thinking with ease, some noble man invented the eraser. These small wondrous pieces of rubber, fiber glass, or steel (yes, steel!) can serve us well.

Figure 6.27 illustrates a few of the erasers we can and should have available. In particular, let us dwell for a moment on the electric eraser. This instrument is essential to the illustrator who anticipates working with ink. *No substitute can be found for the electric eraser for erasing inked lines.*

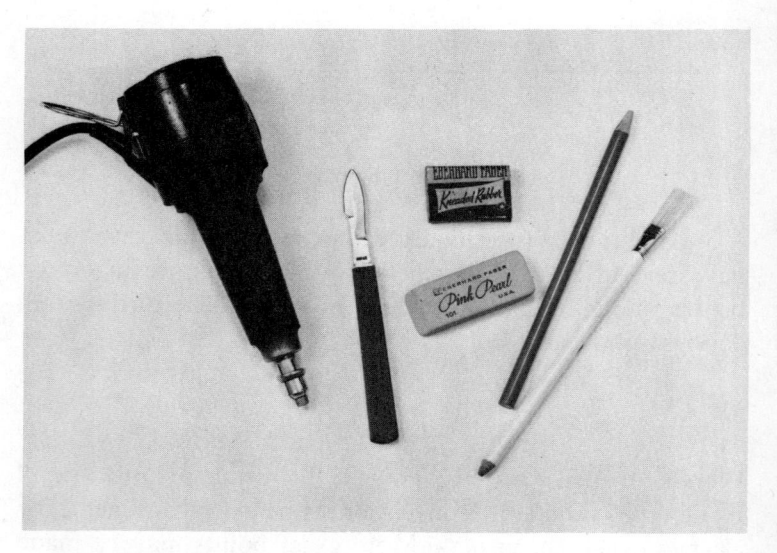

Figure 6.27 Erasers that can be used by an illustrator. (Photo by R.T. Gladin.)

STRAIGHT EDGE

This device is essentially what the name implies: a straight edge of plastic (or metal) equipped with a pulley system that allows it to *move* normal to the straightedge—see Fig. 6.28.

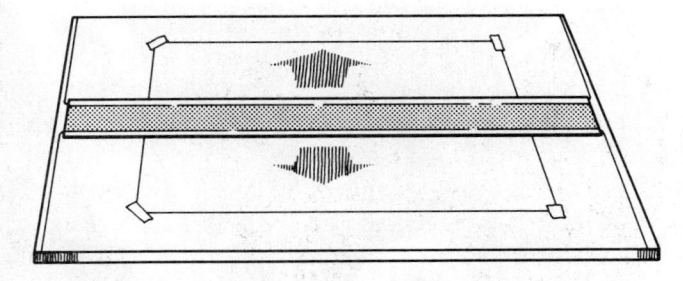

Figure 6.28 Parallel straightedge.

T SQUARE

This drafting aid has been used for centuries and, unless someone thinks of a simpler device, will be used for many more centuries. A T square is simply a straightedged blade attached to a head in such a fashion that the edge of the head and the blade are positioned at right angles (see Fig. 6.29).

T squares can be made from wood, wood–plastic combinations, and metals. They can be purchased at nearly any drafting or art supply store and are available in many blade lengths. One word of caution concerning T squares and their use: *The edge of the drafting board against which the T square head slides must be true.* Irregularity in this edge will cause errors.

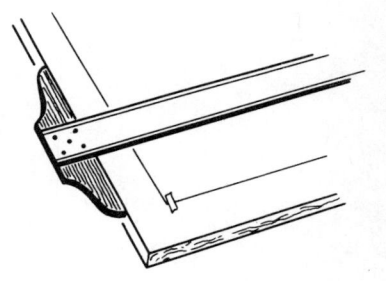

Figure 6.29 A T square.

DRAFTING MACHINES

These instruments are versatile, accurate, long lasting, and expensive. Many different manufacturers market drafting machines and most are excellent pieces of equipment.

A drafting machine combines the functions of a T square (or straightedge), triangle, scale, and circular protractor in one unit. In operation, the scale assembly moves in parallel motion only. When the machine is set so that one scale is horizontal and the other is vertical, we have an equivalent of a T square (horizontal) and a triangle (vertical). The divider head protractor is made such that 15° click stop or fractions of 1° increments may be set. Figure 6.30 illustrates the functions of drafting machines.

Figure 6.30 A drafting machine is a T square, a triangle, and a protractor in one unit (*courtesy K.&E. Co.*).

TEMPLATES

In many instances we will not wish to use a compass or straightedge triangle to draw certain geometric shapes. For example, to draw a blend radius or circular data point using a compass would be too time-consuming for the accuracy demanded. Construction of elliptical shapes would occupy too much of our time. To avoid such costly construction, the illustrator should have a few basic cutout templates (shown in Fig. 6.31) in his equipment inventory. As time passes, the inventory may be added to.

CIRCLE TEMPLATES. Circle templates are available from many suppliers in many forms. We may buy templates with circle diameters measured in either decimals or fractions of an inch or centimeters. Sizes of circles on a template range from $\frac{1}{16}$- to 4-in. diameters. We are able to purchase very accurate or very inaccurate templates.

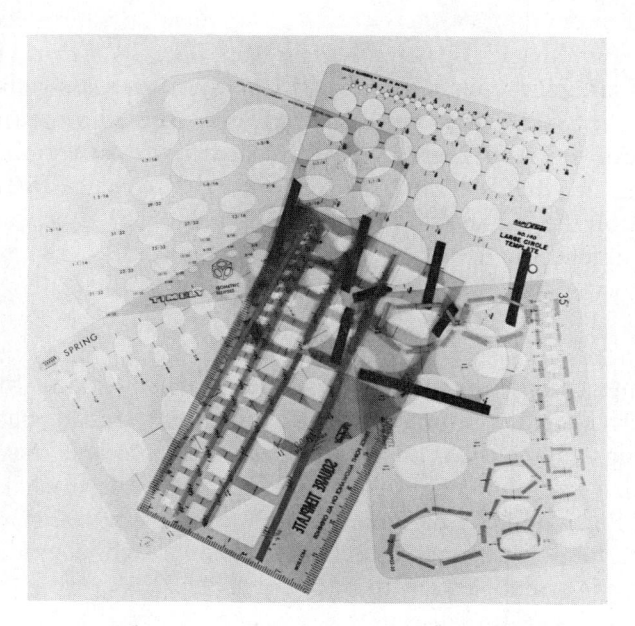

Figure 6.31 Cutout templates. The taped strips allow the template to be held off the drawing surface to avoid smudging. (Photo by R.T. Gladin.)

ELLIPSE TEMPLATES. These templates are necessary if an illustrator is to execute three-dimensional drawings. Manufacturers usually make two sets of ellipse guides: small series and large series. The small series might include templates that may be used to draw ellipses with $\frac{1}{8}$- to 2-in. major-axis length from 10 to 80° angles. The large series might include 10 to 80° angles and $2\frac{1}{8}$- to 4-in. ellipses.

OTHER TEMPLATES. As the equipment inventory of an illustrator grows, many of the additions will be in the form of timesaving templates. Squares, triangles, sine waves, diamonds, hexagons, bolt heads, arrowheads, brackets, rivets, gear teeth, welding symbols, and literally hundreds of other shapes or items may be drawn rapidly if the proper template is at hand.

The beginner must, however, exercise care in his choices and he must never forget the purpose of the template: to aid him in producing his work. If the template will aid and not detract from the overall appearance of the drawing, then it should be used. If using the template doesn't help, don't use it.

INK

Most drawing will be done in black India ink on vellum paper and will be reproduced using some sort of photographic process. For this reason, the illustrator must be certain to use an ink that will spread evenly in a dense, black line. In addition the ink should be thin enough to not clog pens. We recommend the use of Higgins Black Magic Ink.

PAPER

For most work, vellum paper will give excellent results. Most people consider vellum to be a translucent tracing paper, whereas in reality vellum can be defined as paper having a finish resembling eggshell. Vellum is available in slick or matt finish and can be found in the form of thin, translucent sheets or poster board-thick sheets. Using a good grade of vellum is essential. Don't skimp on paper.

6E Specialty Items

ULTRASONIC CLEANERS

In 10 minutes, a technical fountain pen may be disassembled and *thoroughly* cleaned using an ultrasonic cleaner. Running water through a dirty pen point does not dislodge small carbon particles from threads and soaking the pens in cleaning fluid requires time. With the ultrasonic cleaner, ultrasound waves are used to dislodge particles and speed the cleaning process.

The vibrator units used in drafting supplies company models are not large enough to hold up under steady use. By spending an extra few dollars, a unit of proper size can be obtained from electronic supply houses.

CAMERA LUCIDA

This instrument employs mirrors and prisms to "project" a right-side-up image of an object onto a flat plane. Then the image can be traced. A lucida is quite often used in conjunction with a microscope for sketching insects or microscopic objects.

The camera lucida shown in Fig. 6.32(a) is an expensive item because it is part of a binocular (3-D) microscope.

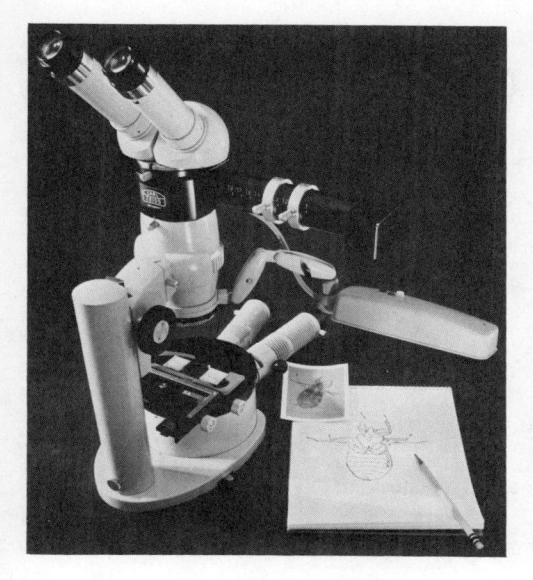

(a) Camera lucida incorporated in a binocular microscope. (*courtesy Carl Zeis, Inc., New York*).

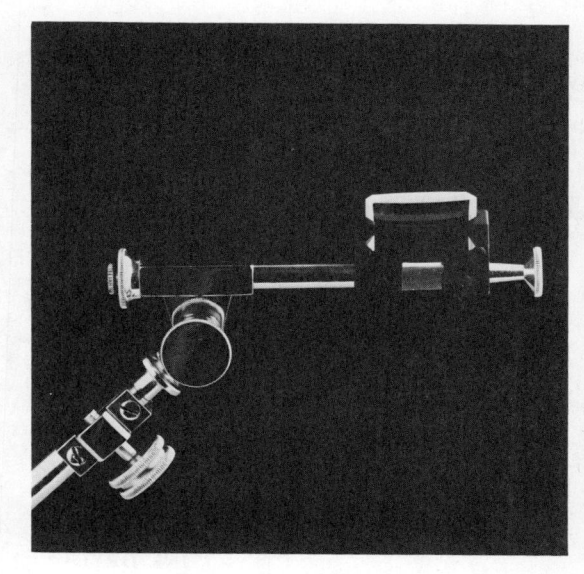

(b) A lucida that requires some practice before mastery of its use is attained. (Photo by R. T. Gladin.)

Figure 6.32 Camera lucidas.

Unless an illustrator intends to specialize in a field (such as entomology) requiring the use of this instrument, he should wait for his first million before buying one.

A less expensive but precise lucida is shown in Fig. 3.32(b). Using such an instrument, an illustrator can enlarge or reduce a drawing, an object, or a photograph. The principle of operation here is simple but practice is necessary before one fully masters the use of such a device.

VISUALIZER

A visualizer is essentially an opaque projector capable of enlarging or reducing copy by accurately controlled amounts. In some models the image is projected onto a ground glass, whereas others project the image directly onto paper for tracing. Figure 6.33 illustrates one model.

Each type has advantages and disadvantages, which should be considered carefully before a purchase is made. As in the case of a microscope camera lucida, an illustrator should be "in the chips" before he considers purchasing a visualizer.

138 / Chap. 6
Essential Equipment

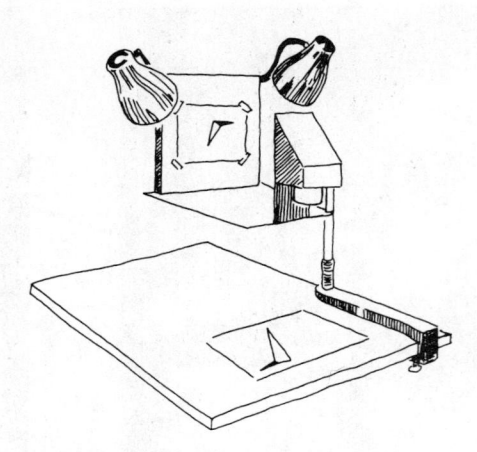

Figure 6.33 A direct image visualizer.

INK DRYER

Although we list an ink dryer as a special piece of equipment, it is so indispensable that it should be a part of an illustrator's initial equipment purchase. Shown in Fig. 6.34 is a hand-held hair dryer that can be used to blow heated or unheated air over ink lines to dry them more quickly. If we stop to consider that a thick line (#3 Rapidograph pen) is drawn in a few seconds and then we must wait for a minute (60 seconds) for the ink to dry, the importance of drying lines quickly becomes relevant.

Even more time can be consumed waiting for large areas that are painted with ink to dry. It may seem to be a small point to consider but when we must wait for ink to dry, we cannot be putting ink lines on the paper—we are losing time and wasting our client's money. In addition, if the ink is dry—we can't smudge it.

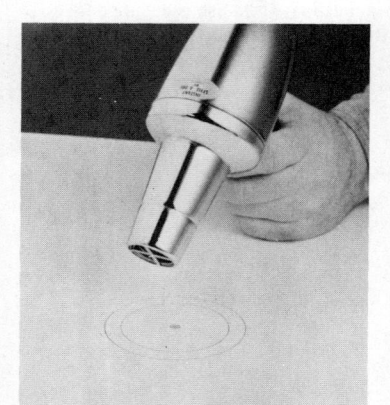

Figure 6.34
A device to dry ink—a hand-held hair dryer. (Photo by R.T. Gladin.)

REDUCING LENS

More often than not, we will execute illustrations to a size larger than the final product. The beginner and his client will have difficulty visualizing what the final product will look like. For purposes of previewing the final product, an inexpensive reducing lens may be purchased. Then by applying a few marks to the lens (as shown in Fig. 6.35) we can actually see a reduced version of the drawing.

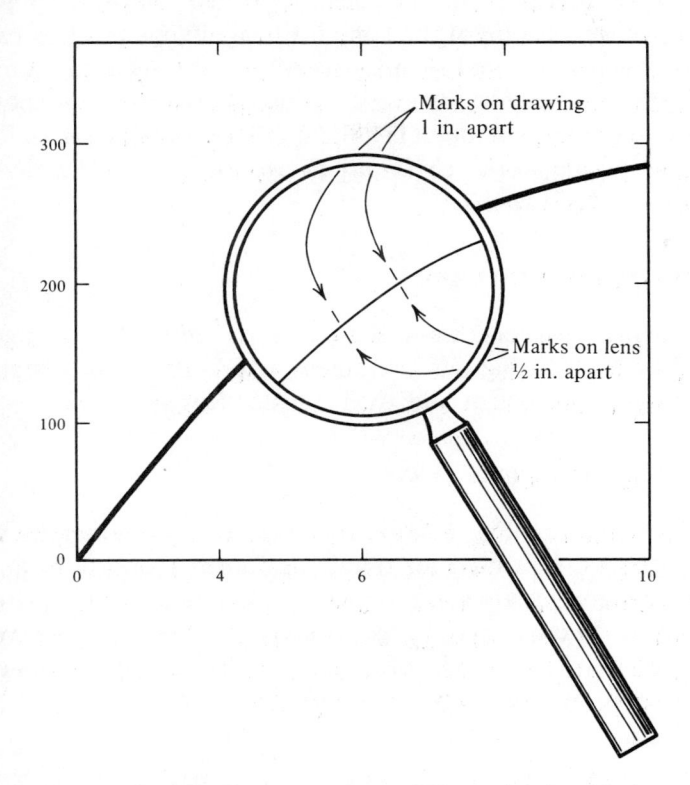

Figure 6.35 Use of a reducing lens to preview a drawing. Mark 1 in. (to the prescribed reduced scale) *on* the lens (use crayon pencil) and a full-size 1 in. on the illustration. Vary the distance the lens is from the art until the two marks match.

LAMPS

Some may say that light is light, which is true—up to a point. They also may say that light sources (lamps) are light sources and that nothing will be lost (or gained) by using one light source as opposed to another. In reality, nothing could be further from the truth.

Incandescent lamps give off a great deal of heat and tend to produce hot spots (areas more highly illuminated than others) on paper, causing eyes to strain. Fluorescent lamps, on the other hand, give off much less heat and produce a more even illumination, thereby causing less eye strain. Because an illustrator uses his eyes at all times during his work, he should protect them.

140 / Chap. 6
Essential Equipment

One useful lamp to consider is the magnifier type. The center portion of the lamp is a magnifying lens that can be changed to change magnification. Although the lamp should not be used for every job because of the "hot spot" nature of illumination, it is quite useful for detail work or for hand stipple work. *Under no circumstances should a high-intensity lamp be used.*

PROPORTIONAL DIVIDERS

In many instances, we will be able to reduce (or enlarge) a drawing by using this instrument, which allows us to make a simple adjustment and then transfer lengths.

LOGARITHMIC SPIRAL CURVE

This curve (see Fig. 6.36) is constructed using principles of logarithms. It is used for obtaining fourth proportions and to perform multiplication and division graphically. Also, because the curvature changes from point to point, this curve can be fitted to *any* part of a given curve. Finding centers of curvature of given curves is simplified.

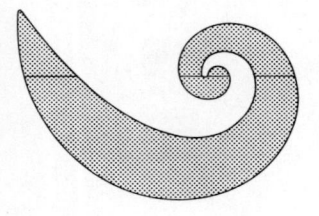

Figure 6.36
A logarithmic spiral curve.

PANTOGRAPH

A pantograph is a device used either to enlarge or to reduce drawings to scale. Structurally, the pantograph is a hinged parallelogram with a tracer point and a drawing point set at the ends of the diagonals of the parallelogram. A *good* pantograph is expensive and an *inexpensive* one is useless.

**6F
Incidental Equipment
and Supplies**

Incidental to every illustrator's equipment and supplies are items such as those listed below. In most cases, individual preferences gained from experience will dictate brands.

Masking tape. Used to secure paper to the drawing surface.

Clear adhesive tape. Used for paste-up or patching drawings.

Pounce. To eliminate oily finger or palm prints.

Pen cleaner fluid. To soften hard carbon deposits in pens or on pen points.

Double-backed tape. A thin, transparent, double-backed tape that can be used to stick lettering or other paste-up parts to a drawing.

Paper (drawing medium). Illustrator's choice for the particular application.

Board brush. Self-explanatory.

Paper cutters. It is best to have a 14-in. scissors for long cuts and to use on thick material, a 6-in. scissors for work fitting that size, and a 1- or 2-in. scissors for small detail work. The small scissors should be made from stainless steel.

Sharp, pointed-blade knife. Here the No. 11 blade and X-Acto knife is best.

Burnishing tool. A tool used to rub acetate overlay patterns or transfer letters.

Tweezers. The three point types shown in the illustration will serve the purpose in most instances. *Always* buy stainless steel tweezers.

Pica Scale. This scale, usually an inexpensive plastic type, is used to lay out copy in pica measure rather than in inches or centimeters. It is indispensable when working with publishers or typographers; they *never* use inches.

Paint brushes. Good grade sable brushes are needed to paint in large areas, to do lettering, or to opaque negatives.

Circular protractor. A 6-in. circular protractor (full 360°) should be available.

Elliptical protractor. If much isometric, dimetric, and trimetric work is to be done, an ellipse protractor for the various angle ellipses is useful.

Percentage protractor. A circular protractor marked in percentages of full circular measure (instead of degrees) is useful for making "pie" charts.

Arkansas oil stone. To sharpen knife blades, rather than buy new ones, the Arkansas oil stone is a must. Note that the Arkansas oil stone (and only that one) is recommended. Don't accept substitutes.

Tape dispensers. Rather than peel tape from a roll, buy two or three weighted dispensers.

Scales. Here the illustrator should have scales marked off both in fractions of an inch ($\frac{1}{32}$), in decimal parts of an inch ($\frac{1}{50}$), and in centimeters. Accuracy is a matter of price.

QUESTIONS

1. What is a technical fountain pen? What is the *main* purpose of using such a pen?
2. Name and describe the use of the pens listed below:
   (a) Speedball
   (b) Osmiroid
   (c) Crow quill
3. List several reasons why Leroy equipment is useful to have and advantageous to use.
4. What does a slant–height scriber do?
5. What is a stencil-like lettering device?
6. Name three types of compasses.
7. Why is it important to check the accuracy of a triangle?
8. What is a drafting machine? Explain the operation of this device.
9. Is a drafting machine more versatile than a parallel straightedge? Why or why not?
10. In what cases would a cutout template be used?
11. Do you consider paper an important part of your supplies? Why or why not?

Part III

Using Skills and Tools

In the American way of life, visual communication (both the written word and illustrations) plays an extremely important role. We have merely to pick up a newspaper, a magazine, or a textbook or to watch education-programmed television to realize the importance of visual communication. Each of these items stress seeing.

Newspapers. The primary vehicle for transferring information in a newspaper is the printed word. Illustrations are used, however, in advertising, comic strips, the editorial page (caricatures of politicians is a good example), and certain articles of interest where an illustration will help convey the message.

Magazines. In this medium, illustrations play an important part—usually as important a part as the printed matter. Illustrations are black and white or color line drawings and color and black and white photographs.

Textbooks. For the most part, illustrations in texts are complementary to the text—not supplementary. A picture (or drawing) is literally worth the thousand words it is supposed to be worth. A complex equation can be solved numerically and plotted as a curve to illustrate features that could not be *imagined* from looking at the equation.

Television. Students of today are learning by watching television. For example, children in elementary schools watch television programs in classrooms to learn numbering systems, geography, and many other subjects. Learning programs that use a display screen and a typewriter-like console are in use. The student is asked a question (by a computer program—not the computer); he responds by typing in his answer; he is questioned again (if his answer is wrong); and, ultimately, his answer is correct and he is graded. Many illustrations are used in this type of television programming.

In most cases, in each of the four media listed above, certain illustrations will be done in a recognizable style. For example, political cartoonist Oliphant* uses a particular style that is recognized immediately.

'. . . BUT FIRST, LET'S HEAR YOUR POSITION ON THE ALASKA PIPELINE AND INDEPENDENT GAS DISTRIBUTORS!'

Figure III.1 Political cartoon by Oliphant. (*Editorial cartoon by Pat Oliphant, copyright, The Denver Post. Reprinted with Permission of Los Angeles Times syndicate.*)

*Denver Post newspaper and syndicated.

Fashion illustrations in newspapers and magazines usually show a particular style. Certain textbooks are done in a definite style.

On the whole, not many types of styles exist. In this text we will discuss two types—freehand and mechanical. Before discussing them, however, we will examine criteria for any type of style or drawing. For any illustration to be worth the paper it is drawn on, we must answer yes to five questions.

1. *Is the illustration executed well?* Independent of the style used, an illustration must be executed well. The drawing in Fig. III.2(a) is done poorly and is unsuitable for use anywhere, whereas the same drawing redone in Fig. III.2(b) is well done and could be used nearly anywhere. The point to be made is simple: If the illustrator was happy with (a), he should re-examine his criteria for choosing good work.

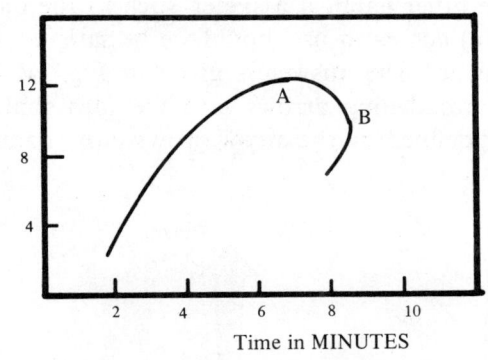

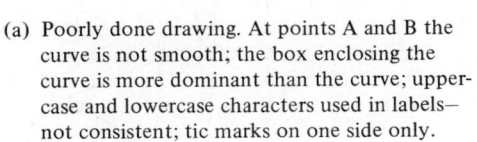

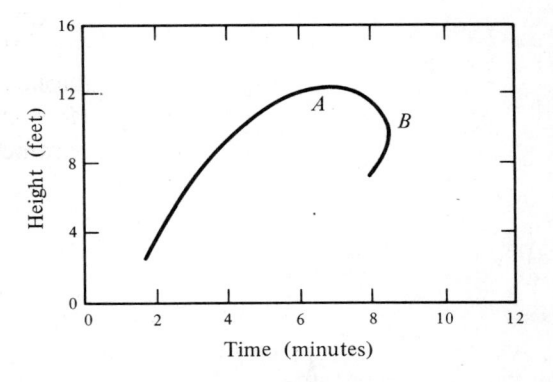

(a) Poorly done drawing. At points A and B the curve is not smooth; the box enclosing the curve is more dominant than the curve; uppercase and lowercase characters used in labels—not consistent; tic marks on one side only.

(b) Part (a) redrawn correctly

Figure III.2 Comparison of (a) a poor drawing and (b) a good drawing.

2. *Is the illustration descriptive?* Note and note well that descriptive does not mean detailed. In Fig. III.3(a) an extremely detailed representation of a machine part is given. In Fig. III.3(b) the same drawing has been redone and, although not detailed, the drawing is descriptive. Never include detail that is superfluous.

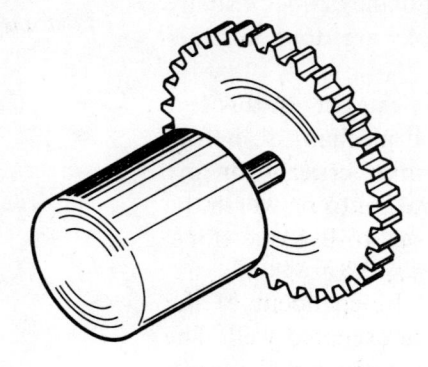

(a) A detailed gear 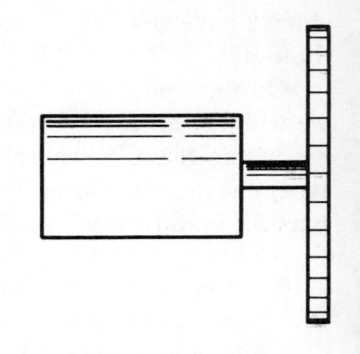 (b) A descriptive version

Figure III.3 A drawing can be (a) detailed and (b) not be as effective as one that is descriptive. The amount of detail in (a) does not assist the reader in seeing how the device operates.

Why have someone (a reader or buyer) sort through detail to get to the meat of the drawing?

On the other hand, if a sketch such as the one in Fig. III.4(a) comes to us, should we be satisfied with duplicating it? The answer is given in Fig. III.4(b). Here the broadening arrows give the idea that the parameter defined by the arrow grows more complex

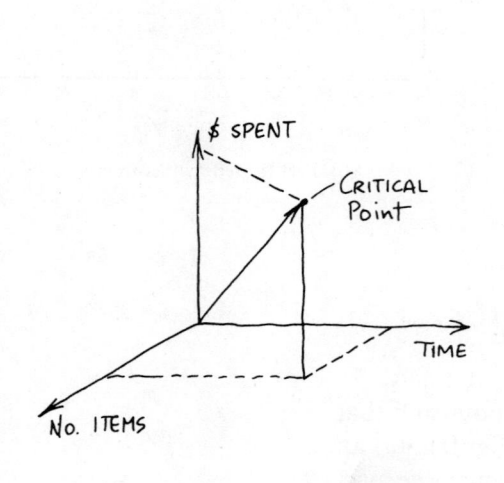

(a) An author's sketch 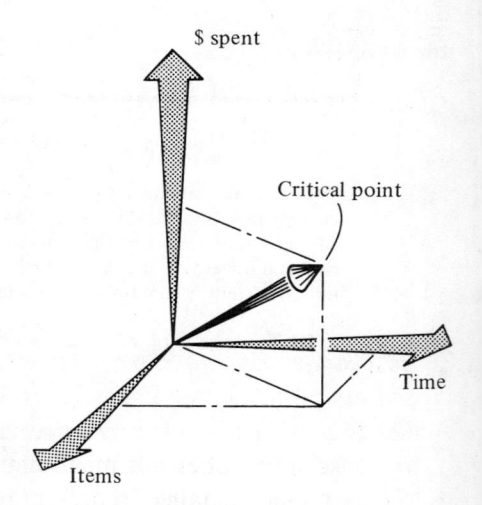 (b) An artist's version

Figure III.4 A descriptive drawing adds flavor to an otherwise bland presentation.

146

as we proceed from the origin of the plot. The illustration is descriptive.

3. *Is the illustration realistic?* We can mean one of two things when we talk about realism. If the object or idea we are illustrating is something we can see and relate to, we should execute the illustration so that our audience can recognize immediately what we have drawn. For example, the chemical apparatus in Fig. III.5(a) is drawn in Fig. III.5(b). We can see the likeness. The drawing is realistic.

(a) Chemical apparatus as a photograph

(b) Chemical apparatus as a drawing

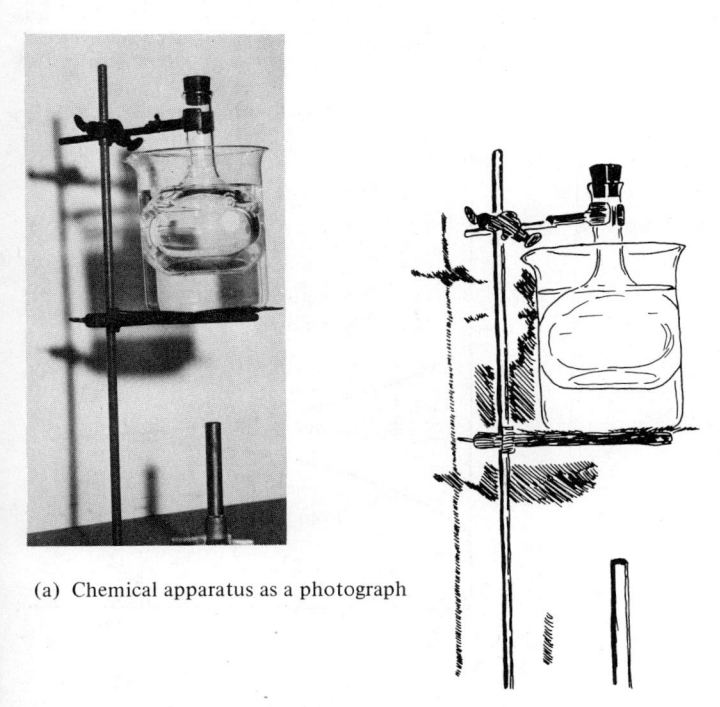

Figure III.5 To be realistic, a photograph is not always necessary.

Now assume that we must prepare an illustration showing a single molecule bouncing around in a box. Because we have never witnessed this phenomenon, we must abstract the drawing and hope that everyone who looks at the drawing will be happy with our interpretation.

4. *Have we addressed the audience properly?* If we are preparing an illustration to be used to explain a concept

148 / Part III
Using Skills and Tools

of physics to grammer school students, we might wish to use a cartoon. The drawing in Fig. III.6(a) would be suited to youngsters, whereas the drawing in Fig. III.6(b) would be used to explain the same concept to a college physics student.

Man (warm) and bed (cold)

The concept being illustrated is that a warm body and cold body in contact eventually reach the same temperature.

Man and bed (same temperature)

(a) For youngsters

(b) For college students

Figure III.6 The cartoons in (a) would be suitable for explaining a concept to youngsters; in (b), the same concept would be explained to college physics students by using a more technical approach.

The point to be made is that we must always be aware of the audience to whom the illustration is addressed. If we are not, the act of illustrating can become an exercise in futility.

5. *Are we proud of the drawing?* If we are willing to sign our name to the drawings we execute and tell the world that we did them, the illustrations will probably have

met the criteria above. On the other hand, if we are reluctant to sign our name, we should re-examine the effort. We may rightly be proud of *good* work but we should be willing to alter work of questionable quality. In addition, we should *always* be looking for ways to be a better illustrator.

With these thoughts in mind, let us proceed to a discussion of the two basic types of technical illustrations.

7

Styles

7A Freehand

First of all, we should make a distinction between freehand and mechanically drawn illustrations. Freehand drawings are executed using no mechanical aids such as triangles, compasses, and ellipse guides. Mechanically drawn illustrations are executed using the aids mentioned above.

When we speak of a freehand style, we speak of executing a drawing in one of two ways: totally freehand or semifreehand. Figure 7.1 shows an illustration done totally freehand. In other words, no mechanical aid was employed during any phase of preparing the drawing.

In Fig. 7.2 are shown two drawings made using mechanical aids in the layout phase but not in the inking phase. These are semifreehand drawings that *appear* to have been done completely freehand.

The most difficult task facing the illustrator, if he wishes to consider using the freehand style, is when to use the style. Chances are good that scientific journals, such as the *Journal of Applied Physics*, would not accept freehand-style drawings. By the same token, a publisher may accept the style for a liberal arts and sciences (LAS) chemistry textbook. Journals dealing with anthropology, entomology (insects and suchlike), or biology will readily accept the freehand

Figure 7.1 A drawing made completely freehand. All lines are guided by the hand.

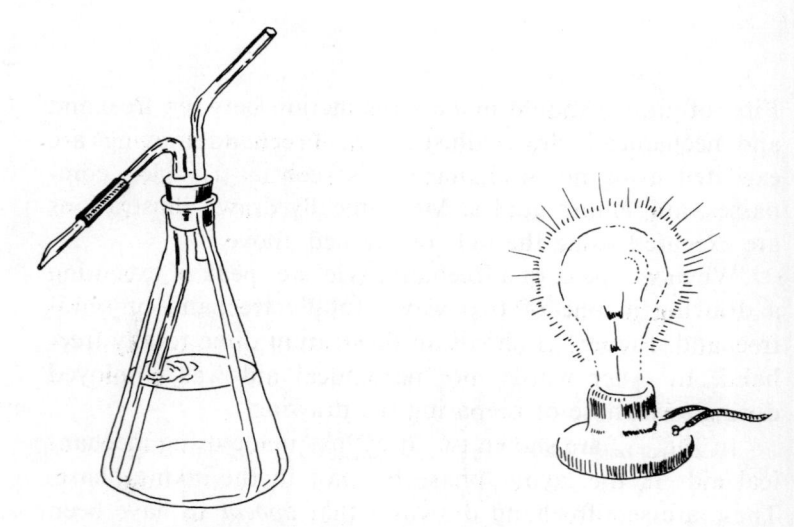

Figure 7.2 Semifreehand drawing. Each drawing *appears* to have been done using no mechanical drawing aids. Aids were used in the layout stage.

style. In fact, such journals will be less likely to accept mechanically drawn illustrations.

We see, therefore, that to a large degree our decision as to when to use the freehand style for an illustration is based upon the following question: For what audience is the illustration intended? Keeping in mind that we are, in all cases, speaking of technical illustrations, we can make a general statement about the freehand style. The more technically skilled audience (scientists, professors, graduate engineers) will not appreciate freehand illustrations as much as the less technically skilled audience (high school, junior college, and nonscience college students).

If we examine a copy of *Scientific American* (*SA*) magazine, we see that the illustrations used in the main articles are drawn mechanically. Toward the back of this magazine is a section called "The Amateur Scientist." The drawings in this section are in a freehand style. Next, consider the audiences to which the main articles and the "amateur" section are directed. Clearly, the amateur section is provided for people less technically oriented.

The "Amateur Scientist" column in *SA* provides an example of another point concerning the freehand style. Mr. Hayward, who illustrated that section for many years,

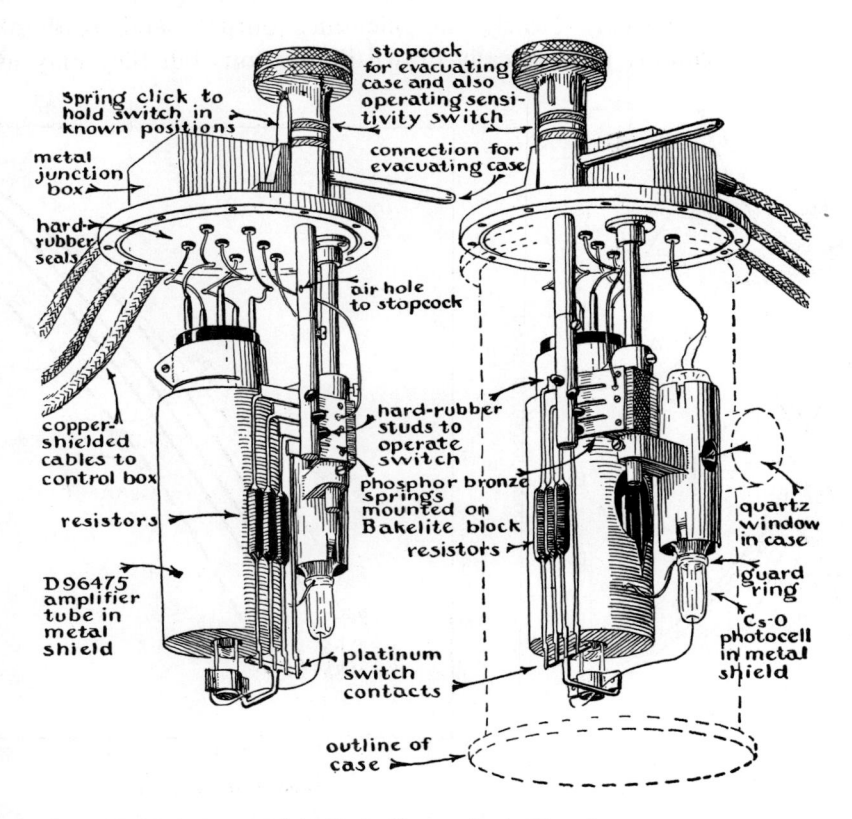

Figure 7.3 An example of the Roger Hayward style (*from Strong, Procedures In Experimental Physics, Prentice-Hall, Inc., Englewood Cliffs, N.J., 1938*).

developed a style that is recognized immediately as being his. He developed this style, used it consistently, and, as a result, his work is distinctive from other freehand styles. See Fig. 7.3 for an example.

An illustrator may wish to develop a style that will be so distinctive that contracts for work will come to him *because* of the style. The use of one style thus can provide benefits. The illustrator will (or can) become an expert and execute the drawings rapidly. His accounts may grow (in number and in size) because his style is well-known.

7B Mechanical

Mechanically drawn illustrations are those made using triangles, T squares, circle and ellipse templates, and compasses during the inking phase. We will refer to lines in such drawings as rigidly controlled lines or machine-drawn lines, inferring that machines draw perfectly straight lines with no "jittering." Nearly all scientific journals and textbooks employ mechanically drawn illustrations but they may use

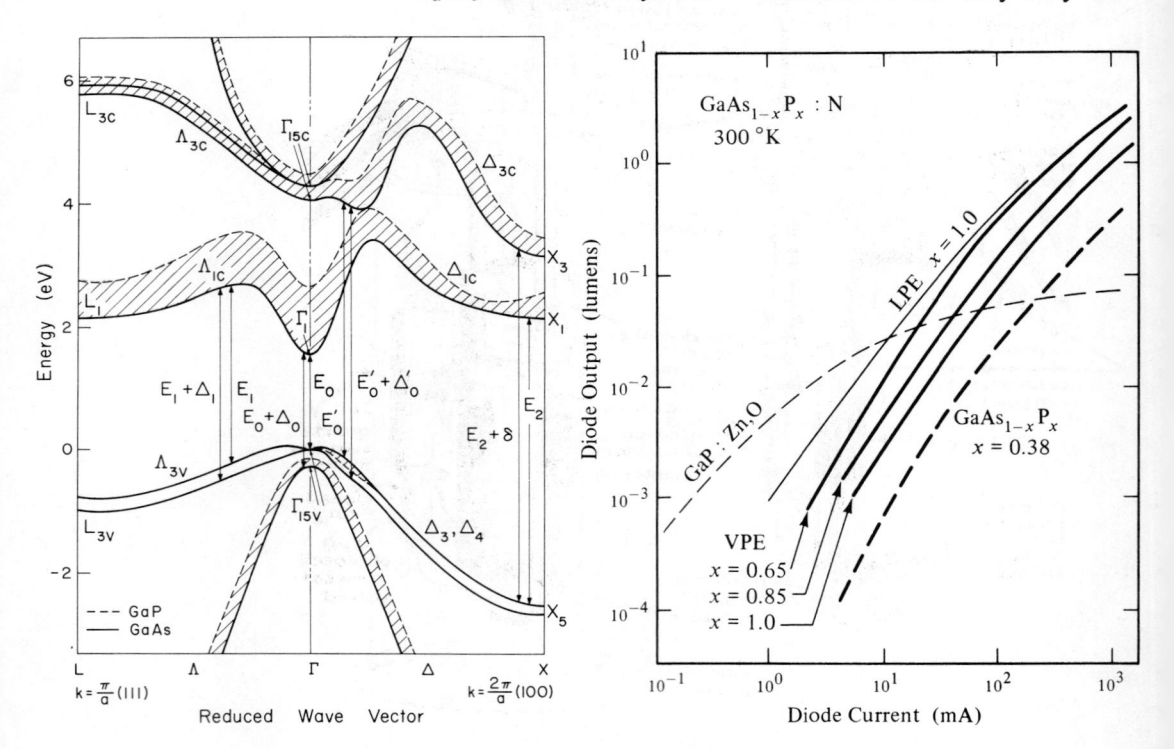

Figure 7.4 The two most popular lettering styles.

one of two basic lettering styles in conjunction—Leroy or typeset. Figure 7.4 illustrates these two types of lettering.

LEROY LETTERING

In Chapter 6 we briefly discussed a mechanical lettering set called Leroy, manufactured by the K.&E. Company. This lettering style has been and continues to be popular and, in the case of scientific journals, the standard lettering. Many journals, in their style manuals, state that Leroy lettering must be used.

TYPESET LETTERING

Over 75 percent of the lettering for illustrations in textbooks is done in typeset style. By using this lettering, the publisher assures that illustration callouts can match the text material exactly. This point (matching) is of vital importance when a book is mathematical in nature and is laden with equations. As an example, compare the two parts of Fig. 7.5.

Vector addition: **A + B = C**   Vector addition: **A + B = C**

(a) Leroy lettering   (b) Typeset lettering

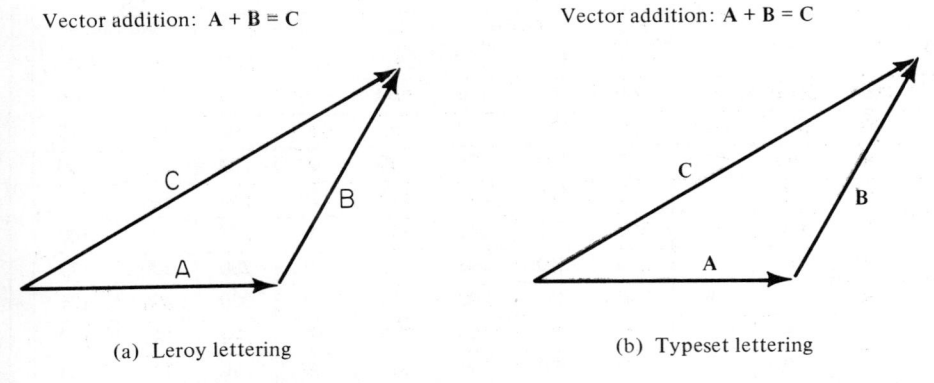

Figure 7.5 The use of lettering with equations.

In Fig. 7.5(a) the text material above the figure matches exactly the vector notation in the figure, whereas in Fig. 7.5(b) the text and figure callouts do not match. Clearly, a student who must study from a book would prefer the matching style. To match the text in (b), where Leroy lettering was used, will require additional study time.

Noting that the two basic styles are audience-dependent and that the mechanically drawn style is by far more popular for technical illustrations, we present the following discussion as a guide to choosing lettering and line sizes. A formula approach to sizing features of a drawing is presented and can be used without fear of mistaken or improperly chosen line weights or letter sizes.

7C The Formula Approach to Sizing

Scientists, engineers, and other professionals report results of their research and experience in journals. These journals (*Journal of Applied Physics*, *IEEE*, *ASME*) are laid out (usually) in a two-column format. Each column is approximately 3 in. wide by 9 in. high.

A question arises. If a 3-in. column is nearly universal,

Table 7.1 SCALING INFORMATION USED TO PREPARE ILLUSTRATIONS FOR 3-INCH JOURNAL COLUMNS SO THAT ANY TWO OR MORE ORIGINALS OF DIFFERENT WIDTHS WILL BE SCALED IDENTICALLY IN THE JOURNAL.

						Column Number							
1	2	3	4	5	6	7	8	9	10	11	12	13	14
Drawing Size (in.)		Ruling Pens‡			Lettering Pen	K.&E. Leroy Lettering Guide Size							
						Lettering			Sub & Supers			Axis Numbers	
Width	Max. Height	Heavy	Med.	Light		Std	Greek		Std	Greek			
						ULC	UC	LC*	ULC	UC	LC*	Std	S&S
3	9	0	00R	000R	000	100	100	120	060	060†	080†	080	060
4	12	1	00	000	000	120	120	140	080	080†	100	100	080
5	15	2	1R	000	00	140	140	175	100	100	120	120	100
6	18	3R	1	00R	0	175	175	200	120	120	140	140	120
7	21	3	2	00	0	200	200	240	140	140	175	175	140
8	24	4	3R	00	1	240	240	290	175	175	200	200	175
9	27	4R	3R	0	1	240	240	290	175	175	200	200	175
10	30	4R	3	1R	2	290	290	350	200	200	240	240	200
11	33	5	3	1R	2	290	290	350	200	200	240	240	200
12	36	6R	4	1	3	350	350	425	240	240	290	290	240
13	39	6	4	2½R	3	350	350	425	240	240	290	290	240
14	42	7	4R	2½R	3	425	425	500	290	290	350	350	290
15	45	7R	4R	2	4	425	425	500	290	290	350	350	290

*Except $\beta, \delta, \zeta, \theta, \lambda, \xi, \phi$, and ψ for which the templates listed in column 8 and/or 11 are used.
†Use K.&E. Height & Slant Control Scriber.
‡Suffix R denotes RAPIDOGRAPH pen; no suffix indicates K.&E. pen.
Abbreviations: ULC = UPPERCASE and lowercase; UC = UPPERCASE; LC = lowercase.
S&S = subscripts and superscripts; Std = K.&E. Leroy standard lettering template.

can we devise a system that will eliminate guesswork sizing of material to be used for illustrations? In other words, can a system provide that *all* illustrative material be size-consistent when reduced into the 3-in. format? The answer to each question is yes.

The author of a technical paper provides the illustrator with a series of sketches for use with the text material. Some drawings can be made by tracing the sketches (curves representing data), whereas other sketches will require expert attention. In either case, a formula is required to size the illustrations properly. Such a formula is provided by Table 7.1. To use this table we must

1. Determine the drawing width, which then determines the correct *row* in the table to use.
2. Check to be certain that the drawing height does not exceed the height listed in column 2.
3. Proceed across the row to find properly sized pens and letter heights for callouts. Note that Table 7.1 has been prepared for use with Leroy lettering equipment. If typeset lettering is to be used, we must refer to Table 7.2.

Referring to Fig. 7.6, let us retrace the path followed in Table 7.1 to properly size features on the drawings.

1. First we measure the sketch, which, in this case, was 7 in. wide.
2. Entering Table 7.1 at 7-row (column 1), we find that the maximum permissible drawing height in column 2 is 21 in. Our sketch is shorter than 21 in. so we proceed to the right.
3. In columns 3, 4, and 5 are given the pens for heavy, medium, and light lines—K.&E. No. 3, K.&E. No. 2, and K.&E. No. 00, respectively. Note that the heaviest lines are the most important lines, medium lines are next in importance, and light lines are the least important on the drawing.
4. All lettering was done using a K.&E. No. 0 pen, as indicated in column 6.
5. Proceeding to the right (still in 7-row) we find the proper sizes for lettering (columns 7, 8, and 9), the proper sizes for subscripts and superscripts (columns

Table 7.2 SCALING INFORMATION USED TO PREPARE ILLUSTRATIONS FOR THREE-INCH JOURNAL COLUMNS SO THAT ANY TWO OR MORE ORIGINALS OF DIFFERENT WIDTHS WILL BE SCALED IDENTICALLY IN THE JOURNAL.

1	2	3	4	5	6	7	8	9	10	11	12	13	14
\multicolumn{2}{Drawing Size (in.)}	\multicolumn{3}{Ruling Pens*}	Lettering Pen	\multicolumn{6}{Type Size (in *actual* points)}	\multicolumn{2}{Axis Numbers}
						\multicolumn{3}{Lettering}	\multicolumn{3}{Subs & Supers}		
						Std	\multicolumn{2}{Greek}	Std	\multicolumn{2}{Greek}		
Width	Max. Height	Heavy	Med.	Light		ULC	UC	LC	ULC	UC	LC	Std	S&S
3	9	0	00R	000R	000	7	7	8	4	4	6	6	4
4	12	1	00	000	000	8	8	10	6	6	7	7	6
5	15	2	1R	000	00	10	10	12	7	7	8	8	7
6	18	3R	1	00R	0	12	12	14	8	8	10	10	8
7	21	3	2	00	0	14	14	18	10	10	12	12	10
8	24	4	3R	00	1	18	18	20	12	12	14	14	12
9	27	4R	3R	0	1	18	18	20	12	12	14	14	12
10	30	4R	3	1R	2	20	20	24	14	14	18	18	14
11	33	5	3	1R	2	20	20	24	14	14	18	18	14
12	36	6R	4	1	3	24	24	30	18	18	20	20	18
13	39	6	4	2½R	3	24	24	30	18	18	20	20	18
14	42	7	4R	2½R	3	30	30	36	20	20	24	24	20
15	45	7R	4R	2	4	30	30	36	20	20	24	24	20

*Suffix R denotes RAPIDOGRAPH pen; no suffix indicates K.&E. pen.
Abbreviations: ULC = UPPERCASE and lowercase; UC = UPPERCASE; LC = lowercase.
S&S = subscripts and superscripts; Std = English alphabet and Arabic numbers.

10, 11, and 12), and the proper sizes for axis numbers (columns 13 and 14). Note that the sizes in columns 7 to 12 are in thousandths of an inch and correspond to numbers engraved on K.&E. lettering templates.

Several features of Fig. 7.6 ordinarily escape detection. Although each is a small item, each is important.

1. Vertical and horizontal scale lines are not ruled the entire height and width of the drawing. Tic marks are replacements for these cluttering lines. Because a journal illustration is 3 in. wide, a reader should not suppose he can make accurate readings from the figure. So, why add confusion?
2. Uppercase and lowercase letters both are used throughout, consistent with the fact that few of us write using

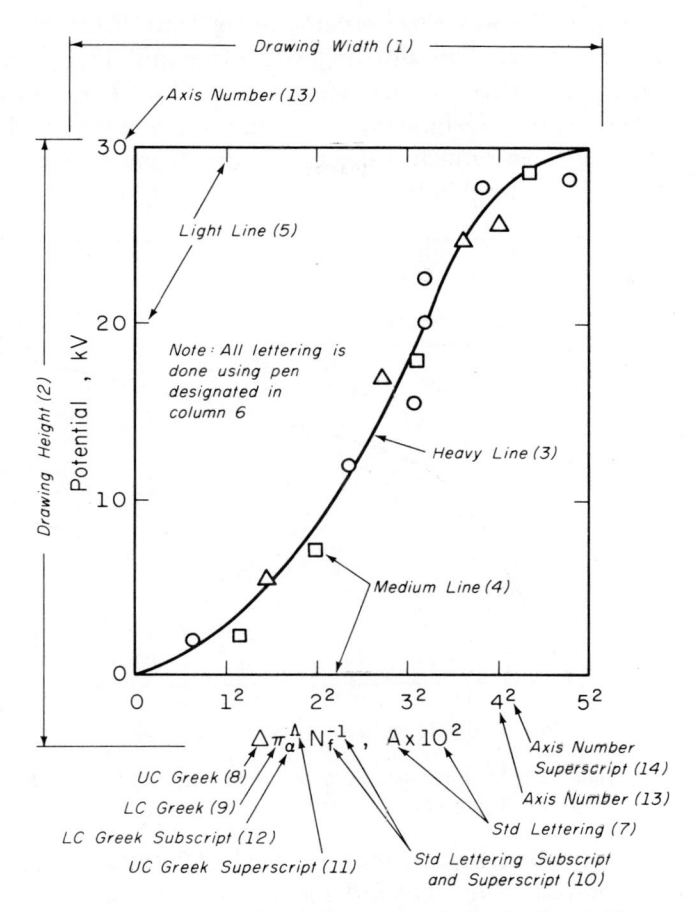

Figure 7.6 A fully annotated illustration prepared using Table 7.1 as a guide for choosing inking pens and Leroy template sizes.

uppercase (all caps) exclusively. The text of an article, of which the illustration is a part, is set in uppercase and lowercase letters. Why be different in the figures and illustrations? If an acronym or designator requiring all caps is used, it can be spotted immediately.

3. The Arabic number one (1) is distinctly different from a lowercase "el."
4. *All* decimal values less than unity are preceded by zero and the decimal point is large and does not get lost in reduction or reproduction.
5. The curve is the dominant feature of the drawing and is so denoted by using the heavy pen size.

Figure 7.7 was also prepared using Table 7.1. One difference is noted: This drawing was originally 12 in. wide—5 in. wider than the drawing in Fig. 7.6. Trace through Table 7.1 for a 12-in. wide drawing, noting how much larger lettering is and much thicker lines are. Then note the final sizes of comparable features.

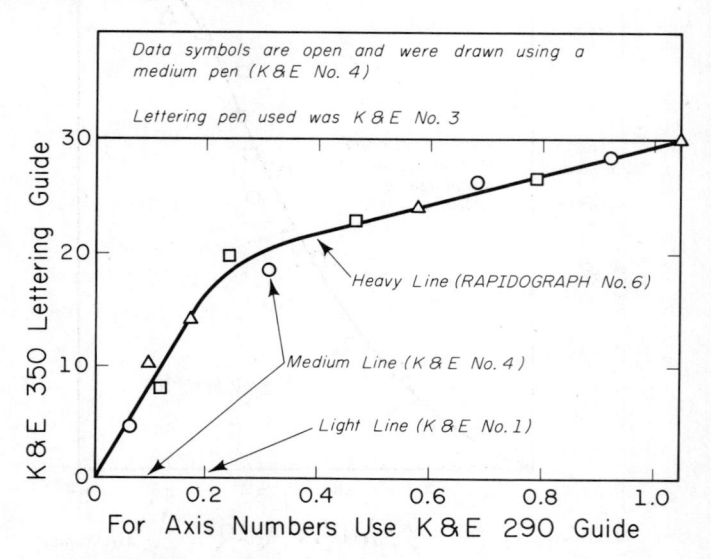

Figure 7.7 An illustration prepared using Table 7.1 as a guide. Original drawing was 12 in. wide.

As stated earlier, we may use Table 7.2 if typeset lettering is employed. The only difference between Tables 7.1 and 7.2 is that letter heights in Table 7.2 are given in actual point sizes* rather than thousandths of an inch. We will be better off, however, if when we use typeset lettering, we pick *one* drawing width. The cost of type makes it too expensive to consider using a different size for each drawing.

7D Closure

As we discussed earlier, illustrations are abundant in many places. We, as illustrators, must continually be on the alert to find ways to improve our product—drawings. We must never pass up an opportunity to examine good work.

Comic books are an excellent source of ideas. *Mad* magazine is superbly illustrated. *Popular Mechanics* is another good source. When we come across a good illustra-

---

*See Appendix C for the explanation of actual point size.

tion, catalog it. It is a good idea to keep a card index of where to find a certain illustration, style, or idea. Always be looking. The list of books that follows contains excellent references. The serious student should study illustrations from them.

For freehand style

REFERENCES

1. G. S. Christiansen and P. H. Garrett, *Structure and Change: An Introduction to the Science of Matter*. San Francisco: W. H. Freeman and Company, 1960.

    In addition to demonstrating a distinctive style, the illustrator (Evan L. Gillespie) makes drawings come alive with the use of two colors. This book is an excellent reference.

2. J. Strong, et al., *Procedures in Experimental Physics*. Englewood Cliffs, N.J.: Prentice-Hall, Inc., 1938.

    The illustrator here (Roger Hayward) uses a distinctive style that has been used effectively in the "Amateur Scientist" section in *Scientific American* magazine for many years. Truly a collector's item. Many fine examples.

3. C. L. Stong, *The Scientific American Book of Projects for the Amateur Scientist*. New York: Simon & Schuster, Inc., 1960.

    This book is available in paperback and is an excellent source of reference materials.

4. J. E. Hammesfahr and C. L. Stong, *Creative Glass Blowing*. San Francisco: W. H. Freeman and Company, 1968.

    The illustrator (Wayne Gallup) uses a distinctive style that is attractive and well suited to the text material. Note that a sans serif typeface is used in the illustrations, whereas a serif typeface is used for the text.

5. C. S. Papp, *Scientific Illustration Theory and Practice*. Dubuque, Iowa: Wm. C. Brown Company Publishers, 1968.

    This book, illustrated by the author, is of great value to the biological illustrator. The freehand *style* here is not inventive. It records exactly what the artist sees. An excellent reference.

6. J. D'Amelio, *Perspective Drawing Handbook*. New York: Tudor Publishing Company, 1964.

7. C. A. Lawson, et al., *Laboratory Studies in Biology: Observations and their Implications*. San Francisco: W. H. Freeman and Company, 1955.

    The distinctive style of Evan Gillespie is noted here, in a somewhat different (from conventional techniques) approach than most biological drawings follow.

8. G. Hardin, *Biology: Its Principles and Implications*. San Francisco: W. H. Freeman and Company, 1961.

   This book is an outstanding source of ideas. The illustrator uses two colors to good advantage. The style is flamboyant but pleasant and informative.

9. J. Strong, *Concepts of Classical Optics*. San Francisco: W. H. Freeman and Company, 1958.

   Roger Hayward has done an outstanding job in presenting his style. This book is an excellent reference for ideas.

10. G. E. Owen, *Introduction to Electromagnetic Theory*. Boston: Allyn and Bacon, Inc., 1963.

    The author illustrated this work. It is a pleasing respite from the mechanical style.

11. J. Gilluly, A. C. Waters, and A. O. Woodford, *Principles of Geology* (2nd ed.). San Francisco: W. H. Freeman and Company, 1959.

12. B. G. King and M. J. Showers, *Human Anatomy and Physiology* (5th ed.). Philadelphia: W. B. Saunders Co., 1963.

    An extremely detailed and excellent job by Lucille Cassell, the artist. Most drawings in the book were done by her, and her initials (L. C.) are included in the drawings. Those drawings done by other artists are easily distinguished from the feminine style of the primary artist.

13. A. M. Elliott, *Zoology* (2nd ed.). New York: Appleton-Century-Crofts, Inc., 1957.

    Several artists contributed to this book. One style predominates.

14. T. I. Storer and R. L. Usinger, *Elements of Zoology* (2nd ed.). New York: McGraw-Hill Book Co., 1961.

    The artist for this work was Mrs. Emily E. Reid. A conventional treatment but well done.

15. *The Drawings of Heinrich Kley*. New York: Dover Publications, Inc., 1961.

16. *More Drawings by Heinrich Kley*. New York: Dover Publications, Inc., 1962.

    Neither of these two paperback volumes deals with technical illustrating. Certain aspects of the work can, however, be of use to any illustrator. We learn a bit of history and have fun at the same time.

17. W. Rummer, *Art Anatomy*. New York: Dover Publications, Inc., 1962.

    We should learn a little history here. Some of the art appears gruesome but we must attend to details to see the essence of the work.

18. J. Hamm, *Drawing The Head and Figure*. New York: Grosset & Dunlap, Inc., 1963.

19. J. Hamm, *Cartooning the Head and Figure*. New York: Gosset & Dunlap, Inc., 1967.

    Both books are inexpensive paperbacks that will serve many useful purposes. Have fun with these.

20. L. Pauling, *College Chemistry: An Introductory Textbook of General Chemistry* (2nd ed.). San Francisco: W. H. Freeman and Co., 1955.

    Many examples of the unique style of Roger Hayward.

21. M. G. Gross, *Oceanography A View of the Earth*. Englewood Cliffs: Prentice-Hall, Inc., 1972.

    Many of the illustrations in this book are done white on black, rather than the standard black on white. Roger Hayward has demonstrated versatility in doing so.

For mechanical style

1. H. Frauenfelder and E. M. Henley, *Subatomic Physics*. Englewood Cliffs: Prentice-Hall, Inc., 1974.

   A fairly standard treatment of drawings in a technical textbook. Special attention should be given the line weight consistency and the sizing of drawings. The artist chose all sizes from three categories. Typeset lettering was used in callouts. The artist was George Morris.

2. B. G. Steetman, *Solid State Electronic Devices*. Englewood Cliffs: Prentice-Hall, Inc., 1972.

   Illustrations in this book make use of Leroy lettering. Note that some of the letters are italicized. Of special interest is the fact that circuit elements such as resistors, capacitors, batteries, and inductors are drawn in heavy, whereas the lines connecting (wires) the elements are light lines. The artist was George Morris.

3. W. F. Stoecker, *Design of Thermal Systems*. New York: McGraw-Hill Book Company, 1971.

4. D. D. Meredith, et al., *Design and Planning of Engineering Systems*. Englewood Cliffs: Prentice-Hall, Inc., 1973.

   The typeface used to letter the callouts in this book was IBM Univers. It contrasts with the Times Roman used for the text material. Such a tact is often used in designing a textbook. Artist: George Morris.

5. N. Narayana Rao, *Basic Electromagnetics With Applications*. Englewood Cliffs: Prentice-Hall, Inc., 1972.

   This textbook is an extremely mathematical one. As a result the typeface for callouts is *identical* to that for the text material. Just glancing at the formidable equations indicates why this is done.

Little of the zip-a-tone or other shading media are used. Artist: George Morris.

6. C. N. Herrick, *Color Television: Theory and Servicing*. Reston: Reston Publishing Company, 1973.

   A good source of electronic circuit drawings, by Robert MacFarlane.

7. V. Robinson, *Electronic Concepts: A Self Instructional Programmed Manual*. Reston: Reston Publishing Company, 1973.

   A source of electronic circuit drawings by Robert MacFarlane.

8. R. Didday and R. Page, *Fortran for Humans*. St. Paul: West Publishing Company, 1974.

   This book makes use of two styles of drawings: cartoons and "plain old" line art. A pleasant departure from normality. Line art by Jeffrey Mellander and Tom Paxton.

9. D. Ewen, et al., *Physics for Career Education*. Englewood Cliffs: Prentice-Hall, Inc., 1974.

   The illustrations in this book incorporate two styles: freehand and mechanical—mostly mechanical. Rulings, zip-a-tone, and hand stipple techniques are used. Many everyday objects are used as illustrative examples. Two artists, George Morris (mechanical) and Carol Coope (freehand), merge two styles well.

10. A. W. Bennett, *Introduction to Hybrid Computers*. St. Paul: West Publishing Co., 1974.

    A relatively bland set of illustrations of computer symbols are given character by a good choice of line weights and careful attention to quality. Artist was Ronald Kempke.

QUESTIONS

1. In your own words, answer the following questions.
   (a) Why must an illustration be executed well?
   (b) What is meant by a descriptive illustration?
   (c) What is meant by a realistic illustration?
   (d) Why is it important to consider an audience when an illustration is prepared?
   (e) Why should pride enter into illustrating?

2. Explain the difference between freehand and semifreehand styles.

3. What is a mechanical style?

4. Describe LEROY lettering. Why would you think that this style of lettering is important?

5. Why is typeset lettering important?

6. The formula approach to size-consistent lettering was explained in detail. Why do you feel that this approach is good? Bad?

8

Techniques and Media for Shading

Bar charts, circuit diagrams, flow diagrams, and data curves may be represented on a flat plane easily because each is two-dimensional. Any one view of a multiple view drawing is also two-dimensional and can be represented easily on a plane. If we follow the rules for isometric, oblique, and the other three-dimensional drawing schemes, we can represent any object on a plane. Our problem (in some cases) will be to represent an object such that it appears more lifelike than simple construction lines allow.

For example, we know that if we look at a sphere from any angle, the outside diameter of the sphere projects as a circle. Although by the rules of orthographic projection we have drawn a sphere (the projection of the outside diameter) in Fig. 8.1(a), we have not conveyed to the casual reader the

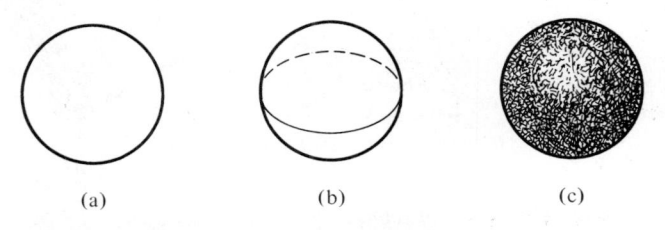

Figure 8.1 Shading a sphere to give it character.

entire message. In Fig. 8.1(b) we give a better indication of a sphere by drawing a great circle trace. In Fig. 8.1(c) we add shading to the surface of the sphere and do a better job. The point to be made here is *if an object is to be drawn, make the object appear realistic—show depth and give the object character.*

As illustrators we must continually search for ways and means to make our work better. When drawing a three-dimensional object we are limited to *working* in two dimensions. We must synthesize depth, the third dimension.

The task confronting us, however, is not so difficult as it might seem. By observing details carefully and appreciating the problem, we can perform the task successfully. When an object "jumps out of the paper at you," the job has been well done. The big question is how to accomplish our goal.

The four methods most often used to accomplish the "jumping out" drawing are

1. Rulings drawn on a surface.
2. Shade.
3. Shadow.
4. Surface texture.

It is possible to subdivide these four methods but we gain nothing by doing so. Before proceeding to actual techniques and media, we will define and show examples of the four methods.

1. Rulings on a surface are nothing more than lines drawn to influence the reader's interpretation of

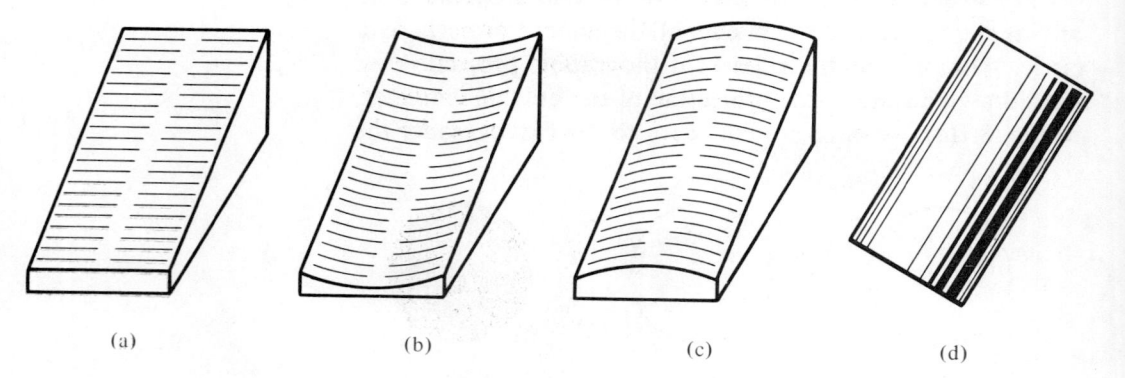

(a) (b) (c) (d)

Figure 8.2 The use of rulings influence a reader's interpretation of contours.

surface contours. In Fig. 8.2 we see rulings used to indicate a flat, sloping surface (a), a concave surface (b), a convex surface (c), and a cylindrically shaped surface (d).

2. Shade is usually not defined as a quantity. Shade *exists* on a surface when that surface is turned away from a light source. In other words, if light does not strike a surface, the surface is in shade. Note the shade lines in Fig. 8.3(b) and (c). A shade line is the boundary line between shade and light.

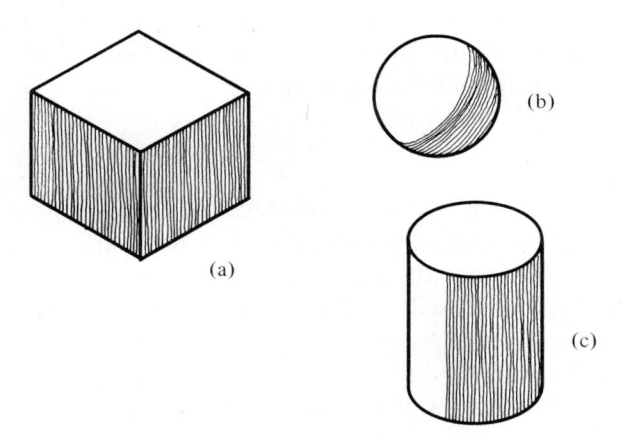

Figure 8.3 The use of shade to show shape.

Figure 8.4 The use of shadows gives an illustration meaning and the reader a feeling of "being there."

168 / Chap. 8
Techniques and Media for Shading

Figure 8.5 Surface texture can give the reader an idea of materials.

3. Shadow, like shade, is not a quantity. Shadow *exists* on a surface when another object prevents light from striking the surface. Shade and shadow are shown clearly in Fig. 8.4.
4. Surface texture is a more subtle indicator of depth or shape and is ordinarily used by experienced illustrators. In Fig. 8.5 an example is presented.

With these definitions in mind, we may proceed to study the techniques and media used to obtain our desired result. Examples from several sources will be used. Each example was chosen carefully and for a reason. In some cases the reason will be apparent or will be discussed. In other cases, the reader will learn by studying the illustration to *discover* the reason.

8A Rulings

As discussed earlier, rulings influence the reader to interpret contours and shapes. Hopefully, the illustrator will use rulings to influence the *proper* interpretation. Improper use of rulings can and will be detrimental to the illustration.

The intersecting cylinders in Fig. 8.6(a) are faceless representations. To add feeling to this illustration we add a few rulings as shown in Fig. 8.6(b). Observe that the rulings

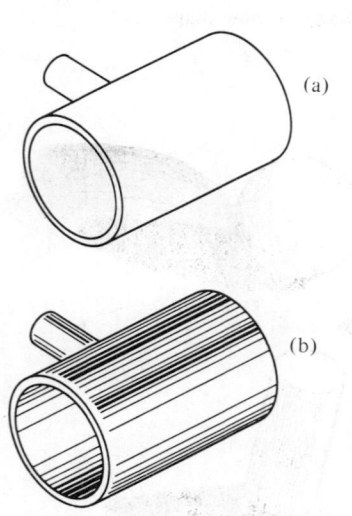

Figure 8.6 Rulings make the drawing better. Compare (a) to (b).

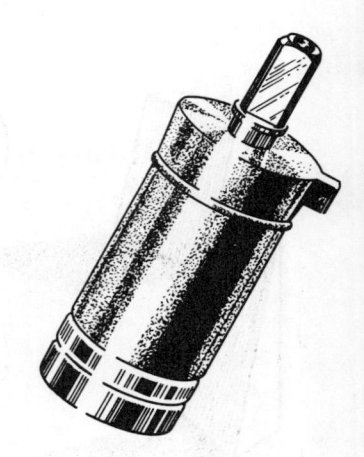

Figure 8.7 Note the use of rulings and where highlights are located.

are drawn parallel to the axes of the cylinders. We can see that the shape is circular in cross section—an ellipse guide was used to represent the circle. Further emphasis of the circular shape is unnecessary.

It should be noted that when rulings are used on certain shapes (such as spheres and cylinders), we should strive to reproduce natural highlights. Pick up a shiny object and hold it close to a bare light bulb. Certain areas of the object will reflect enough light to make these areas appear to have no

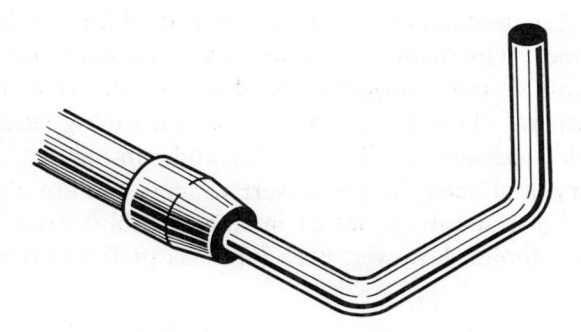

Figure 8.8 Rulings used to show contours and surface texture.

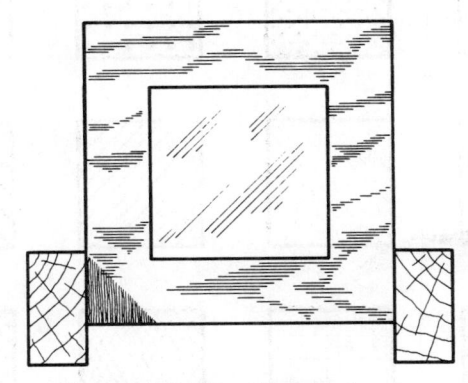

Figure 8.9 Rulings show wood grain.

Figure 8.10 Note how rulings stop short of end points to show contours. Also, the springs that are coiled around each shaft, stand out.

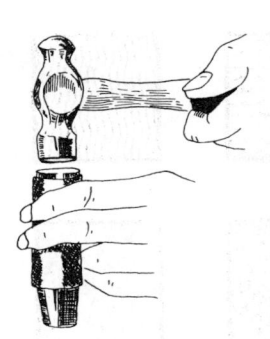

Figure 8.11 Rulings give an indication of depth and texture.

color or texture. These areas are called *highlights*. In viewing the illustrations in this chapter, attention should be given to defining highlights, which are real and exist in nature: They should exist in illustrations also. Figures 8.7 through 8.11 show examples of the use of rulings. Each figure warrants careful attention. Note that rulings indicate texture (glass, wood grain), shape (curved, flat), shade, shadow, and highlights.

8B
Acetate Sheets

The most often used name for acetate sheets used for shading is "zip-a-tone." This name, however, is a trade name for a specific manufacturer's product and does not describe the sheets in general. Two basic types of acetate toning sheets are available: pressure-sensitive overlay and rub-on.

In theory, and according to advertisements, we are able to use overlay and rub-on sheets interchangeably. From a practical standpoint, however, each type has preferred uses.

Figure 8.12 Some of the many patterns available in acetate sheets. All patterns shown here full size.

For example, if we wish to use a fine screen pattern (60 line, 10 percent of black) to cover a 40-sq. in. area, we would be better off using an overlay. If we wished to shade a small sphere and show highlights, we could do the job better with the rub-on type. The primary reason for using an overlay on large areas is that it is much less difficult to apply.

The patterns available in the rub-on type are essentially the same as those available in overlay sheets. About the only difference between the two types is the method of application for each.

Figure 8.12 illustrates a few of the screened, lined, and miscellaneous patterns available. In defining a screened

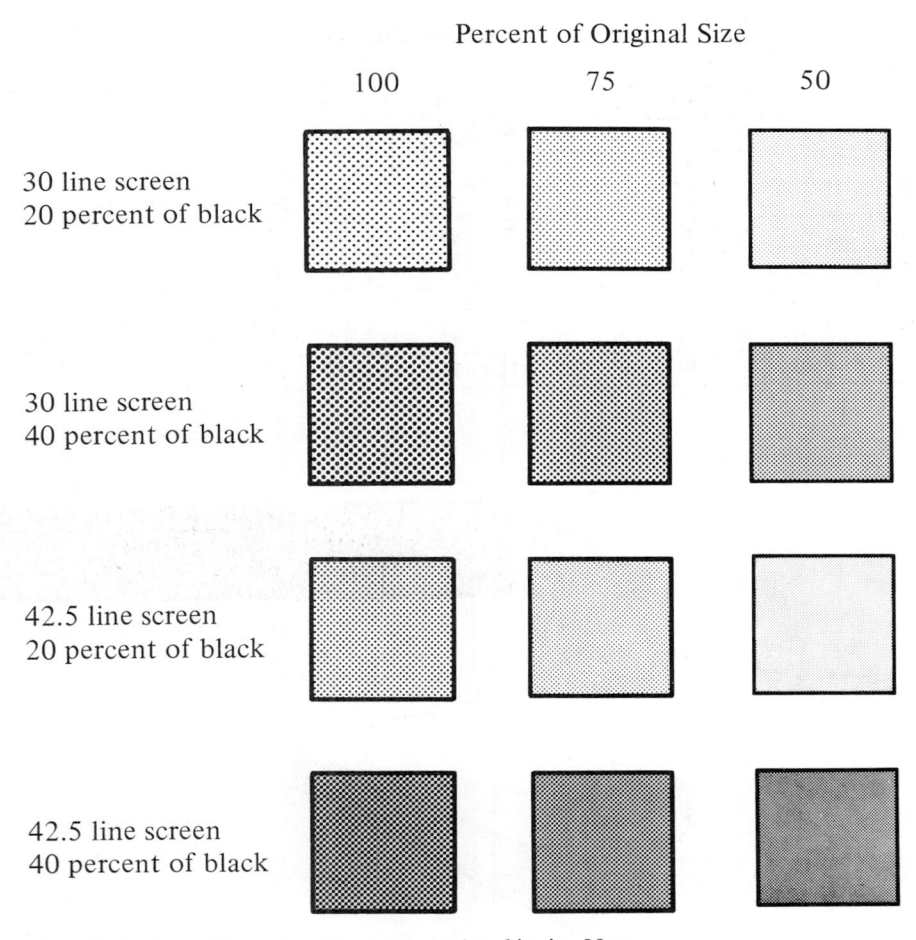

Figure 8.13 Comparison of screen patterns reduced in size. Note that the percent of black does not change.

pattern we must specify lines and percent. The lines designation is the number of lines of dots per linear inch, whereas the percent designation is the percent of total black. In other words, if a square is nearly totally black, a 90 percent designation might apply.

When we use acetate screen patterns, we must *always* be

Table 8.1 LINES PER INCH—REDUCTION CHART

Pick a row agreeing with the choice of screen pattern. Then pick the column headed by the percent of original size to which the illustration will be reduced. The square on which the row and column intersect gives the lines per inch screen pattern in the reduced illustration. For example, an illustration using a 30-lines-per-inch screen is to be reduced to 65 percent of original. Enter Table 8.1 at row 2 and column g. The intersection of this row and column gives the number 46. The *reduced* illustration will have a 46-lines-per-inch screen pattern.

		a	b	c	d	e	f	g	h	i	j	k	l	m	n
		95	90	85	80	75	70	65	60	55	50	45	40	35	30
Rows (Lines/inch)	1	27.5	29	31	32	34	37	39	42	45	50	55	61	69	78	92
	2	30	32	33	35	37	40	43	46	50	54	60	67	75	86	100
	3	32.5	34	36	38	41	43	46	50	54	59	65	72	81	93	108
	4	42.5	45	47	50	53	57	61	65	71	77	85	94	106	121	142
	5	55	58	61	65	69	73	78	85	92	100	110	122	137	157	183
	6	60	63	67	71	75	80	86	92	100	109	120	133	150	171	200
	7	65	68	72	76	81	87	93	100	108	118	130	144	162	186	216
	8	85	90	94	100	106	113	121	131	142	154	170	189	212	243	283

Columns (Percent of Original Size)

(a) 27.5 line, 10-90 percent of black
Reduced to 75 percent of original.

(b)

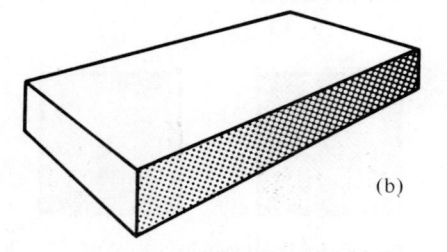

Figure 8.14 Graduated density screens are useful.

aware of the final size of the artwork. If we do not take into account the final drawing size, the pattern we end up with may be too light, too small, or too dense. Figure 8.13 and Table 8.1 give an indication of what to expect when reducing screen patterns. Keep in mind that the number of lines per inch changes in direct proportion to the percent reduction but the percent of black does not change.

In addition to the black screen patterns of one density, acetate sheets are available in graduated screens—27.5, 32.5, 55, and 65 lines per inch ranging in percent of black from 10 to 90. A portion of one of these sheets is shown in Fig. 8.14 along with an illustration that has used the sheet. In many instances, such a graduated tone is useful to illustrate depth or changing density.

Another useful screen pattern is the opaque white dot screen, which can be used to screen a black area. These screens are available in several lines-per-inch, percent *of white* configurations. Figure 8.15 illustrates the use of the white dot pattern.

An inventive illustrator will recognize that certain screen patterns may be overlaid to obtain a pattern completely different from the patterns used in the overlay. For example, carefully examine the patterns in Fig. 8.16. Each pattern was made by laying one screen on top of another. Many beautiful and different effects can be realized by such a scheme.

Figures 8.17 through 8.20 are included here to show the use of acetate overlays in technical illustrations. Each figure deserves careful attention.

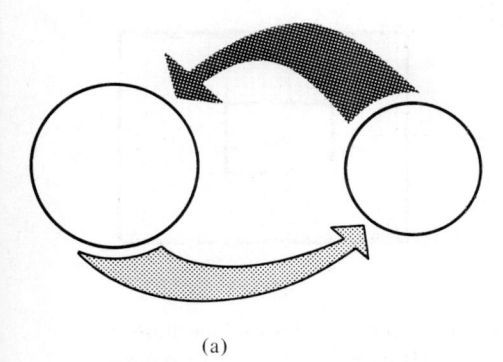

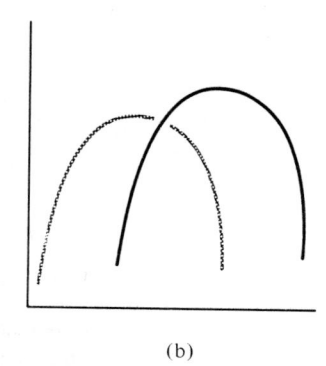

Figure 8.15 White dot patterns can be used to show (a) contrasts or (b) ghost in an image.

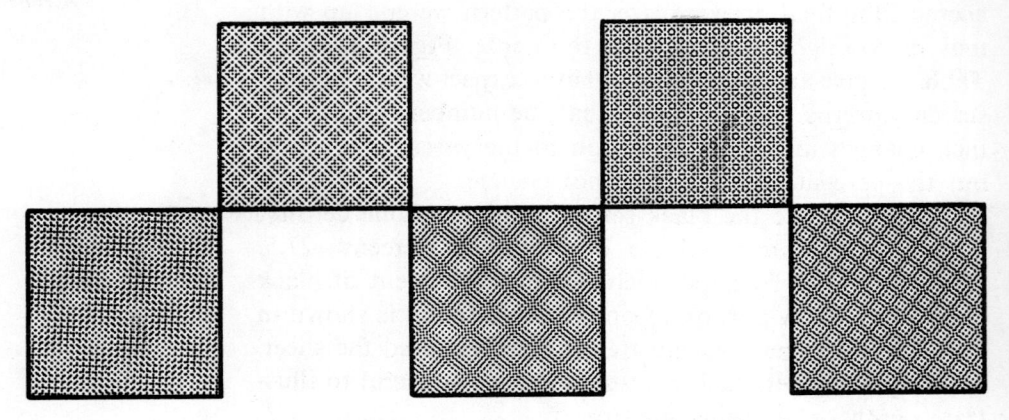

Figure 8.16 Overlay patterns can be created and used in situations in which other patterns are not suitable.

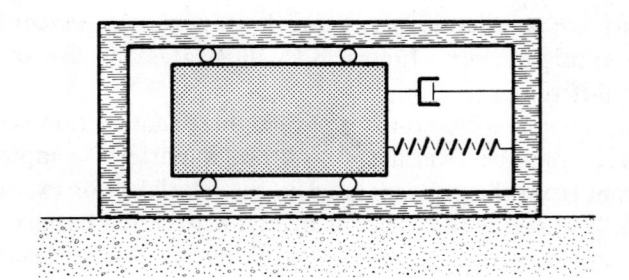

Figure 8.17 Three different patterns are used in this illustration to delineate three different parts of the scene. Also, note that rulings are used.

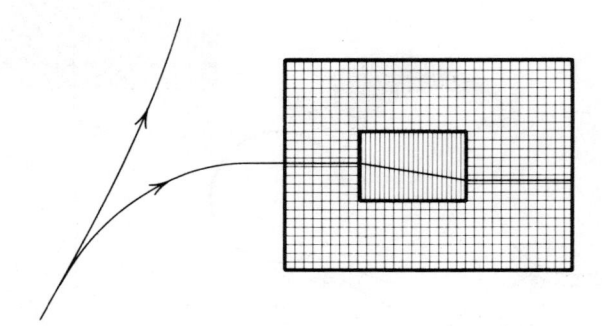

Figure 8.18 No amount of patience would reward the illustrator who attempts to make a square pattern or line pattern as regular and perfect as those provided on overlay sheets.

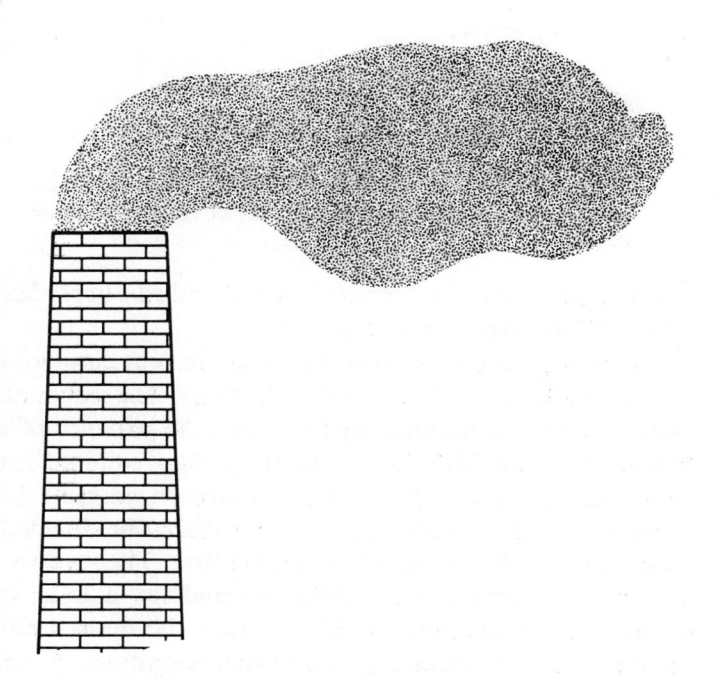

Figure 8.19 The smoke coming from the brick chimney is formed by cutting a shape from an overlay pattern. In addition, the bricks are another pattern available.

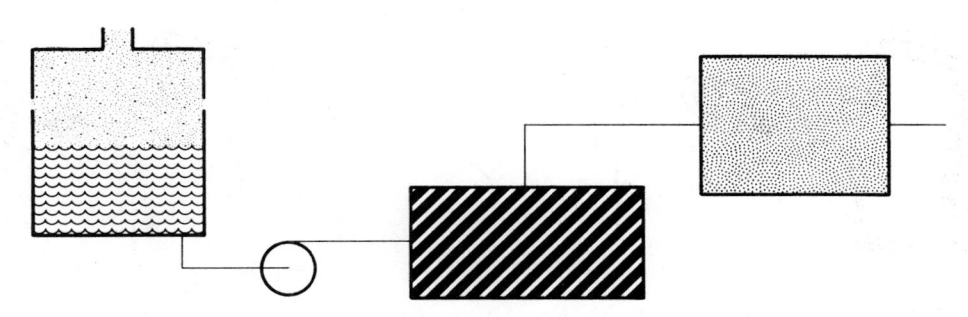

Figure 8.20 Each pattern used here is available as an overlay sheet.

8C
Hand Stipple

Webster defines *stipple* as follows: *to make* (*as in paint or ink*) *by small touches that together produce an even or softly graded shadow.* Translated by means of Fig. 8.21, to stipple is to shade, show curvature, or show texture by using small dots or lines. To hand stipple is to make the dots by hand,

176 / Chap. 8
*Techniques and
Media for Shading*

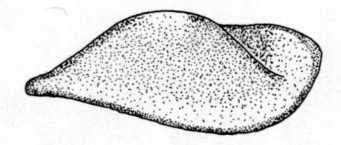

Figure 8.21 The small dots give an impression of varying density shading of the object. Stippling is the act of making the small dots.

as opposed to using a prepared surface called *stipple board*, which will be discussed in Sec. 8D.

Hand stippling is used often in fields such as entomology, botany, zoology, medicine, and archeology. The technique is extremely time-consuming and requires the patience of Job (the hero of an Old Testament story who endured much with great patience). If it were possible to describe hand stippling as a procedure, we would probably be directed to shade areas with nonreproducing blue first. Then we would dot the blue area nearly uniformly and, as a final step, graduate the separation of dots to gain the desired effect. Figure 8.22 is a three-step example illustration. A small hand-held magnifying glass is a useful item to have available when hand stippling is anticipated. Figures 8.23 through 8.26 are example illustrations that should be studied carefully.

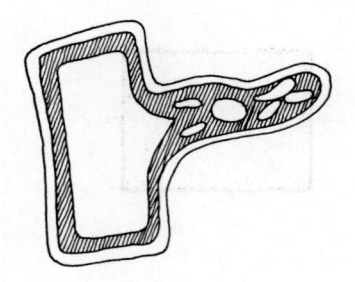

(a) The ruled areas are to be shaded in light blue.

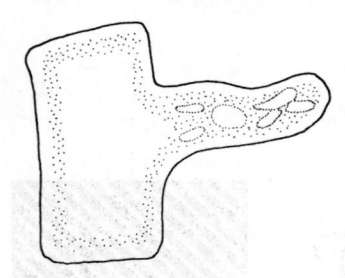

(b) The general pattern is stippled, not showing density changes.

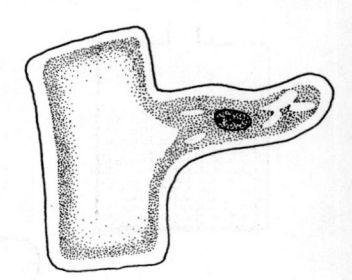

(c) The final drawing.

Figure 8.22 Three stages involved in stippling.

Sec. 8C / 177
Hand Stipple

50 percent of original

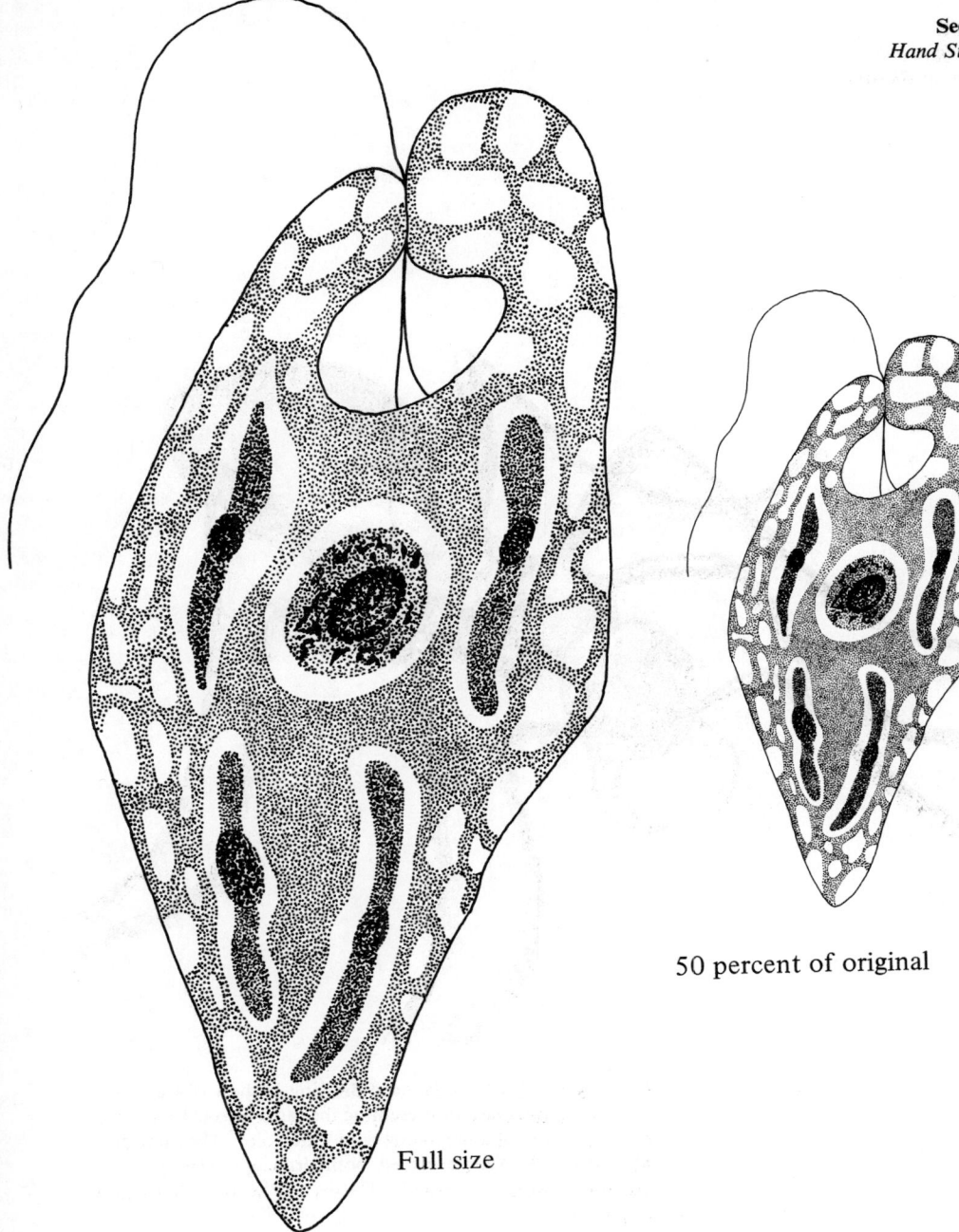

Full size

Figure 8.23 One interpretation of *Euglena*. Stippling this drawing required in excess of five hours. Hand stippling is a slow, laborious process that cannot be done hastily if good results are expected. The full-size version as well as one at 50 percent of original size are shown.

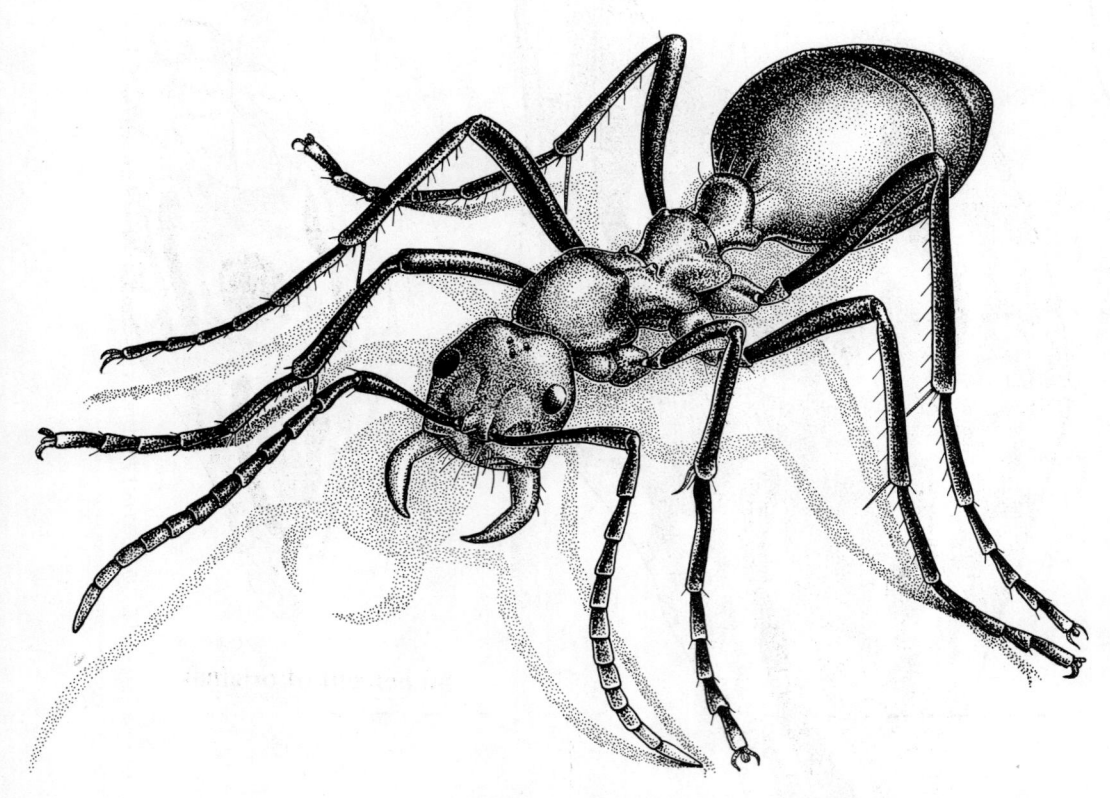

Figure 8.24 This hand-stippled drawing is shown here to illustrate two techniques for presenting the same insect. Figure 5.1 is a reproduction of a fire ant done in watercolor. The same artist, Mrs. Alice Prickett, executed both drawings. (Permission to use this drawing was given by Darius E. Phebus, who owns the original.)

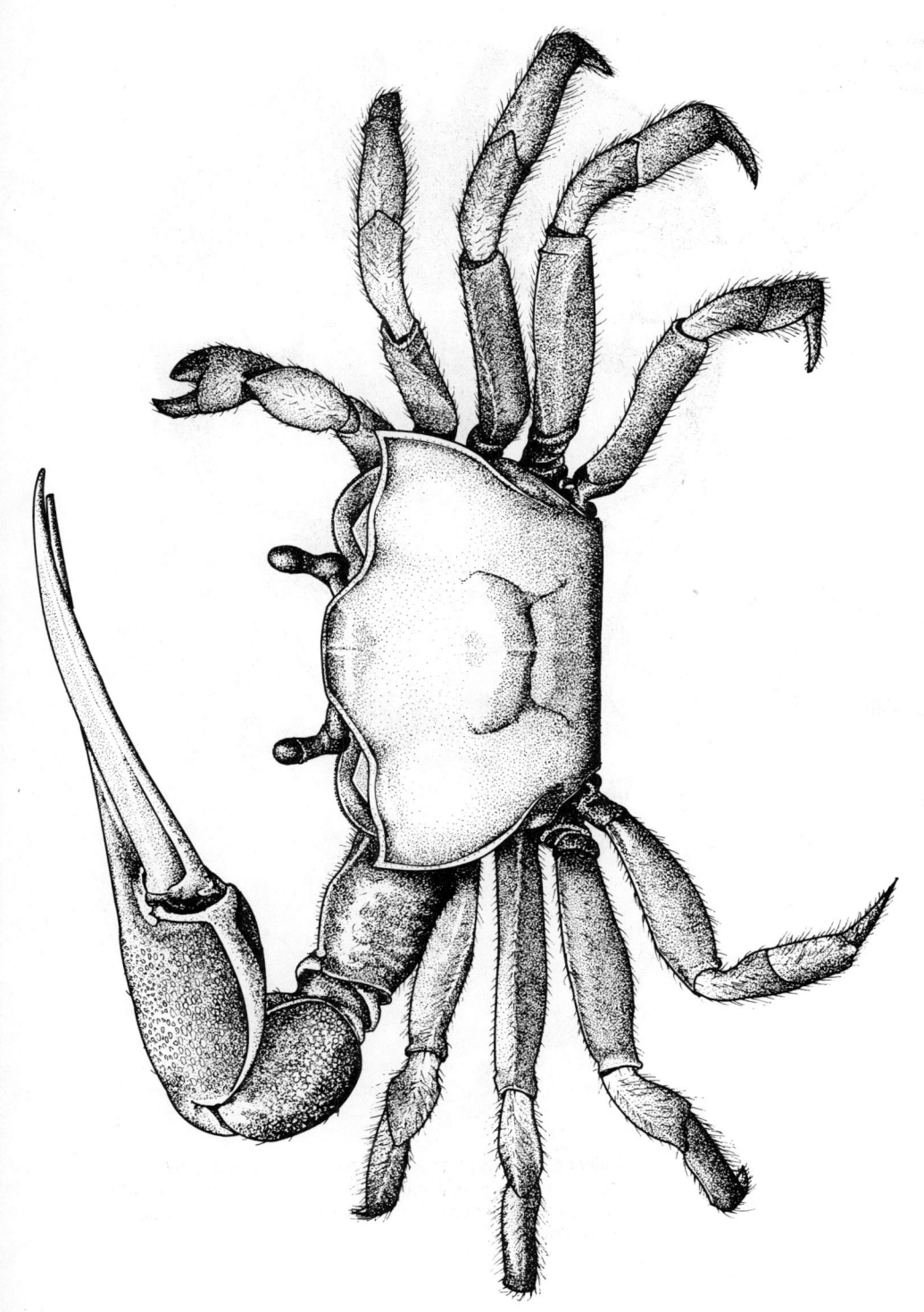

Figure 8.25 A small crab was viewed through a magnifying lens to capture the detail shown here. It should be noted that a very fine pen was used. To stipple this drawing, Carol Arian was the artist.

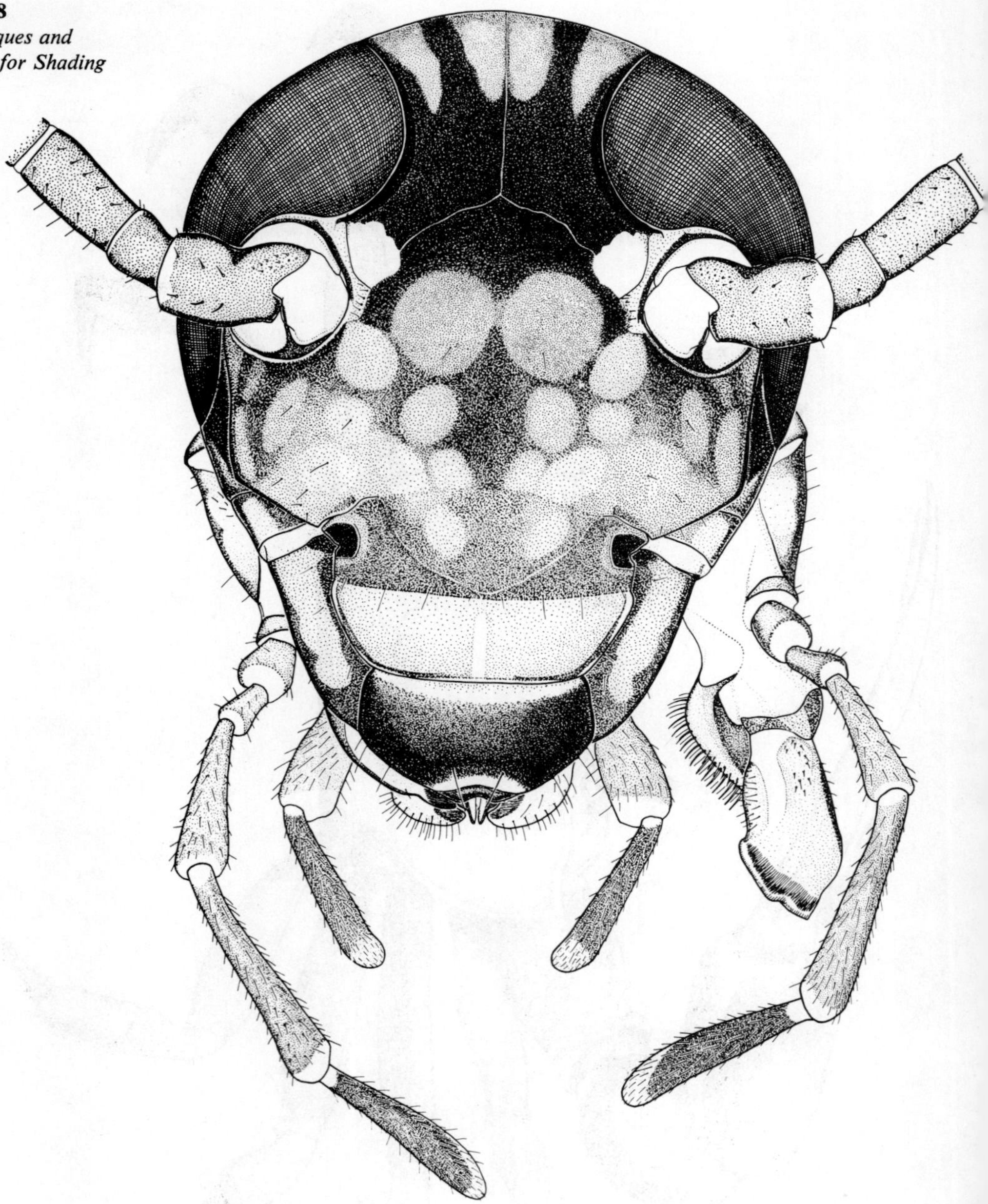

Figure 8.26 This greatly enlarged head of a cockroach is one of the best examples of hand stippling technique that you will ever see, even if the subject matter is not appealing. Artist: Mrs. Alice Prickett.

8D
Stipple Board

A stipple board drawing is one prepared on a surface that, when the finished drawing is examined, gives the appearance of having been hand stippled. Upon close examination, however, the pattern regularity shows clearly that hand stippling was not used. Other names applied to this board are halftone board, ross board, and croquil board. The board surface is a series of raised shapes over which the illustrator shades with crayon, charcoal, or pencil. By regulating the pressure on the pencil, the artist controls the density of the pattern.

One advantage gained by using stipple board (rather than hand stippling) is the time savings: Stipple board is much faster. Another feature of stipple board drawing (that applies to hand stippling as well) is that continuous tones may be reproduced as line copy using this technique. This point is of such importance to publishers and printers that we will discuss it here.

When we rule a line in ink or when we make a drawing using black ink lines exclusively, we have produced *line copy*.

(a) Line copy. Artist: Karol Goebel.

(b) Continuous tone copy.

Figure 8.27 (a) Line copy does not need special photographic treatment. (b) Continuous tone copy does. Notice the dot pattern in (b).

Chap. 8
Techniques and Media for Shading

When we take a snapshot photograph at a family reunion, we have produced continuous tone copy. Note the two parts of Fig. 8.27: (a) is line copy; (b) is continuous tone copy produced by a halftone process. Using a magnifying glass we see that the line copy is not broken into pieces but the continuous tone copy is a series of dots. The process used to produce Fig. 8.27(b) requires special considerations in printing and is costly. As a result, publishers and printers attempt to use such copy sparingly. The actual process is discussed in Appendix B.

Figures 8.28 through 8.30 are examples of uses of stipple board in technical illustrating.

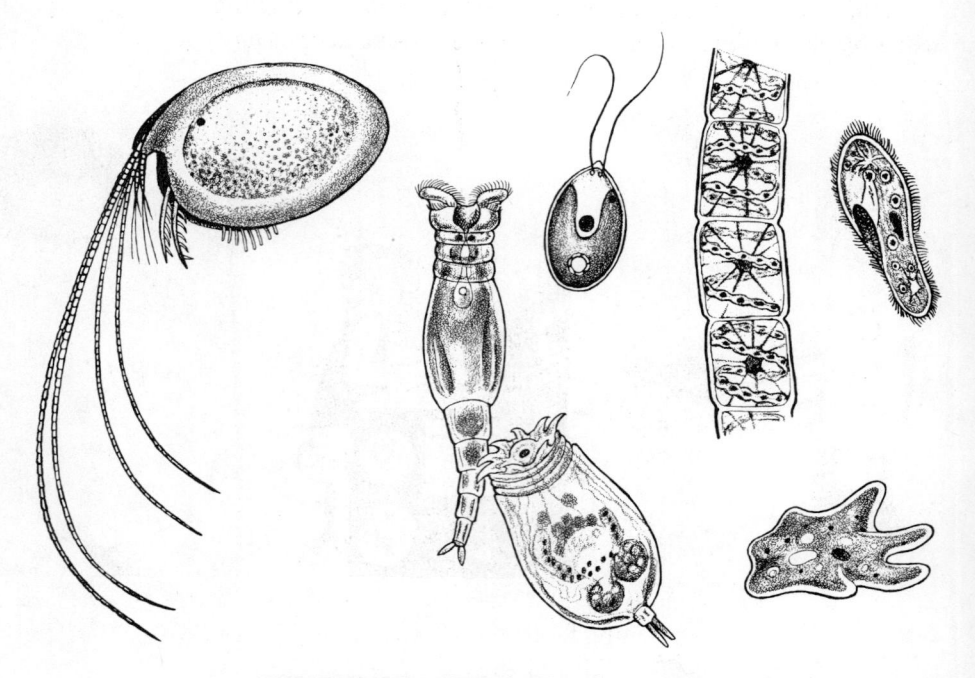

Figure 8.28 The small biological specimens shown here are well done examples of the use of stipple board. Note the detail and, in one instance, the transparent quality of the specimen. Artist: Mrs. Alice Prickett.

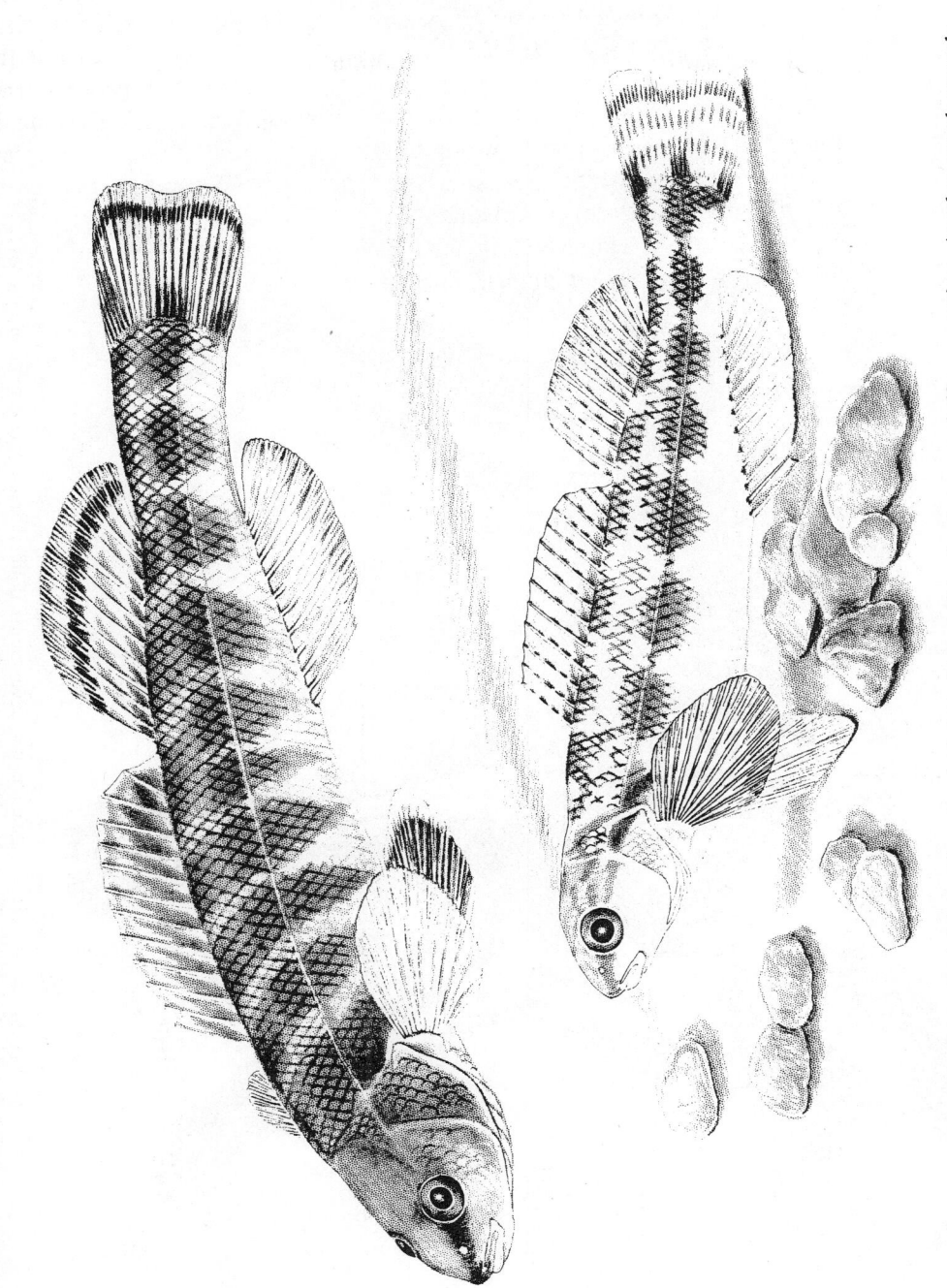

Figure 8.29 This pair of fish was done in stipple board to avoid having to prepare halftone negatives. Another superb example of the technique of Mrs. Alice Prickett.

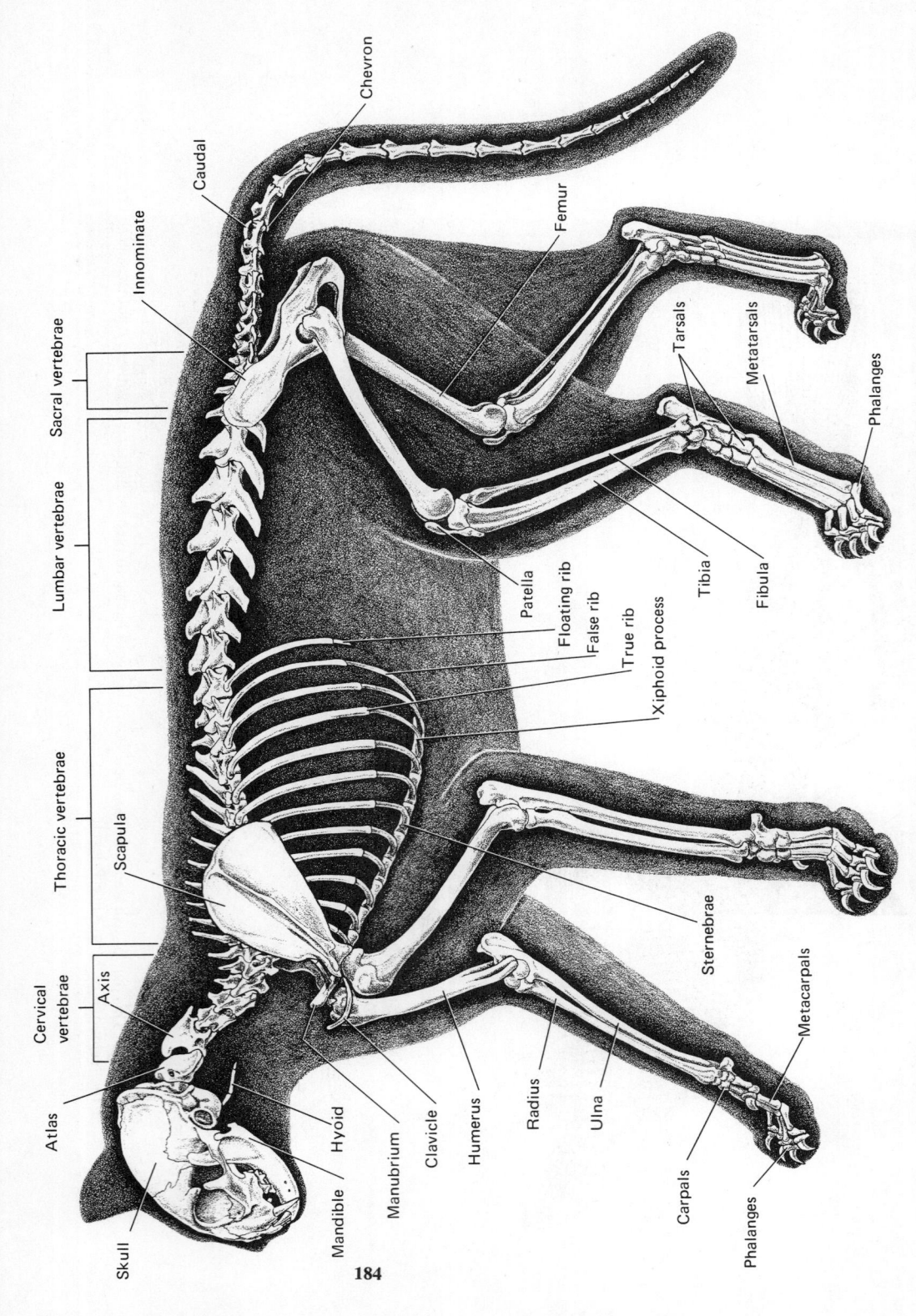

Figure 8.30 A superb example of stipple board art. No one can doubt the enormous amount of time saved by using this medium rather than hand stippling. Artist: Mrs. Alice Prickett. [From Harrison, Bruce M.: Dissection of the cat, ed. 7, St. Louis, The C. V. Mosby Co. (in press)]

Scratch board, as the name implies, is a special smooth-surfaced illustration board that is painted with ink and then scratched with a tool to produce a drawing. The technique

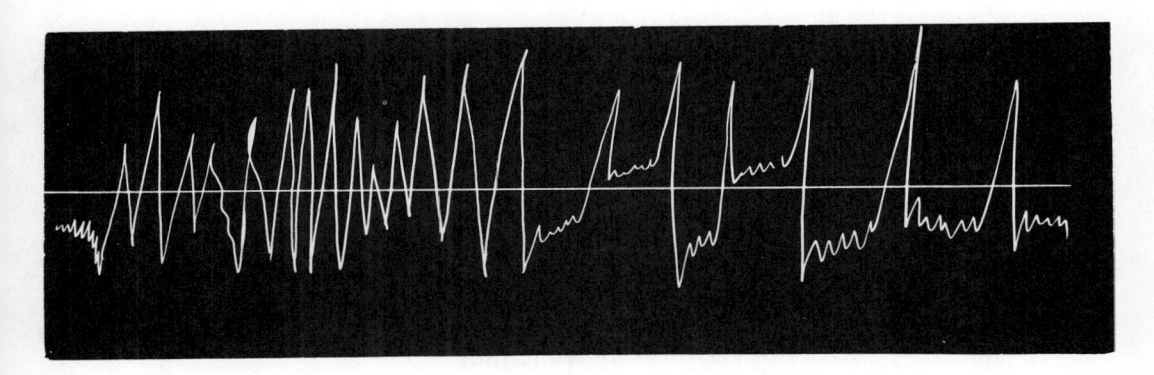

8E
Scratch Board

Figure 8.31 A scratch board was used to "rule" white lines on a black background here. By doing so, an intermediate reversal negative was avoided and cost savings were realized for the publisher.

Figure 8.32 A scratch board drawing of a seal (from Charles S. Papp, *Scientific Illustration*, Wm. C. Brown Company Publishers, Dubuque, Iowa, 1968, p. 39).

is useful, tedious, and time-consuming and is most often used by experienced illustrators in special instances.

Scratch board drawings are shown in Figs. 8.31 and 8.32. Note that they are reproduced as line copy.

8F
Ink Wash

Although we are concerned primarily with ink drawings, wash drawings can be made with a brush and *any* water-soluble material, such as India ink or tempera. For beginners, India ink thinned with water is a good starting point.

Four basic shades shown in Fig. 8.33 are mixed in separate containers. The surface, a good three-ply Strathmore paper, should be kept moist while working. Applying the ink solution to a dry surface will result in uneven shading and different shades will not blend—see Fig. 8.34. Highlights may be added using white ink.

Figure 8.33 Four basic shades of India ink–water mixtures.

Figure 8.34 Application of ink–water solution to a dry surface gives uneven shading.

It should be noted that wash drawings are continuous tone copy and require halftone plates for reproduction. The illustrations used in Figs. 8.35 through 8.37 are wash drawings.

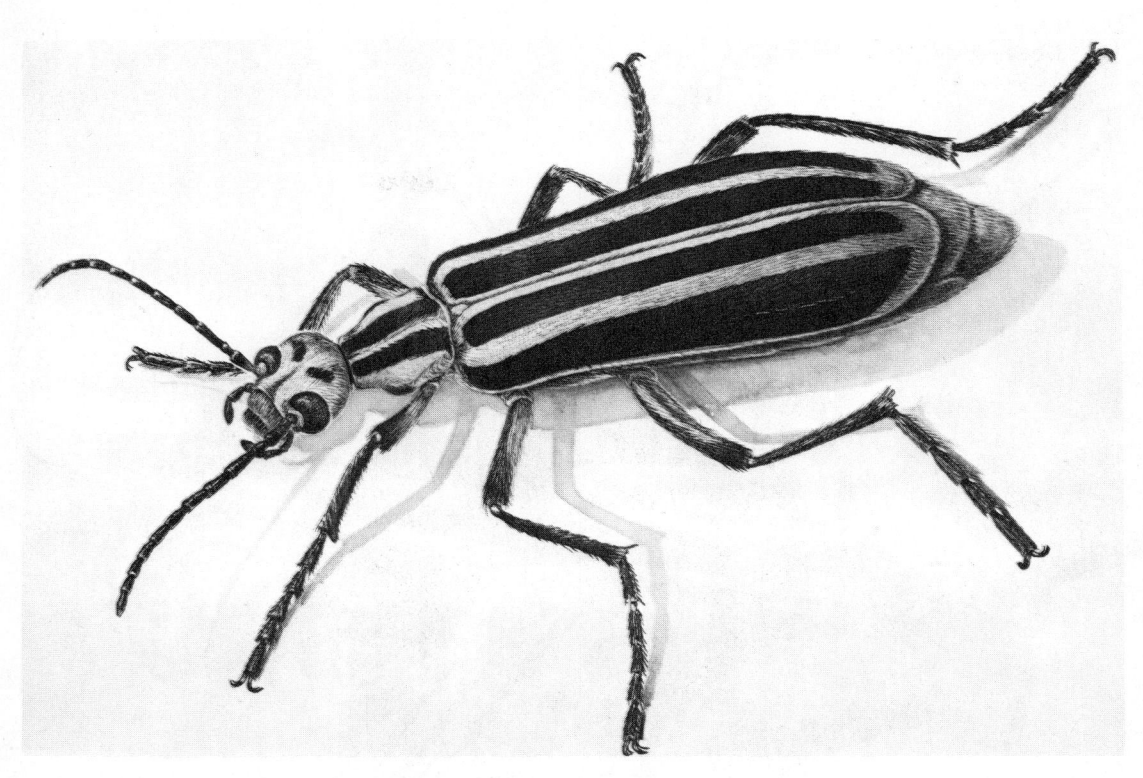

Figure 8.35 An ink wash drawing of a male blister beetle is shown here. Note the detail possible. Artist: Mrs. Alice Prickett. (The originals for this figure and for Fig. 8.36 were executed as part of the research of Dr. Richard Selander at the University of Illinois. We thank Dr. Selander for allowing them to be used here.)

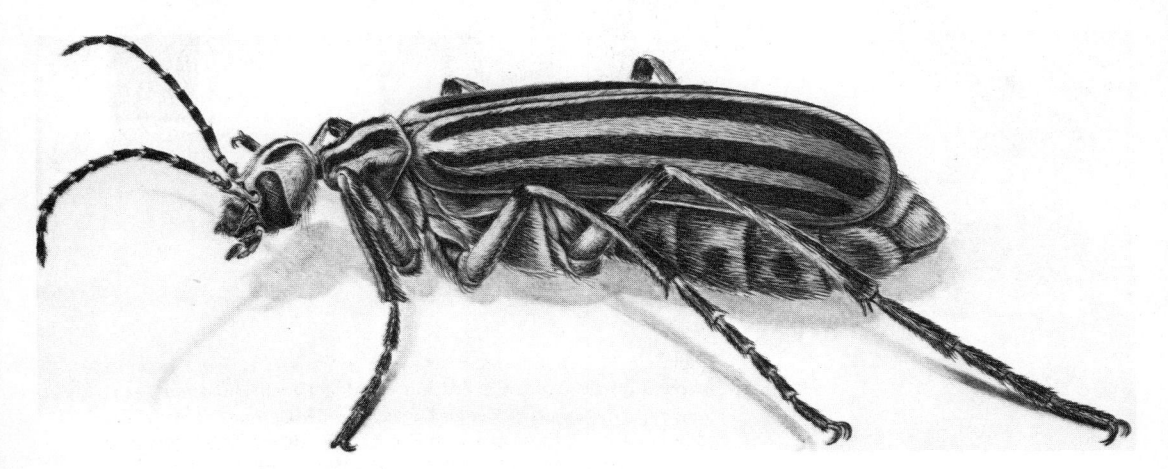

Figure 8.36 A female blister beetle.

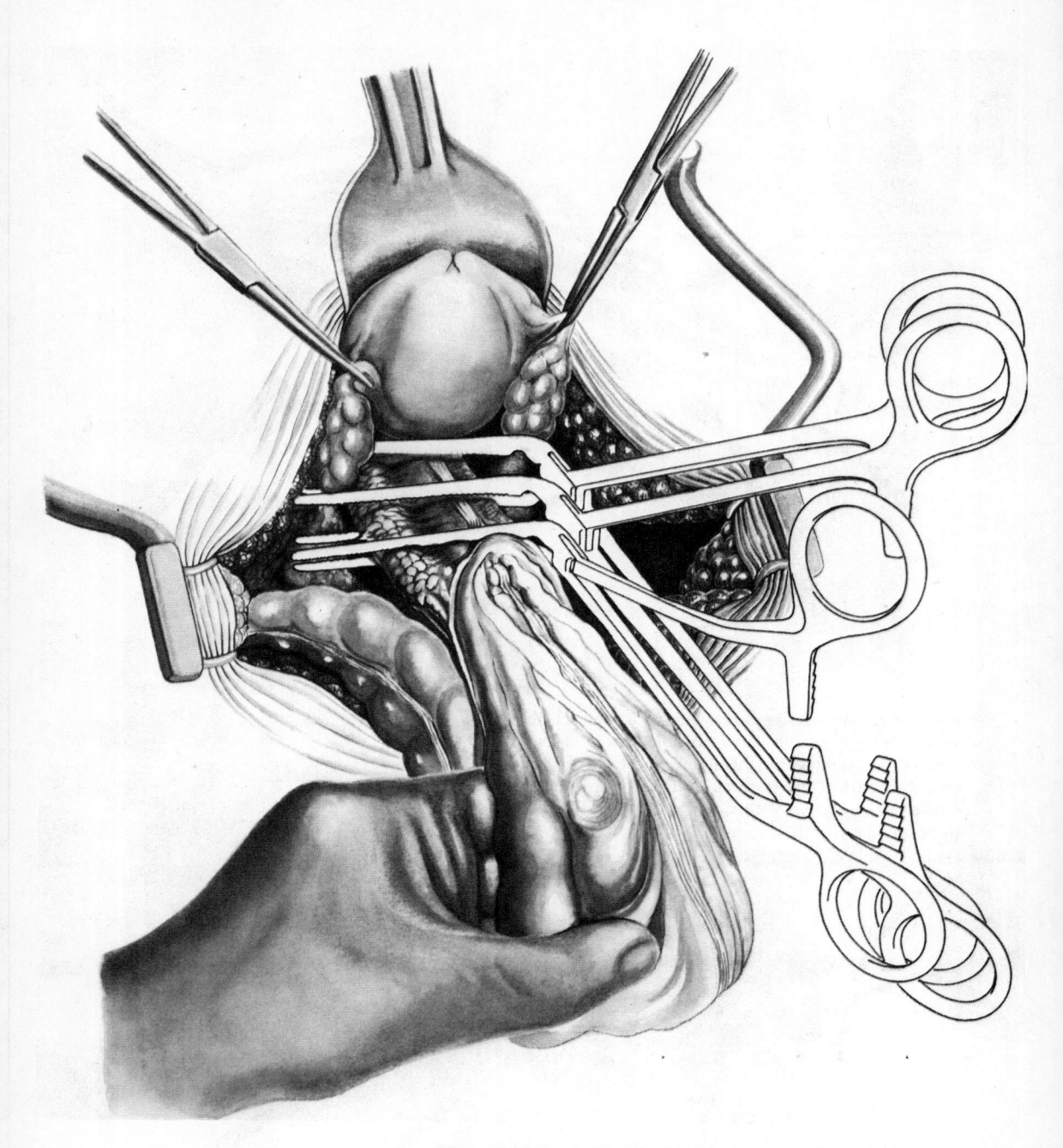

Figure 8.37 An ink wash drawing is used effectively here to show a portion of an operation entitled *Clamp Isolation Technique for Resection of Rectal Cancer with Anastimosis:* A procedure being used and perfected by Dr. G. Bruce Thow of Carle Clinic. Artist: Mrs. Alice Prickett. (We thank Dr. Thow for allowing this reproduction of his original to be used.)

In Fig. 8.38, we show a type of shading that is often used in textbooks and magazines. This one illustration is the product of *three* separate sub-illustrations. Let's see the procedure used in making a tint screen illustration.

First of all, all work is done on a drafting *film*, which is a plastic-base material that is dimensionally stable. In other words, changes in temperature and humidity do not make the film change in size (stretch or shrink).

The first sub-illustration to be made is shown in Fig. 8.39(a). Note that all lines on this drawing appear as black lines and letters in Fig. 8.38. Also note the *three* asymmetric crossmarks. These are called *registration marks*, and are used to line up the sub-illustrations. These marks *must* be asymmetric to assure only one alignment of overlays. Symmetry would allow overlays to be placed upside-down.

The next sub-illustration, Fig. 8.39(b), is a single line drawn in the proper position with respect to the axes. This curve will drop out (become white) in the screened background. The *same* registration marks made on the first sub-illustration are made on the second one. This is of utmost importance.

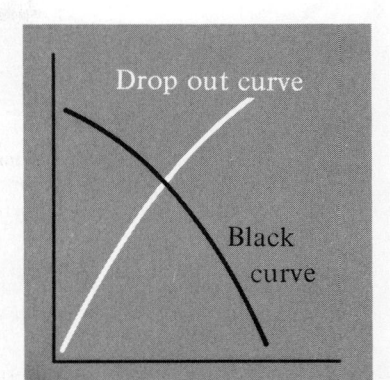

8G
Tint Screen

Figure 8.38
A tint screen drawing that employs black, a 40-percent-of-black screen, and a drop out white curve.

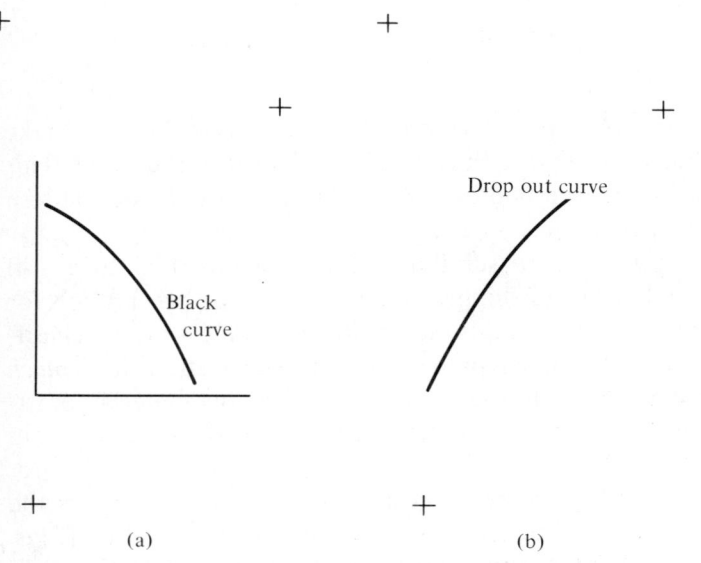

Figure 8.39 The component parts of Fig. 8.38. Part (a) is the drawing that contains all black lines; (b) is the drawing that contains drop out white features; and (c) is the window area for the screen pattern. Note that each is prepared in black ink. The rest is done by the photographic processes.

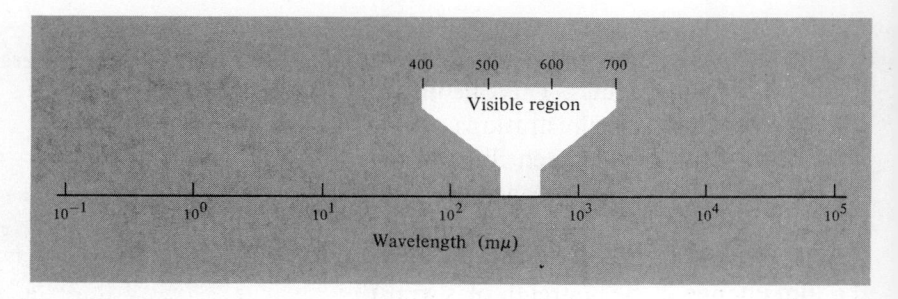

Figure 8.40 A tint screen that is comprised of three sub-illustrations: black, drop out white, and screen. It should prove to be interesting to figure out and sketch the three sub-illustrations.

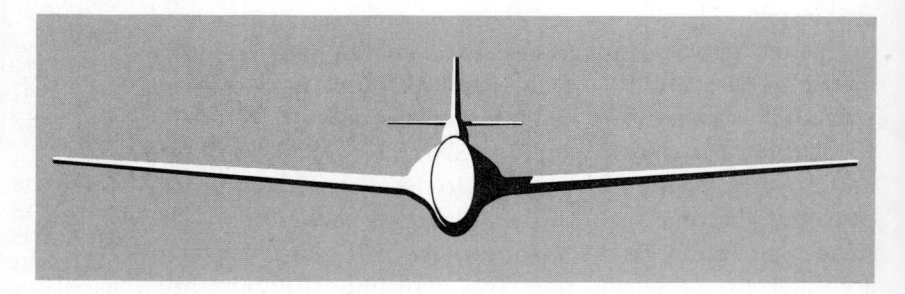

Figure 8.41 The drop out here demonstrates the visible part of the spectrum. A good use of tint screen.

Figure 8.42 In some instances, a drop out can be used to trace a flow of some substance. Here the flow of blood in the human arm is shown effectively.

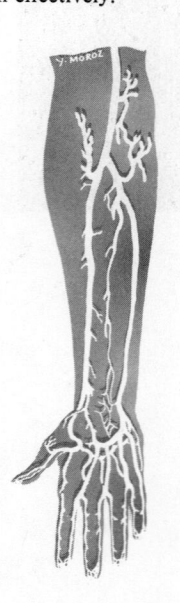

The last step is to use *red* zip-a-tone, Fig. 8.39(c), to make a "window" that is the size of the shaded background. This area is screened photographically to produce the dot pattern that appears grey in Fig. 8.38.

Now all three sub-illustrations are mounted to a stiff poster board and shipped to an engraver for preparation for printing. Although this illustrating technique is not much different from that of preparing a line illustration, it is *much* more expensive to the client. First of all, the material (drafting film) is costly; second, the time required to make certain the lines on overlay sheets are in register is costly; and third, the engraving process is costly. For these three reasons the technique is used sparingly. The figures that follow (Figs. 8.40, 8.41, 8.42, and 8.43) illustrate the power of the technique. It is not difficult to imagine other uses of tint screening in other figures in this book. For the reason above—cost—it was used sparingly.

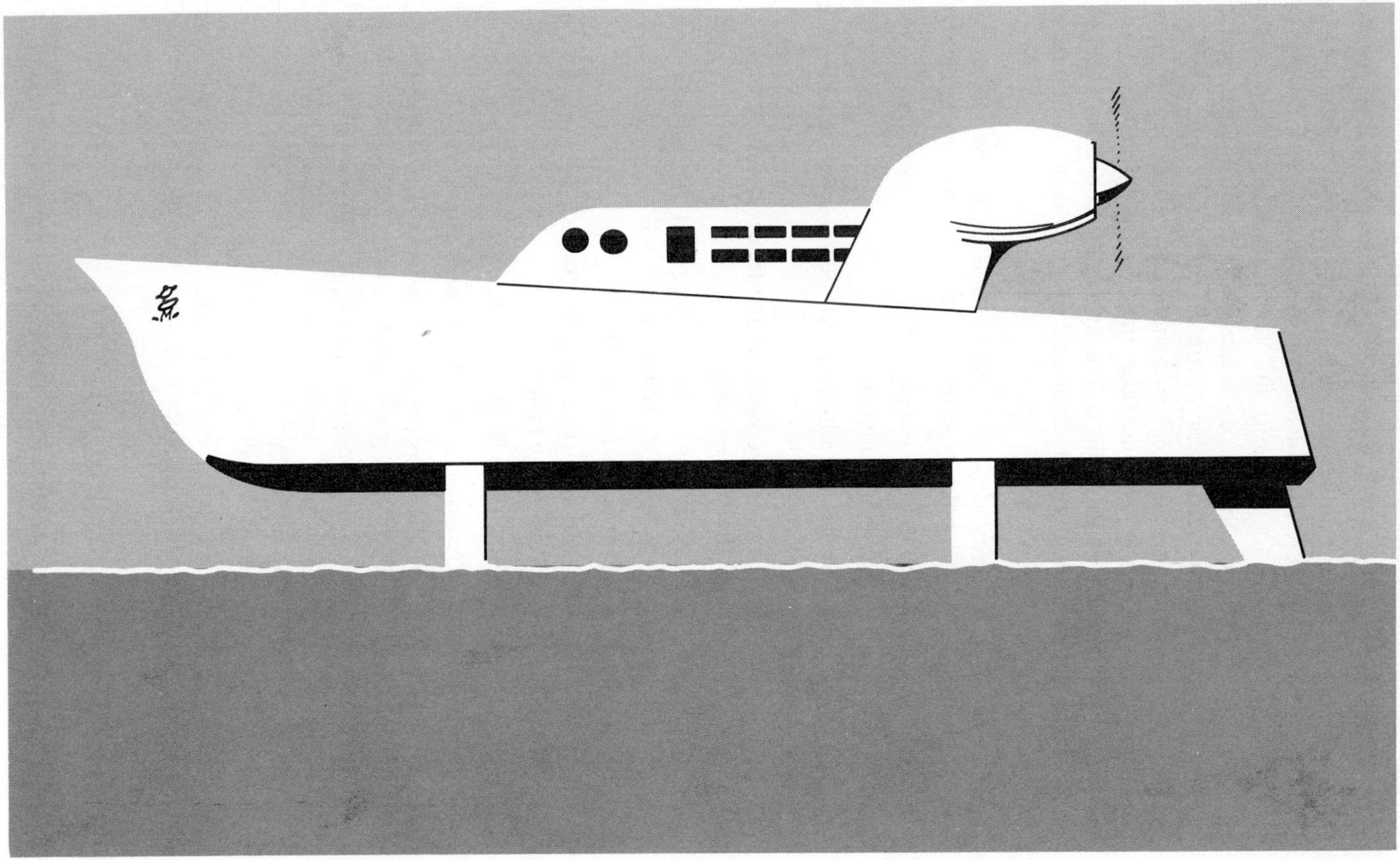

Figure 8.43 Try to figure this one out.

8H
Closure In closing, we mention that we have at our disposal *any* of the techniques mentioned above—plus others not mentioned—to use for illustrating. We should not limit our considerations to pen and ink if another technique will serve the purpose better. By settling into a routine we may be stifling creativity. We can become addicted to one style or technique and miss the real enjoyment and challenge of illustrating—showing an audience the best possible representation of data or an object. We urge the reader to experiment with each technique. Time and practice alone will make an expert.

QUESTIONS
1. Name the four methods most often used to shade drawings and make them more realistic. Explain each method briefly.
2. What is the purpose of rulings on a surface?
3. What is a highlight?
4. What is the difference between pressure-sensitive overlays and rub-on sheets?
5. How is a screened pattern (dot) designated? Explain each part of the designation.
6. Why is it important to consider the reduction in size of a drawing when we use screen patterns?
7. What is a graduated tone?
8. If you are asked to hand stipple a drawing, how do you accomplish the task?
9. Name three fields in which hand stippling is used extensively.
10. What is stipple board? How is it used?
11. Why is stipple board often used rather than hand stippling? (*Hint*: Two major reasons.)
12. Describe briefly the techniques below:
    (a) Scratch board
    (b) Ink wash
    (c) Air brush
13. What is the major disadvantage of using the three methods listed in Questions 12?

REFERENCES *For the use of stipple board*

1. B. M. Harrison, *Dissection of the Cat*. St. Louis: The C. V. Mosby Company, 1973.

2. J. R. Larson, Jr., *A Laboratory Manual in Biology*. Champaign: Stipes Publishing Co., 1973.

   These two textbooks were illustrated by the same artist, Mrs. Alice Prickett. She has done a masterful job in the first book—an extremely detailed treatment that shows the full power of stipple board. Parts of the second entry (the parts illustrating the dissection of the fetal pig) are excellent examples as well.

3. Jack Hamm, *Drawing the Head and Figure*. New York: Grosset and Dunlap, Inc., Publishers, 1963.

   Many fine examples of the use of stipple board and the versatility of the medium are included here. No directions are given for the procedure. A fun book.

4. D. H. Andrews, and R. J. Kokes, *Fundamental Chemistry*. New York: John Wiley & Sons, Inc., 1962.

   Atomic structures drawn using stipple board are superb.

5. D. R. Corson, and P. Lorrain, *Introduction to Electromagnetic Fields and Waves*. San Francisco: W. H. Freeman and Co., 1962.

   A good example to demonstrate a technique that is lacking. Some good ideas are available, but the overall quality of illustrations, caused in large part by the poor lettering, is not professional.

6. W. J. Luzzader, *Fundamentals of Engineering Drafting for Design, Communication, and Numerical Control* (6th ed.). Englewood Cliffs: Prentice-Hall, Inc., 1971.

   Halftone board (raised dots) is used in this book. It compares favorably with other stipple board techniques.

7. C. S. Papp, *Scientific Illustration Theory and Practice*. Dubuque: Wm. C. Brown Company Publishers, 1968.

   Excellent examples of the use of stipple board. The author attempts to teach the reader how to use the medium.

For the use of acetate sheets

1. H. W. Frantz, and L. E. Malm, *Chemical Principles in the Laboratory*. San Francisco: W. H. Freeman and Co., 1966.

   Some double overlay patterns were created by the artist.

2. G. Hardin, *Biology: Its Principles and Implications*. San Francisco: W. H. Freeman and Co., 1961.

   The artist demonstrates some novel uses of tone sheets and patterns. For example, see pp. 80 and 81.

3. G. S. Christiansen, and P. H. Garrett, *Structure and Change: An Introduction to the Science of Matter*. San Francisco: W. H. Freeman and Co., 1960.

   Many examples of the use of the medium in a rather flamboyant style.

4. H. Frauenfelder, and E. M. Henley, *Subatomic Physics*. Englewood Cliffs: Prentice-Hall, Inc., 1974.

5. D. Ewen, et al., *Physics for Career Education*. Englewood Cliffs: Prentice-Hall, Inc., 1974.

   These last two books, illustrated by the author of *Technical Illustrating*, make use of acetate sheets in many figures. Note the use of a dot pattern that fits the reduction: 75 percent of original in these cases.

For the use of tint screens

1. J. L. Meriam, *Statics and Dynamics* (2nd ed.). New York: John Wiley & Sons, Inc., 1971.

   There are not enough superlatives to describe the art work in this book. It is one of the best examples of craftsmanship in illustrating that can be purchased. Ingenious uses of tint screens abound. A must for every serious illustrator.

2. J. V. Quagliano, and L. M. Vallarino, *Chemistry* (3rd ed.). Englewood Cliffs: Prentice-Hall, Inc., 1969.

   Tint screens are used effectively in this text, which is done in two colors. Air brush renderings are used as well. A good exercise for students is to figure out how many sub-illustrations are used to make up each completed illustration. Some have as many as five sub-illustrations.

3. B. Rodin, *Calculus With Analytic Geometry*. Englewood Cliffs: Prentice-Hall, Inc. 1970.

   A superbly illustrated mathematics book. Two colors are used with many tint screens.

4. T. D. Brock, and K. M. Brock, *Basic Microbiology With Applications*. Englewood Cliffs: Prentice-Hall, Inc., 1973.

   A well-illustrated book which uses tint screens and hand stippling to good advantage. Comparing this book (done in black) with books of two-color illustrations shows how versatile and attractive black alone can be if used properly. The style of illustrations is uncluttered and attractive.

5. A. L. Ruoff, *Materials Science*. Englewood Cliffs: Prentice-Hall, Inc., 1973.

   In many respects this is a poorly illustrated text. Tint screens are used effectively in few places and ineffectively in most places. Leroy lettering is employed. Line weights appear to have been chosen at random.

6. Old World Archaeology: Foundations of Civilization, Readings from *Scientific American*. San Francisco: W. H. Freeman and Company, 1972.

   This book, an inexpensive paperback, contains an invaluable collection of excellent illustrations. Tint screens of color and black are used well. Many examples of freehand and hand stippling techniques are included.

7. *Oceanography, Readings from Scientific American.* San Francisco: W. H. Freeman and Co., 1971.

    Another inexpensive source of examples of the tint screen technique, each in the tradition of *Scientific American.*

8. D. Halliday, and R. Resnick, *Fundamentals of Physics.* New York: John Wiley & Sons, Inc., 1970.

    Although individual illustrations are well done, the mixing of media (stipple board, tint screens, and acetate sheet screening) tends to detract from an *overall* design.

9. L. D. Leet, and S. Judson, *Physical Geology* (4th ed.). Englewood Cliffs: Prentice-Hall, Inc., 1971.

    The tint screens in this book are of the two-color variety. Also included is line art and hand stippling. A well-illustrated book. Although the material in the text is dull to most, an illustrator could learn much from studying the figures.

10. R. Mitchell, *Introduction to Environmental Microbiology.* Englewood Cliffs: Prentice-Hall, Inc., 1974.

    Many curves in drop out white. Many stylized organism drawings. An excellent reference.

For use of scratchboard

1. M. Cutler, *How To Cut Drawings On Scratchboard.* New York: Watson-Guptill Publications, Inc., 1960.

2. M. Cutler, *Scratchboard Drawings.* New York: Watson-Guptill Publications, Inc., 1949.

    The examples in these two books are, for the most part, "arty," as opposed to practical. Both illustrate the technique, however, and attempt to give basic directions.

3. C. S. Papp, *Scientific Illustration Theory and Practice.* Dubuque: Wm. C. Brown Company Publishers, 1968.

    The author, who illustrated the book, is a superb practitioner of the use of scratchboard. Examples are from the life sciences and are excellent. Much detail in how to do the drawing described is presented.

For use of hand stippling

1. N. H. Russell, *Introduction to Plant Science: A Humanistic and Ecological Approach.* St. Paul: West Publishing Co., 1974.

    The artist, Carol Coope, has done a superlative job in using hand stippling in conjunction with tint screens. The subject field (plant science) makes use of this technique often.

2. W. H. Johnson, et al., *Biology*. New York: Holt, Rinehart and Winston, 1961.

   An example of stippling that leaves one with the impression of blandness. Too small and too tight drawings result in a crowding of the art. Stippling shows little of the changing density that it should.

3. D. C. Braungart, and R. H. Arnett, *An Introduction to Plant Biology*. St. Louis: The C. V. Mosby Company, 1965.

   One of the better collections of hand stippling under one cover.

4. A. M. Elliott, *Zoology* (2nd ed.). New York: Appleton-Century-Croft, Inc., 1957.

   The art is well done, as is the stippling. Somehow the figures do not look real. An unnaturalness prevails.

5. N. D. Buffaloe, *Principles of Biology*. Englewood Cliffs: Prentice-Hall, Inc., 1962.

   A two-color printing that uses many well-executed, hand-stippled drawings. Many excellent examples.

6. C. A. Villee, *Biology*. Philadelphia: W. B. Saunders Company, 1962.

   For the most part, the art in this book is good. There are, however, a few superb hand-stippled figures and several extremely poor ones.

7. W. D. McElroy, and C. P. Swanson, Editors, *Foundations of Biology*. Englewood Cliffs: Prentice-Hall., Inc., 1968.

   A two-color treatment of artwork is well done here. Hand stippling is excellent. In addition, the artist has used several wash drawings of complex structures.

8. W. A. Jensen, and F. B. Salisbury, *Botany: An Ecological Approach*. Belmont: Wadsworth Publishing Co., 1972.

   An excellent collection of examples. Although a traditional treatment, the serious artist can obtain many ideas here.

9

Projection Slides

In many cases an illustration will be used in two ways—as a figure in a book (or journal article) and as copy for a projection slide for a talk to be delivered. In other cases the illustration will be used *only* to make a projection slide: a popular 2 × 2 (35 mm) size, a $3\frac{1}{4}$ × 4 (lantern glass slide or Polaroid) size, or an 8 × 10 overhead projection size. The slide can be in color, black and white line copy, or continuous tone. In preparing illustrations to be used in making projection slides, we must be aware of certain restrictions and principles that are not applicable to preparing illustrations for other uses.

9A Format

We noted three sizes of slides: 2 × 2, $3\frac{1}{4}$ × 4, and 8 × 10. These dimensions are given in inches and are related to the *overall* size of the slide. Table 9.1 shows the actual dimensions within which the final copy must fit in order to mount the transparency in a frame.

When we prepare illustrations to be used in any of these formats, we must execute the drawing within a box whose sides are multiples of these sizes. Table 9.2 gives the dimensions required to be whole-number multiples of the basic dimensions in Table 9.1.

198 / Chap. 9
Projection Slides

Table 9.1. Projection slide formats.

Slide Size height × width (inches)	Usable* Dimensions	
	Width (inches)	Height (inches)
2 × 2	$1\frac{1}{4}$	$1\frac{13}{16}$
$3\frac{1}{4}$ × 4	$3\frac{1}{2}$	$2\frac{3}{4}$
8 × 10	9	7

*By usable, we mean that area of the slide that is projected onto a screen.

Table 9.2. Dimension for multiples of basic slide dimensions.

Multiple of Basic Dimension from Table 9.1	Dimensions within which Drawing Must Fit (inches)			
	2 × 2		$3\frac{1}{4}$ × 4	
	Width	Height	Width	Height
2	$2\frac{1}{2}$	$1\frac{5}{8}$	7	$5\frac{1}{2}$
3	$3\frac{3}{4}$	$2\frac{9}{16}$	$10\frac{1}{2}$	$8\frac{1}{4}$
4	5	$3\frac{1}{4}$	14	11
5	$6\frac{1}{4}$	$4\frac{1}{16}$	$17\frac{1}{2}$	$13\frac{3}{4}$
6	$7\frac{1}{2}$	$4\frac{7}{8}$	21	$16\frac{1}{2}$
7	$8\frac{3}{4}$	$5\frac{11}{16}$	$24\frac{1}{2}$	$19\frac{1}{4}$
8	10	$6\frac{1}{2}$	28	22
9	$11\frac{1}{4}$	$7\frac{5}{16}$	$31\frac{1}{2}$	$24\frac{3}{4}$

After we have determined the size drawing we intend to make, a determination of line widths and letter heights must be made.

**9B
Letter Sizes and Line Widths**

As we saw in Chapter 7 (Table 7.1, p. 156), a formula approach to making size-consistent drawings is a reality and a timesaving device. We can, with slight modification, prepare tables to provide the same information for making slide drawings. The tables that follow may be used for sizing slides.

Example (using Table 9.3)

If we use Table 9.3, we have decided that the finished product will be a 2 × 2 slide. Assume we will be using a drawing that is five times as large as the basic $1\frac{1}{4}$ × $1\frac{3}{16}$ dimensions. We enter the table on the 5-row and note that the maximum dimensions (columns 2

Table 9.3. SCALING INFORMATION USED TO PREPARE ILLUSTRATIONS FOR 2 × 2 SLIDES SO THAT ANY TWO OR MORE ORIGINALS OF DIFFERENT WIDTHS WILL BE SCALED IDENTICALLY IN THE SLIDE.

\multicolumn{15}{c}{Column Number}
1	2	3	4	5	6	7	8	9	10	11	12	13	14	15
Dimension of Drawing (inches) (from Table 9.2)			Ruling Pen*			Lettering Pen	K.&E. LEROY Lettering Guide Size						Axis Numbers	
							Lettering			Subs & Supers				
							Std	Greek		Std	Greek			
Multiple	Width	Height	Heavy	Medium	Light		ULC	UC	LC†	ULC	UC	LC†	Std	S&S
2	$2\frac{1}{2}$	$1\frac{5}{8}$	0	00R	000R	000	100	100	120	060	060‡	080‡	080	060
3	$3\frac{3}{4}$	$2\frac{9}{16}$	0	00R	000R	000	100	100	120	060	060‡	080‡	080	060
4	5	$3\frac{1}{4}$	1	00	000	000	120	120	140	080	080‡	100	100	080
5	$6\frac{1}{4}$	$4\frac{1}{16}$	1	00	000	000	120	120	140	080	080‡	100	100	080
6	$7\frac{1}{2}$	$4\frac{7}{8}$	2	1R	00	00	140	140	175	100	100	120	120	100
7	$8\frac{3}{4}$	$5\frac{11}{16}$	3R	1	00R	0	175	175	200	120	120	140	140	120
8	10	$6\frac{1}{2}$	3	2	00	0	200	200	240	140	140	175	175	140
9	$11\frac{1}{4}$	$7\frac{5}{16}$	4	3R	00	1	240	240	290	175	175	200	200	175

*Suffix R denotes Rapidograph pen; no suffix indicates K.&E. pen.
†Except $\beta, \delta, \zeta, \theta, \lambda, \xi, \phi$, and ψ for which the templates listed in column 8 and/or 11 are used.
‡Use K.&E. Height & Slant Control Scriber.
Abbreviations: ULC = UPPERCASE and lowercase; UC = UPPERCASE; LC = lowercase; S&S = subscripts and superscripts; Std = K.&E. LEROY standard lettering template.

and 3) are $6\frac{1}{4} \times 4\frac{1}{16}$. Then we proceed to the right (still in row 5) and read pen sizes and letter heights. Note that letter heights are given in thousandths of an inch for Leroy letters. Figure 9.1 has been prepared using Table 9.3 and is annotated to show uses of the various columns.

If we were to have chosen a $3\frac{1}{4} \times 4$ format, rather than a 2 × 2 format, we would use Table 9.4 for pen sizes and letter heights as in Fig. 9.2. This table is used exactly the same as Table 9.3.

Sizes used for 8 × 10 overhead projection slides are not too critical. The main caution here is to not crowd too much material onto one slide. We will discuss this aspect (crowding) of preparing slides later in this chapter.

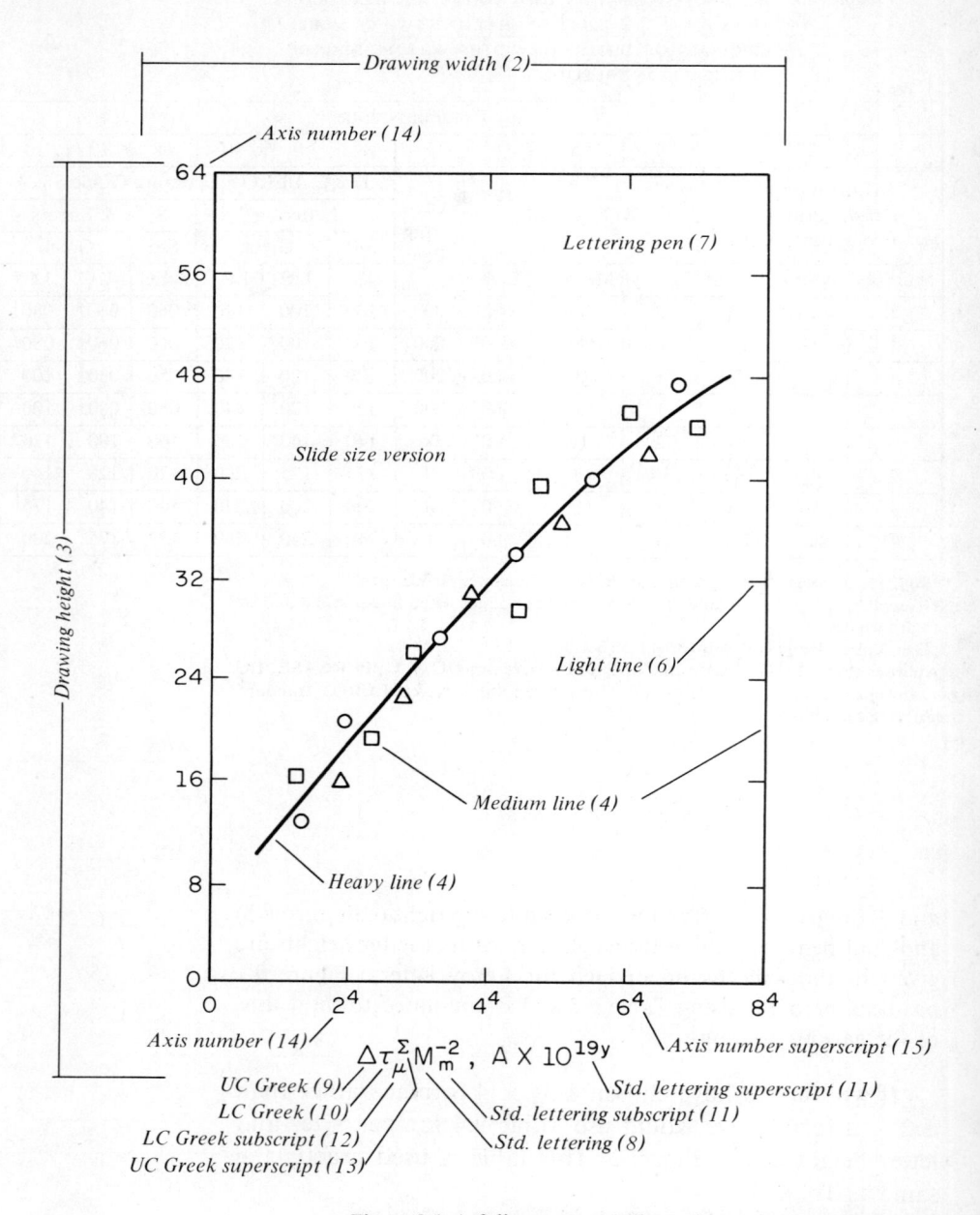

Figure 9.1 A fully annotated illustration prepared using Table 9.3. Numbers in parentheses refer to column numbers in the table. All columns are employed.

Sec. 9B / 201
Letter Sizes and Line Widths

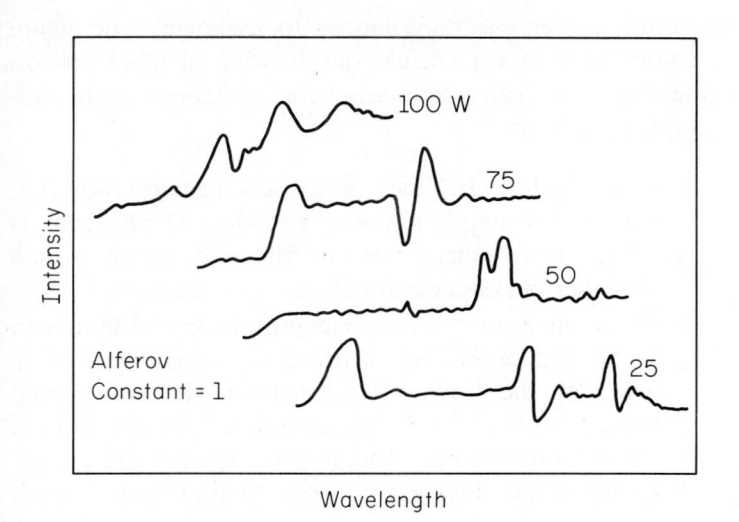

Figure 9.2 A slide-size illustration prepared using Table 9.4.

Table 9.4. SCALING INFORMATION USED TO PREPARE ILLUSTRATIONS FOR $3\frac{1}{4} \times 4$ SLIDES SO THAT ANY TWO OR MORE ORIGINALS OF DIFFERENT WIDTHS WILL BE SCALED IDENTICALLY IN THE SLIDE.

Column Number														
1	2	3	4	5	6	7	8	9	10	11	12	13	14	15
Dimension of Drawing (inches) (from Table 9.2)			Ruling Pen*			Lettering Pen	K.&E. LEROY Lettering Guide Size						Axis Numbers	
							Lettering			Subs & Supers				
							Std	Greek		Std	Greek			
Multiple	Width	Height	Heavy	Medium	Light		ULC	UC	LC†	ULC	UC	LC†	Std	S&S
1	$3\frac{1}{2}$	$2\frac{3}{4}$	1	0R	000	000	120	120	140	080	080‡	100	100	080
2	7	$5\frac{1}{2}$	3	$2\frac{1}{2}$R	00	0	200	200	240	140	140	175	175	140
3	$10\frac{1}{2}$	$8\frac{1}{4}$	5	3	1R	2	290	290	350	200	200	240	240	200
4	14	11	6	4R	$2\frac{1}{2}$R	3	425	425	500	290	290	350	350	290
5	$17\frac{1}{2}$	$13\frac{3}{4}$	8	6R	3R	4	500	500	700	350	350	425	425	350
6	21	$16\frac{1}{2}$	8R	7	3	5	500	500	700	425	425	500	500	425
7	$24\frac{1}{2}$	$19\frac{1}{4}$	9R	7R	4	6	700	700	1000	500	500	700	700	500

*Suffix R denotes Rapidograph pen; no suffix indicates K.&E. pen.
†Except $\beta, \delta, \zeta, \theta, \lambda, \xi, \phi,$ and ψ for which the templates listed in column 3 and/or 11 are used.
‡Use K.&E. Height & Slant Control Scriber.
Abbreviations: ULC = UPPERCASE and lowercase; UC = UPPERCASE; LC = lowercase; S&S = subscripts and superscripts: Std = K.&E. LEROY standard lettering template.

9C
Black and White or Color 2 × 2 Slides

As stated earlier, we may choose to use black and white or color slides. If we execute the drawing in black ink on white paper, we can produce several variations with photographic processes.

1. Slides with white lines on a black background (Fig. 9.3) are the simplest type to produce. The drawing is copied at a reduced size on litho film, which is then mounted in either cardboard or glass mounts.
2. Black lines on a white background are obtained in a two-step photographic procedure as shown in Fig. 9.4. First the drawing is copied on litho film (giving white lines on a black background). Then the litho is printed on another litho film to reverse the image, giving black lines on a clear (white) background.

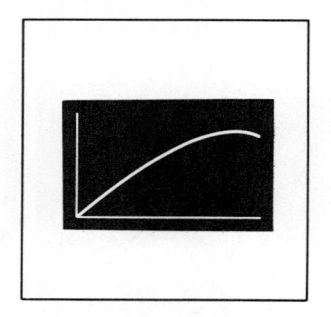

Figure 9.3 A slide that projects as white lines on black background.

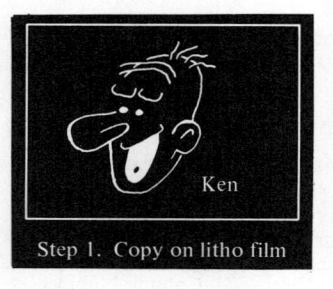

Step 1. Copy on litho film

Step 2. Reverse the image

Figure 9.4 The two-step process employed to produce black lines and a clear (white) background for a projection slide.

3. If we are not satisfied with plain black and white, we can easily provide color for the slides.
    a. *Colored lines on a black background.* First we obtain a litho negative of the drawing—a $3\frac{1}{4} \times 4$ negative. We may then proceed in one of two ways: (1) paint the clear lines with transparent photo dyes or (2) mask the lines with a gelatin filter or colored acetate. After we have applied the color, the $3\frac{1}{4} \times 4$ negative is exposed on 35-mm color film.
    In preparing illustrations for slides that are to be colored as described above, we must keep in mind that in order to paint with the photo dye or mask a line we must allow room to do so. For example, in Fig. 9.5 we could not paint the two

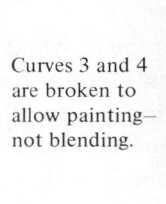

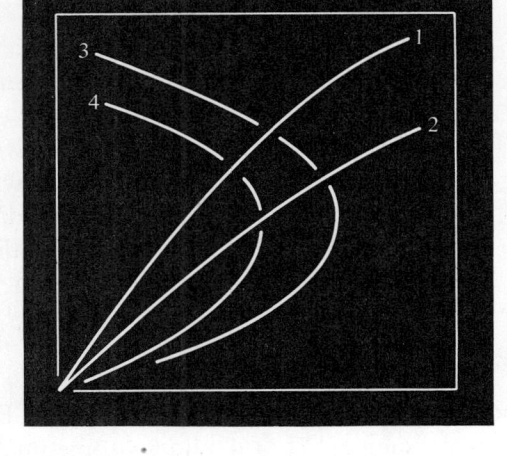

Curves 3 and 4 are broken to allow painting—not blending.

Figure 9.5 Procedure to obtain colored lines on a black background for projection slides.

lines different colors and not have the colors mix if they crossed. We have, however, allowed space to paint and will experience no problems. Always plan ahead.

b. *Black lines on a colored background.* If we wish to put black lines on a colored background, we can do so mechanically or photographically. The simplest method is to make the drawing on colored paper using black ink. Photographing this drawing using color film gives the desired result. By strictly photographic means, we can follow the four-step procedure outlined here. First a litho negative is made and is used to produce a reversal film. The reversal is then exposed on *color* film. The last step is to double expose the frame, masking the camera lens with a color filter.

c. *White lines on a colored background.* To produce white lines on colored background we employ a three-step procedure that is similar to that used in 3.b., Fig. 9.7. We merely expose a litho negative on color film (to give the white lines) and then double expose that frame with a color filter to obtain the background.

Another method is to use a special sensitized film that is developed by exposing it to ammonia vapor in an ozalid machine. A litho negative is "contact printed" on the special film. Several companies manufacture the material in red, blue, green, yellow, and other colors.

d. *Colored lines on a colored background.* Making a drawing in color provides us with colored lines and colored background. In addition to drawing in color, we may use combinations of different filters and multiple exposures to obtain color on color.

9D Black and White or Color $3\frac{1}{4} \times 4$ Slides

Some clients will not want 2×2 slides. For these people we may suggest $3\frac{1}{4} \times 4$ slides—sometimes called *lantern* slides or *standard glass* slides. This type of slide is large and heavy but can be used to good advantage when detail is necessary that would be lost by reducing to 35-mm size.

1. White lines on a black background are produced by merely exposing a litho film and mounting it in the proper frame or between pieces of glass.
2. Black lines on a white background is the result of reversing the image of step 1. The reversal image can be made on another litho film or on a piece of photosensitive glass.*
3. Color in $3\frac{1}{4} \times 4$ slides can also be provided.
   a. *Colored lines on a black background.* Because color film in a $3\frac{1}{4} \times 4$ size is expensive, most clients will not authorize the use. We are, therefore, not likely to provide slides using the litho negative–color filter technique. We can, however, paint litho negatives with transparent photo dyes and obtain excellent results. These negatives should always be mounted between two pieces of glass to protect the negative.
   b. *White lines on a colored background.* A foil-type material is available that can be exposed on an ozalid machine using a litho negative. The result is a colored background–white line slide. The process is inexpensive, is fast, and can be used for 2×2, $3\frac{1}{4} \times 4$, or 8×10 (overhead projection) slides.

*This process gave the name *standard glass slide*.

9E
Notes Concerning Slides

As we mentioned earlier in this chapter, drawings from which slides are made must be treated differently from drawings to be used in other ways. The short paragraphs that follow are notes of caution to the illustrator preparing slide drawings.

CHOOSING A FORMAT

A client will usually have his preference as to format—2×2 or $3\frac{1}{4} \times 4$. If he does not have a preference, the artist should recommend the correct format based on such considerations as drawing size and detail required, where the slides will be shown (the client would not wish to carry 25 glass slides to Europe if he could use 2×2 slides equally well), whether the slide will be color or black and white, and the cost (2×2 slides are normally less expensive than $3\frac{1}{4} \times 4$).

DETAIL ON A SLIDE

A slide is intended to be a device used by a speaker to make a point that cannot be made by speaking. A slide should *never* be a set of notes from which the speaker reads to his audience. The audience will quickly become disinterested. An illustrator must recognize when too much material has been put into a slide and should inform the client. Two short slides are better than one long, crowded slide.

USE OF DUPLICATE SLIDES

In many cases duplicate slides can be put to good use.

1. When a list of items is discussed, each item in its turn, a duplicate slide (perhaps with the point being discussed in color) will preserve the complete list for the audience.
2. If a slide is to be used in two or more places in the presentation, a duplicate slide is a must. A projectionist has difficulty backing up to the original slide and the audience tires of waiting.

TYPEWRITTEN COPY FOR SLIDES.

> If typewritten copy is to be presented, the copy must fit within a 3¾ × 2½ inch area—the area within this box.

LEGIBILITY OF COPY

If a slide cannot be read or understood when projected, the effort to make the slide has been wasted. A rule of thumb to use is: If you can read 2 × 2 slides without a magnifying lens, the print will project well. The slide-size copies below are examples.

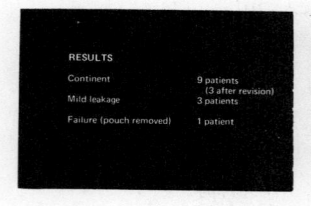

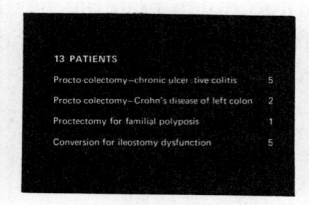

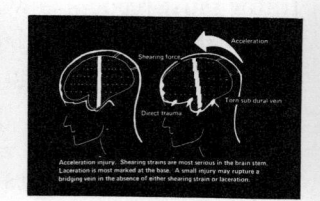

SLIDE TITLES

Avoid using titles, which consume area that could be devoted to making the slide copy more legible. The speaker will ordinarily explain the significance of the slide anyway.

IDEAS PER SLIDE

Limit the number of ideas per slide to *one*. Use several simple slides rather than one complex slide.

PROJECTION OF SLIDES

It is always a good idea to project slides *before* giving them to your client. If mistakes or glaring judgement errors are apparent on the screen, it is possible to make alterations before the client sees the errors—a politically advantageous situation.

USE OF DARK SLIDES

A dark slide is merely an opaque piece of film mounted as a slide. When a speaker wishes no image on the screen, a dark slide is used rather than turning the projector lamp off.

QUESTIONS

1. What are the three most often used formats for projection slides?
2. List the advantages and disadvantages of each format in Question 1.
3. Is it possible to reproduce black ink drawings in color slides? How?
4. List four variations of color slides.
5. Discuss choosing a slide format.
6. How much detail should a slide contain?
7. When should duplicate slides be used?
8. Is typewritten copy suitable for projection slides?
9. In your own words, discuss legibility of slides.

Part IV

Appendices

A. REPRODUCTION PROCESSES 211
    A1. Photographic 211
    A2. Offset Printing 213
    A3. Electrostatic 213
    A4. Blueprint 214
    A5. Ozalid 214
B. HIGH CONTRAST PHOTOGRAPHY 215
    B1. Description 215
C. TYPOGRAPHY 217
    C1. Typefaces 217
    C2. Typesetting Methods 219
    C3. Glossary of Terms 221
D. TYPOGRAPHIC MEASURE 223
E. THE GREEK ALPHABET 224
F. INTERNATIONAL STANDARD PREFIXES 225
G. SYMBOLS AND ABBREVIATIONS 227
H. OBJECT TO DRAW 230

… Part IV

Appendices

A

Reproduction Processes

Nearly every drawing an illustrator makes will be reproduced. In some cases many copies of the work will be made, whereas in other cases the drawing will be reproduced only once. The drawing may be reproduced at the original size or it may be reduced in size. A copy may be a positive or a negative of the original. The short descriptions of processes and the machines that follow give an indication of reproduction processes available to an illustrator.

A1 Photographic

Reproduction of illustrations by photographic means is usually limited to small quantities. In addition, the photograph (whether the end result is a negative or positive film or print) is usually an intermediate product. In other words, the film will be used in the printing or engraving process and the print will be used as a paste-up article.

Photographic films may be any one of four basic types.

1. High contrast (litho) films are used to engrave or print line copy. Figure A.1 illustrates a negative and a positive. Note that the white area in the figure is actually transparent on the film.
2. Continuous tone films are ordinarily negative films of

212 / App. A
Reproduction Processes

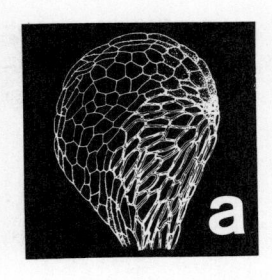

(a) This copy illustrates a negative litho film. In other words, the film image (clear lines, black background) is a reverse, or the negative of, the original.

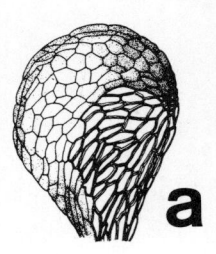

(b) Shown here is a positive litho film. The black lines, clear background film matches the black line, white background of the drawing.

Figure A.1 Positive and negative litho films.

4× enlargement

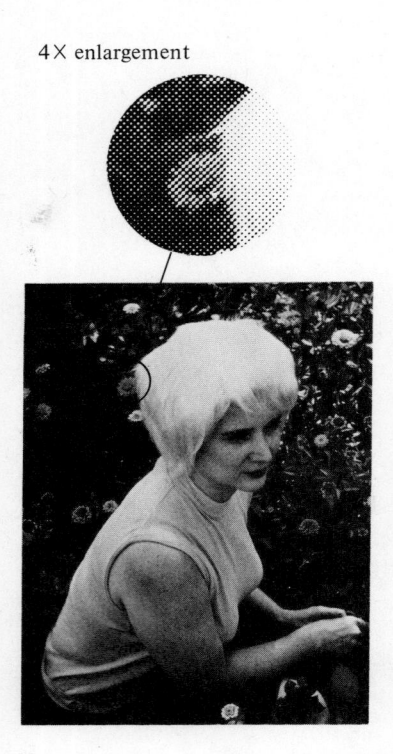

Figure A.2 A continuous tone scene is reproduced here by a halftone process. Note the dot patterns.

a scene (or object). Continuous tone means that all tones from white to black, including grays, are reproduced.

3. Screened films (called *halftones*) are used to *print* continuous tone copy. If we examine Fig. A.2, which is a screened print, we note that the print is actually a series of different size dots. In areas of dark shade, the dots are large: in areas of light shade, the dots are small. The use of screens to demonstrate tone is necessary because the printing press can reproduce black (or a color) only. Tones *between* black and white are simulated by dots of black ink that are sized between the large and small dots used for black or white.

4. Color films are used for special purposes. Reproduction of color is expensive and highly specialized and, ordinarily, used sparingly.

Photographic prints (such as snapshots) are used in many ways by an illustrator. Three basic types exist.

1. Line copy prints are made from high contrast negatives. Such prints are shown in Fig. A.1.
2. Continuous tone prints are made from continuous tone films. If the photo is to be printed, a velox print, which is a print made from a screened film, may be

pasted in with other line copy.* Then, as a final product, the entire copy (including the velox) is photographed using high contrast film.
3. Color prints are expensive and used sparingly.

A2
Offset Printing

Much of the work an illustrator performs will be reproduced using offset printing. The basic idea of offset printing is simple. A master, upon which the copy to be printed is contained, is attached to the impression roller. An ink roller transfers ink to the master. Water washes the ink from all areas of the master, except the copy to be printed. The ink is then transferred from the impression cylinder to a soft blanket roller from which it is then transferred to the paper.

Although black ink is used in most printed matter (such as this page of print), a colored ink can be used. In addition, if several different colors are desired, the page can be run through the press several times—each time using a different color.

Offset presses vary in size from desk-top models to extremely large models that print as many as 64 pages at the same time.

A3
Electrostatic

Two basic types of electrostatic copiers are manufactured. In one type, a drum is charged electrically and a fine thermoplastic powder is deposited on the drum in areas where copy (type or black lines) appears. The paper used is given the opposite charge of the drum. When the paper contacts the drum, the thermoplastic is transferred to the paper, which passes through a heater, where the plastic is melted and becomes bonded to the paper.

The other type of electrostatic copier employs a treated paper and liquid toner (rather than the thermoplastic powder).

Electrostatic copiers are, for the most part, used to make copies rapidly either for proofing purposes or for rough drafts. Copies are not normally suitable for use as a finished product of high quality.

*Remember, *after* the screening process, the film is now *line* copy.

A4
Blueprint A blueprint is made from a vellum tracing—a translucent paper upon which either ink or pencil lines have been drawn. A tracing is laid on top of a sheet of sensitized paper and exposed to light, which passes through the paper but not the lines. A wet bath follows; this develops the blueprint, which derives its name from the fact that white lines on a deep *blue* background is the resulting reproduction. Blueprints are used extensively in manufacturing and in the building trades.

A5
Ozalid An ozalid print of a drawing is made in essentially the same manner as a blueprint. The finished product, however, is a black line on a gray background. Development is accomplished using ammonia fumes and the process is dry.

B

High Contrast Photography

Most of us have heard of lithography but few of us attribute the name to the process of printing using an ink-sensitive, flat metal plate. High contrast photographic films that produced strictly black and white (no intermediate tones) were developed and used extensively in lighography. For that reason, the high contrast film became known as lithographer's film. The name was subsequently shortened to simply litho.

B1 Description

As indicated above, litho film is extremely high contrast. Black and white are (if the film is exposed properly) the only two "shades" reproduced. Intermediate tones are not resolved properly.

If we make a drawing using black ink and if the ink lines are dense, litho photography will reproduce the lines faithfully as in Fig. B.1(a). If, however, we use pencil lines (which are gray) or if the technique used in inking does not produce *dense* black lines, the litho process will yield results shown in Fig. B.1(b).

Litho film "sees" some colors as black. In other words, some colors can be used instead of black ink. Reds and oranges are good examples. Litho film is, on the other hand,

216 / App. B
High Contrast Photography

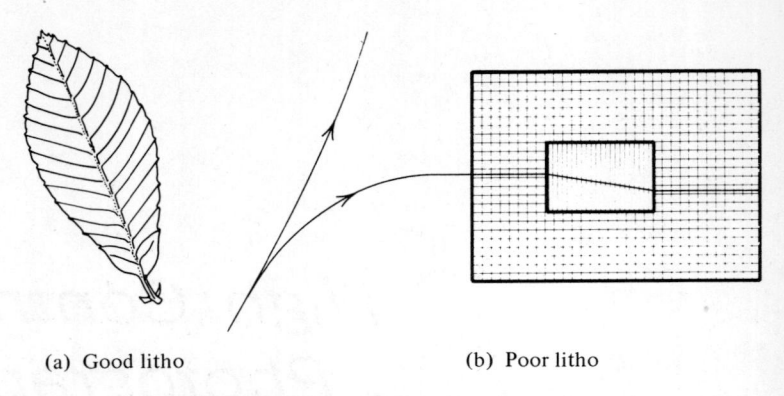

(a) Good litho   (b) Poor litho

Figure B.1 Litho negatives vary in quality.

insensitive to blue and the blue-green area of the color spectrum.

We can deduce, therefore, that if we were executing an illustration to be reproduced using litho film, we *should not* use red as a layout pencil. If we use light blue* lines for layout and construction lines, we need not erase these lines. The film will not "see" them.

---

*Eagle Verithin Sky Blue 740½ pencil works fine.

C

Typography

Printing, as most grammar school students learn, originated in the form of clay tablets, progressed to the papyrus scrolls, and culminated in Gutenberg's invention of movable type. These same students learn that Mr. Gutenberg's invention gave rise to the development of sophisticated and high-speed typesetting machines. As technical illustrators we will, in many cases, be called upon to make use of typeset lettering. To understand, to a limited degree, this facet of illustrating, we must be aware of certain fundamentals.

C1 Typefaces

By most conservative estimates, the number of typefaces in use exceeds 3,000 and the number of different designs that have been used in the past five centuries exceeds 10,000. Typefaces as such are used for three purposes:

1. To attract attention.* Pekin
2. For a special occasion (Old English).   Old English
3. To be readable (Times New Roman).

Few of us would know what a typographer meant if he used the nomenclature of a typeface. For example, what is

*Courtesy Warwick Typographers, Inc., St. Louis, Missouri.

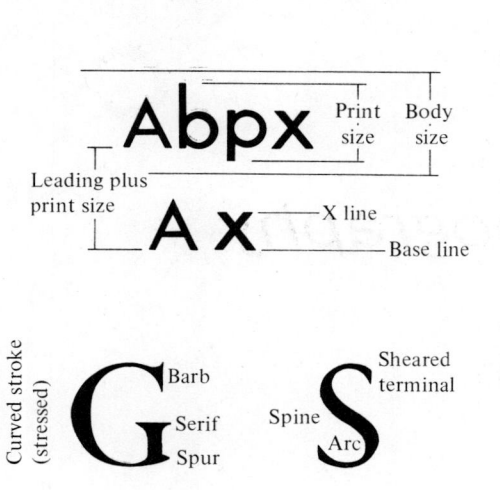

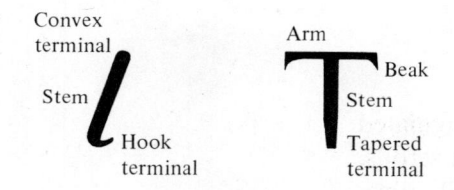

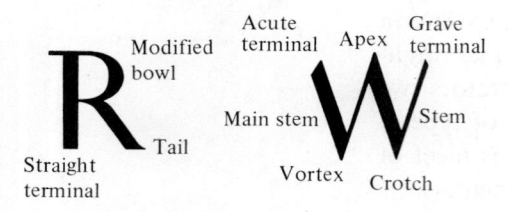

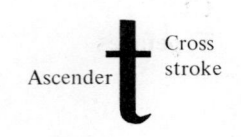

Typeface: The design or pattern of an alphabet of letters to be used together.
Stroke: Any line necessary to basic form of letter.
Curved stroke: A curved necessary line.
Stress: Thickening in a curved stroke.
Monotone or Monoline: All lines same thickness.
Stem: Any vertical or oblique straight stroke.
Main stem: The thicker stem.
Counter: Fully or partly enclosed space within a letter.
Bowl: The line fully enclosing a counter.
Loop: Distinguished from bowl as a flourish rather than necessary part of letter.
Arc: Curved stroke not a bowl, as C, G, bottom of j, t, u.
Spine: Main curved section of S.
Ear: Small stroke extending from bowl of g, stem of r.
Ascender: Part of lowercase letters, b, d, f, h, k, l, t extending above X line.
Descender: Part of lowercase letters g, j, p, q, y and caps J, Q extending below base line.
Extenders: Ascenders and descenders together.
Serif: Line crossing free end of a stroke.
Terminal: Free ending of a stroke with self-contained treatment instead of serif or finial.
Apex: Up-pointing free-ending juncture of two stems.
Vortex: Down-pointing free-ending juncture of two stems.
Crotch: Pointed space where an arm or arc meets a stem.
Arm: Horizontal or upward-sloping short stroke starting from stem, ending free.
Tail: Downward-sloping short stroke or arc starting from stem (or bowl, in Q) and ending free.
Bar: Horizontal or oblique short stroke connected at both ends, as in e, H.
Cross stroke: Short stroke cutting across stem, as in f, t.
Link: Stroke connecting bowl and loop of g.

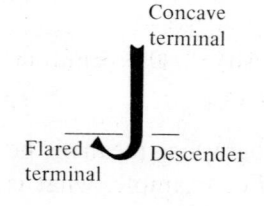

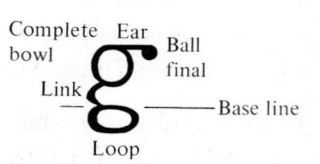

Figure C.1 Nomenclature of a typeface.

a stress? Is the typeface monotone? Sans serif? Point out the link on the letter *g*. The information contained in Figs. C.1 and C.2 is a valuable reference for anyone interested in the nomenclature and definitions of typefaces.

As a part of a typeface, we have type—the individual pieces (letters, numbers, punctuation, ligatures) that make up the typeface. Figure C.2 illustrate the nomenclature of a piece of type, while Fig. C.1 discusses typeface nomenclature.

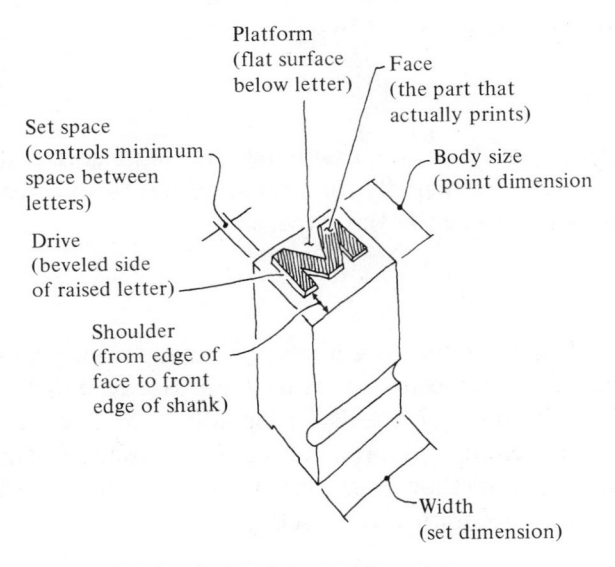

Figure C.2 Nomenclature of type.

C2 Typesetting Methods

Once we have learned what a typeface is and how to specify typeset material, we should have some working knowledge of the methods and machines used to set type.

HAND SETTING

If large sizes or styles that are not ordinarily available, or if an unusual arrangement of type is specified, setting is done by a skilled typographer. The process is manual.

LINOTYPE

A one-piece line of type is cast to any practical width. Linotype is the most extensively used of all typesetting methods. A skilled operator key boards (as we would type on a typewriter) the copy. This method is most widely used to set small and medium sizes.

MONOTYPE

An operator prepares a punched paper tape from a keyboard unit. The tape is then run through a unit that assembles the lines of type. This method is especially useful when setting complex mathematical formulas.

LUDLOW

One-piece type lines are assembled by hand and cast by machine. Used principally for large headings (display copy), the method is versatile but expensive.

PHOTO TYPESETTING

This method is similar to a linotype operation but produces film negatives (or positives) rather than cast type. Sizes are varied easily and quickly. By using photo typesetting, the typographer eliminates proof sheets and extensive camera operation. The method is gaining wide acceptance as a fast, efficient, and accurate way to set type.

PHOTO LETTERING

This method is essentially a photographic means to compete with hand setting. Extensive use of photo lettering is made in setting display composition and special, seldom used typefaces.

COLD TYPE

We seldom think of an office typewriter as a typesetting device but it is. Other cold type typesetters are more sophisticated than an ordinary typewriter but the principle is identical—a character is struck onto a piece of paper. These machines are used primarily for low-cost composition but with costs of other methods as they are, the industry using typesetting products is evaluating cold composition more critically.

COMPUTERIZED TYPESETTING

Basically, a computer is used here with a photo typesetter. The computer is useful in that information retrieval is fast and efficient. For example, if a manufacturer changes prices often, this information can be changed rapidly on the computer and does not disturb the remainder of material to be set.

C3
Glossary of Terms

Agate: A small size of body type, $5\frac{1}{2}$ points tall. Used primarily in classified advertisements in newspapers.

Antique type: A type style in which all parts of the character are uniform in line thickness. Example: **BOOKMAN**

Ascender: The rising strokes on such letters as A, b, d, and h.

Ascending letters: Alphabetic letters such as A, b, d, and h, which occupy the top two-thirds of the type body.

BF: Abbreviation for **boldface** type; a type that is heavier than that used for the text.

Body: The height of type from top to bottom of the letter. Width is called *set width*.

Calligraphic type: A type design based on styles of handwriting rather than a drawn (constructed) letter.

Cap: The abbreviation for capital (uppercase) letter.

Caret (∧): A mark used in proofreading, usually to indicate an insertion.

Cast off: An estimate of the amount of space a manuscript will occupy when set in type.

Ceriphs, cerifs, serifs: Lines or cross strokes at the ends of the stem or a letter (I).

Character: Any single unit of type, such as a letter of the alphabet, a number, or a punctuation mark.

Composition: That part of a manuscript relating to typesetting. Illustrations are not composition.

Compositor: One who sets type.

Copy: The handwritten, typewritten, or printed words given to a compositor.

Descender: The descending strokes on a character, such as on p, q, or y.

Descending letters: Alphabetic characters such as p, q, and y, which occupy the bottom part of the type body.

Display type: A general term applied to type that is used for headlines as opposed to regular reading type.

Drop folio: A page number placed at the bottom of a page.

Face: That part of a piece of type that prints. A shank or shoulder does not print.

Folio: A page number.

Font: A complete assortment of type of one size and face.

Format: The size, form, and proportions of a book or other typeset copy.

Galley: A shallow tray used by compositors to hold type after lines have been set.

Galley proofs: Proof copies made from type standing in a galley. Currently, with the advent of cold composition and photo composition, galley proofs are merely the first copy from composition.

Gutter: The blank space between columns of type.

Halftone: An engraving plate made by photographic means and composed of a series of black dots of various sizes.

Inferior characters: Characters smaller in size than the regular text, set near the bottom of the type line (A_1).

Leading: The white space between lines of type. For example, an 11/13 designation for type means use an 11-point high character with 13 points between base lines of succeeding lines.

Measure: The width of a page of type.

Page proof: A proof copy made after all copy and illustrations have been put into page layout.

Pica: A unit of measure equal to 12 points. Six picas equal 1 inch. This unit of measure is a standard for leading, rules, and lengths and widths of pages.

Point system: Sizes of type cast are graduated on a uniform scale known as the point system. This unit of measure is equal to 0.138 inch. Calculations are usually simplified by assuming 1 point = $\frac{1}{72}$ inch.

Pt: Abbreviation for point.

Recto: Right-hand page, which is odd-numbered.

Sans serif typeface: Typeface with no serifs.

Serif: See Ceriphs.

Subhead: A headline or title of secondary importance.

Superior characters: Characters smaller in size than the regular text, set near the top of the type line (A^1).

Typeface: A particular type design.

Verso: Left-hand page, which is even-numbered.

D

Typographic Measure

Whenever we deal with a typographer or a publisher, we seldom hear of measurements being made in inches. The common terms are picas and points. A point is $\frac{1}{72}$ inch, or it takes 72 points to make 1 inch. There are 12 points in 1 pica so there are 6 picas per inch.

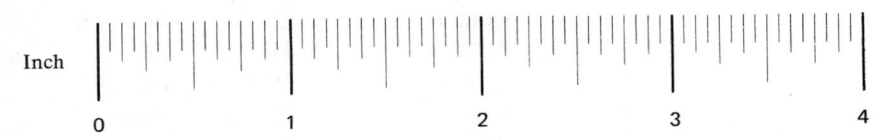

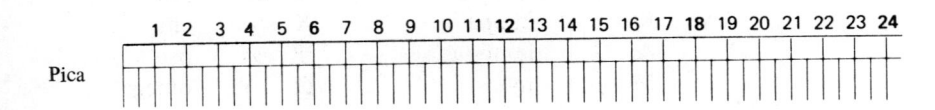

E

The Greek Alphabet

Quite often an illustrator is called upon to use Greek characters in illustrations, especially in scientific work. For the most part, lowercase Greek letters are used.

A	α	alpha	N	ν	nu
B	β	beta	Ξ	ξ	xi
Γ	γ	gamma	O	o	omicron
Δ	δ	delta	Π	π	pi
E	ϵ	epsilon	P	ρ	rho
Z	ζ	zeta	Σ	σ	sigma
H	η	eta	T	τ	tau
Θ	θ	theta	Υ	υ	upsilon
I	ι	iota	Φ	ϕ	phi
K	κ	kappa	X	χ	chi
Λ	λ	lambda	Ψ	ψ	psi
M	μ	mu	Ω	ω	omega

International Standard Prefixes

Prefixes relating to powers of 10 are used extensively in all phases of technical illustrating. For example, rather than indicating a resistor value of 1 million ohms by the following methods (1,000,000 or 10^6), the prefix M is used to indicate million. The list that follows gives recommended prefixes.

Prefix	Power of 10	Symbol
tera	10^{12}	T
giga	10^9	G
mega	10^6	M
kilo	10^3	k
hecto	10^2	h
deka	10	da
deci	10^{-1}	d
centi	10^{-2}	c
milli	10^{-3}	m
micro	10^{-6}	μ
nano	10^{-9}	n
pico	10^{-12}	p or ρ
femto	10^{-15}	f
atto	10^{-18}	a

If we wish to convert one prefix to another, Table F.1 that follows will assist us. For example, suppose we wish

App. F
International Standard Prefixes

to convert microns to millimeters. We enter the table at the *micro* row on the left and proceed to the right until we reach the vertical *milli* column. The number at the intersection is the number of decimal points (in the direction of the large arrow) that we must move the decimal point to obtain milli.

Table F.1 DATA BY WHICH POWER OF 10 PREFIXES MAY BE MANIPULATED.

		SYMBOL	tera	giga	mega	kilo	hecto	deka	UNITY	deci	centi	milli	micro	nano	pico	femto	atto
GIVEN	tera	T		3	6	9	10	11	12	13	14	15	18	21	24	27	30
	giga	G	3		3	6	7	8	9	10	11	12	15	18	21	24	27
	mega	M	6	3			4	5	6	7	8	9	12	15	18	21	24
	kilo	k	9	6	3		1	2	3	4	5	6	9	12	15	18	21
	hecto	h	10	7	4	1		1	2	3	4	5	8	11	14	17	20
	deka	da	11	8	5	2	1		1	2	3	4	7	10	13	16	19
	UNITY		12	9	6	3	2	1		1	2	3	6	9	12	15	18
	deci	d	13	10	7	4	3	2	1		1	2	5	8	11	14	17
	centi	c	14	11	8	5	4	3	2	1		1	4	7	10	13	16
	milli	m	15	12	9	6	5	4	3	2	1		3	6	9	12	15
	micro	μ	18	15	12	9	8	7	6	5	4	3		3	6	9	12
	nano	n	21	18	15	12	11	10	9	8	7	6	3		3	6	9
	pico	p	24	21	18	15	14	13	12	11	10	9	6	3		3	6
	femto	f	27	24	21	18	15	14	13	12	11	10	9	6	3		3
	atto	a	30	27	24	21	18	15	14	13	12	11	10	9	6	3	

TO OBTAIN

Symbols and Abbreviations

When a long phrase or word or a unit of measure is used in technical writing, it is often abbreviated.

Unit or Term	Symbol or Abbreviation	Unit or Term	Symbol or Abbreviation
alternating current	ac	British thermal units	Btu
ampere	A	calorie	cal
ampere-hour	Ah	candela	cd
amplitude modulation	AM	candlepower	cp
angstrom	Å	cathode ray tube	CRT
anno Domini	A.D.	Celsius	C
ante meridiem	a.m.	centimeter	cm
approximate	approx	center of mass	c.m.
atmosphere, standard	A_s	centimeter-gram-second	cgs
atmospheres	atm	centipoise	cP
atomic mass units	amu	continuous wave	cw
atomic weight	at. wt	cosecant	csc
audio frequency	af	cosine	cos
average	av	cotangent	cot
bar	spell out	coulomb	C
barn	b	cubic	cu
bist	Bi	cubic centimeters	cc or cm^3
body-centered cubic	bcc	curie	Ci
boiling point	bp	cycles per second	Hz

227

Unit or Term	Symbol or Abbreviation	Unit or Term	Symbol or Abbreviation
debye	D	logarithm	log
decibel	dB	logarithm, natural	ln
degree	deg	lumen	lm
degrees Baumé	°B	magnetomotive force	mmf
degrees Celsius (centigrade)	°C	maximum	max
degrees Fahrenheit	°F	maxwell	Mx
degrees Kelvin (absolute)	°K	melting point	mp
degrees Rankine	°R	meter	m
diameter	diam	mile	mile
direct current	dc	miles per hour	mph
dyne	dyn	minimum	min
east	E	minute	min
electromotive force	emf	newton	N
electron volt	eV	north	N
equation	Eq.	number	No.
equations	Eqs.	oersted	Oe
exponential	exp	ohm	Ω
face-centered cubic	fcc	ounce	oz
farad	F	page	p.
figure	Fig.	pages	pp.
foot	ft	poise	P
foot-candle	ft-c	post meridiem	p.m.
foot-lambert	ft-L	pound	lb
foot-pound	ft-lb	pounds per square inch	psi
franklin	Fr	radian	rad
frequency modulation	FM	radio frequency	rf
gallon	gal	roentgen	R
gauss	G	root mean square	rms
gilbert	Gi	secant	sec
gram	g	second	sec
henry	H	sine	sin
hertz (cycles per second)	Hz	south	S
hexagonal close packed	hcp	square	sq
horsepower	hp	steradian	sr
hour	hr	tangent	tan
hyperbolic cosecant	csch	tesla	T
hyperbolic cosine	cosh	ultra high frequency	uhf
hyperbolic cotangent	tanh	ultraviolet	uv
hyperbolic sine	sinh	versus	vs
inch	in.	volt	V
joule	J	watt	W
kinetic energy	KE	weber	Wb
lambert	L	west	W
logarithm	log		

We have omitted intentionally a number of entries from this list. For example, we left out millivolt, milliampere, microampere, and such multiples of one unit. By using Appendix F values and the standard abbreviation we can arrive at the correct abbreviations: millivolt = mV; milliampere = mA; microampere = μA.

Some variations will arise, depending on which agency's list you use. The abbreviations used here are those suggested by the American Institute of Physics. Other agencies (IEEE, ANSI, or ASME) will have their own list. Nearly *all* entries in *all* lists will be the same.

The best approach to using a particular list is to see what your client wishes. Use *his* list.

H

Objects to Draw

Figures H.1 to H.75 that follow are a compilation of problems that may be assigned. Objects shown in pictorial views may be drawn in orthographic or shade and shadow may be added. Those objects shown as orthographic drawings may be assigned to be drawn as a pictorial illustration. The instructor may wish for the student to add rulings or use some other shading technique. In addition, the student may find that he will wish to practice using some of the drawings.

These drawings are done in a "less than finished" style to avoid having the student influenced by the illustration. Don't be concerned that dimensions and directions are missing. In the learning process the reader will be rewarded by obtaining proper (or, at least, acceptable) proportions. *Exact* dimensions are unimportant.

The student is encouraged to make up his own dimensions and obtain a pleasing finished product. He should always keep in mind that finished drawings are *his* job—not the job of his client or instructor. Working from "rough" drawings is excellent practice—rough drawings will be the rule and not the exception. Get used to it.

H.1 H.2 H.3 H.4 H.5

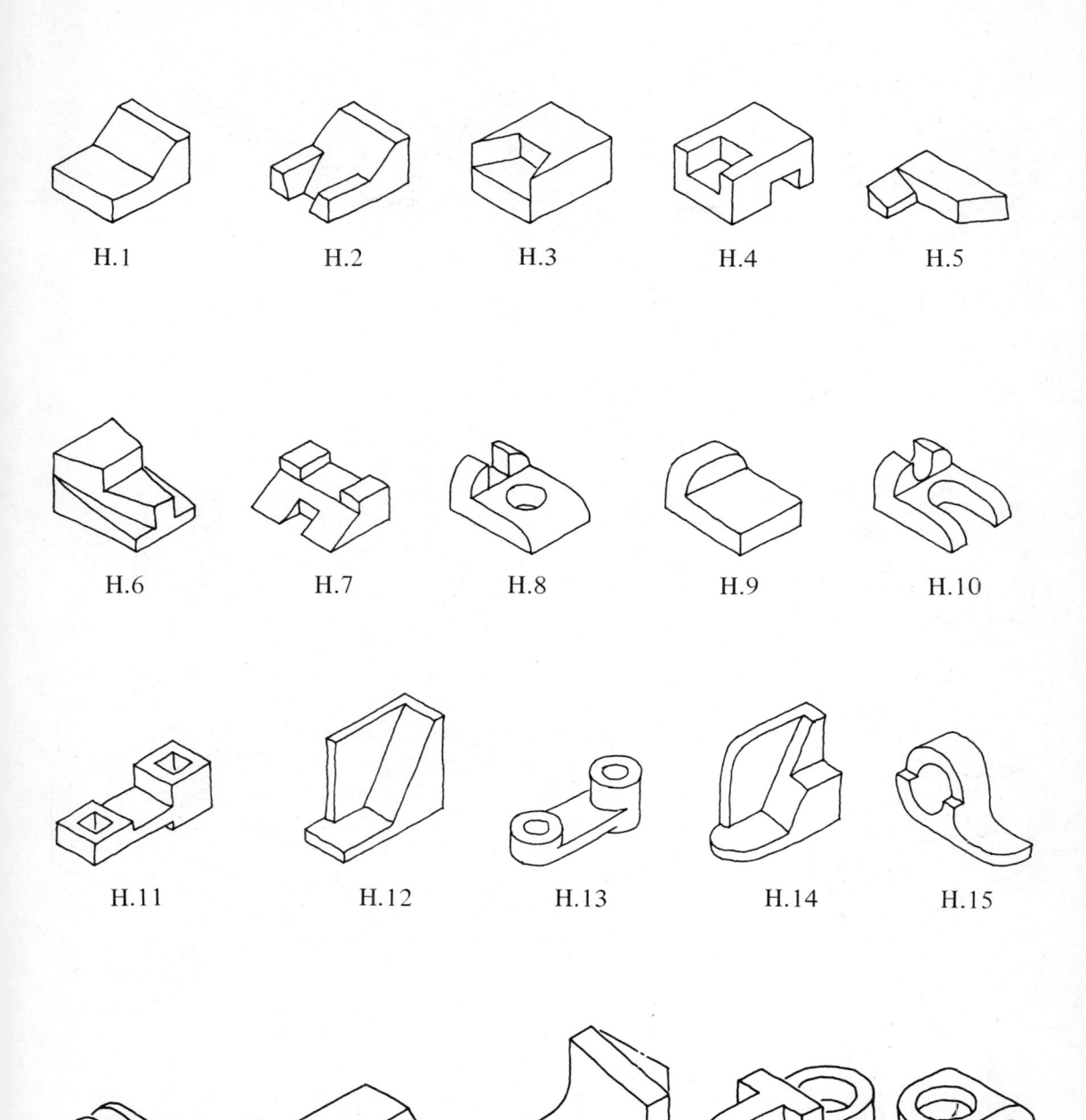

H.6 H.7 H.8 H.9 H.10

H.11 H.12 H.13 H.14 H.15

H.16 H.17 H.18 H.19 H.20

H.21 H.22 H.23 H.24

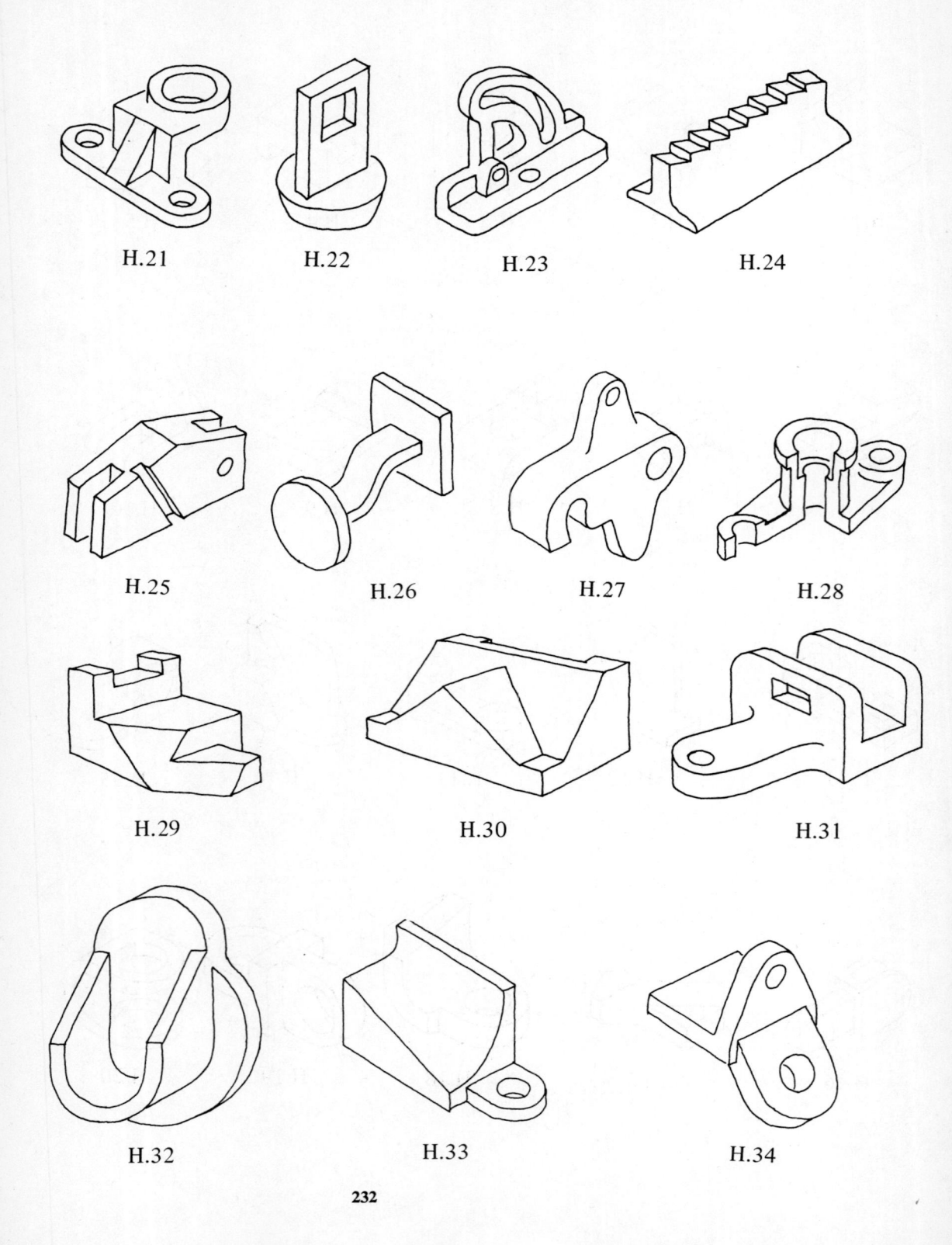

H.25 H.26 H.27 H.28

H.29 H.30 H.31

H.32 H.33 H.34

232

H.35

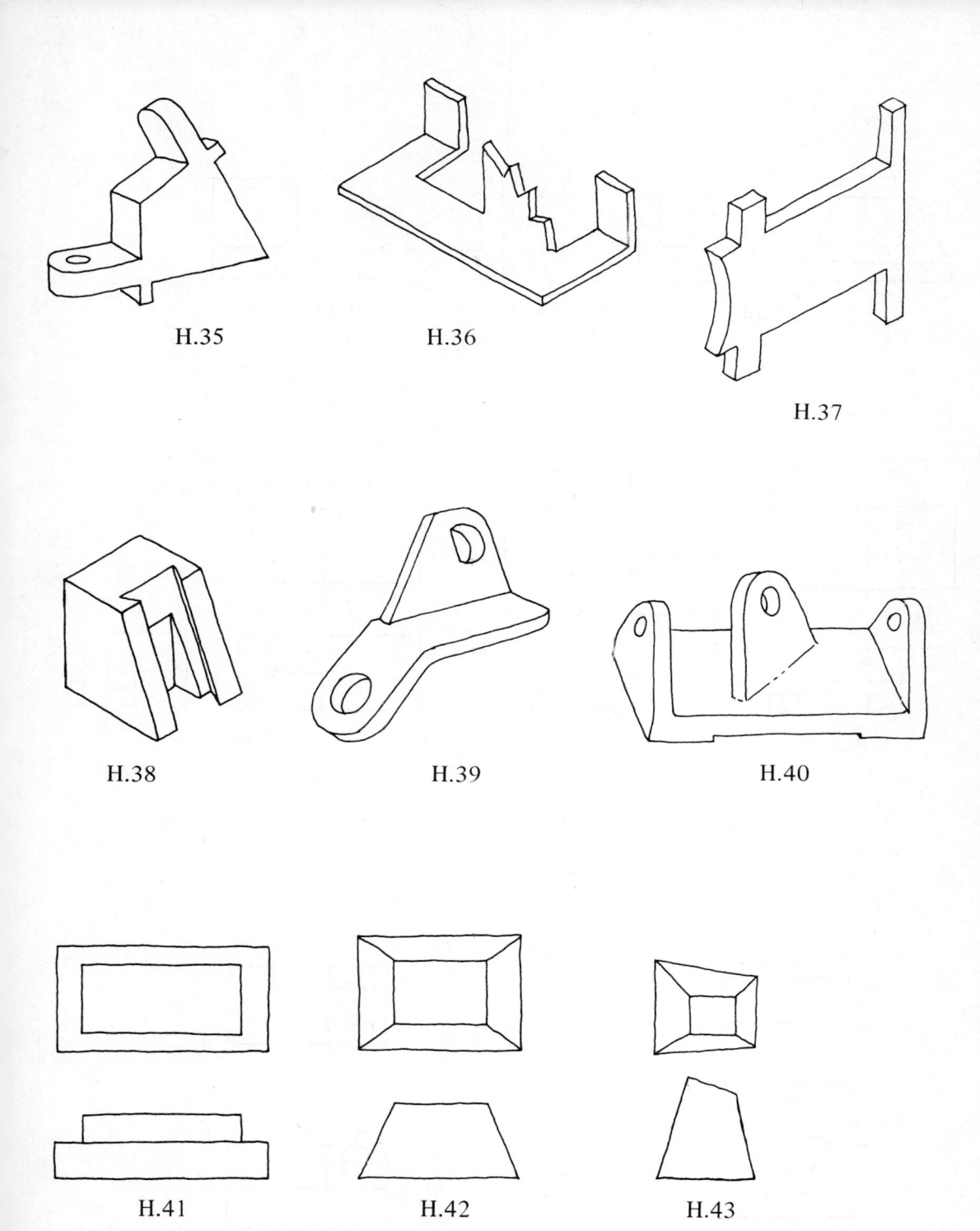

H.36

H.37

H.38

H.39

H.40

H.41

H.42

H.43

H.44

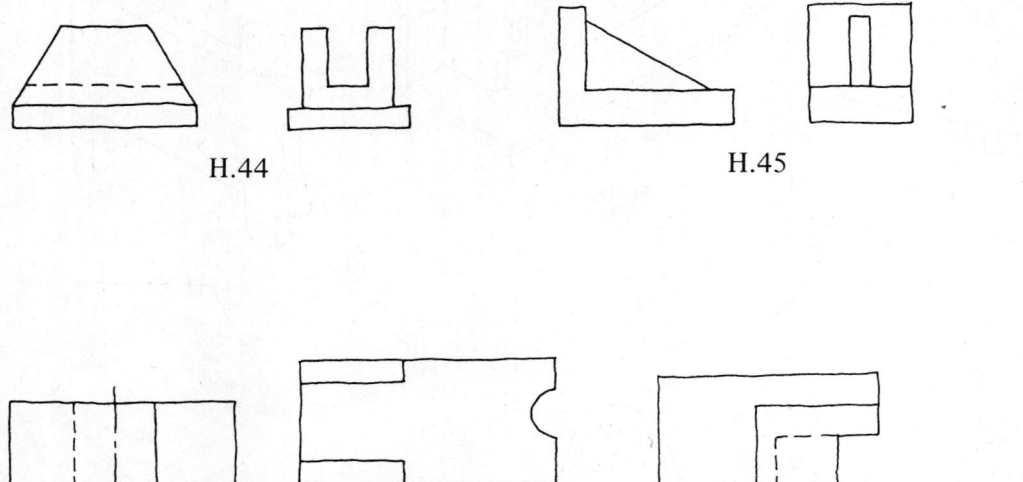

H.45

H.46

H.47

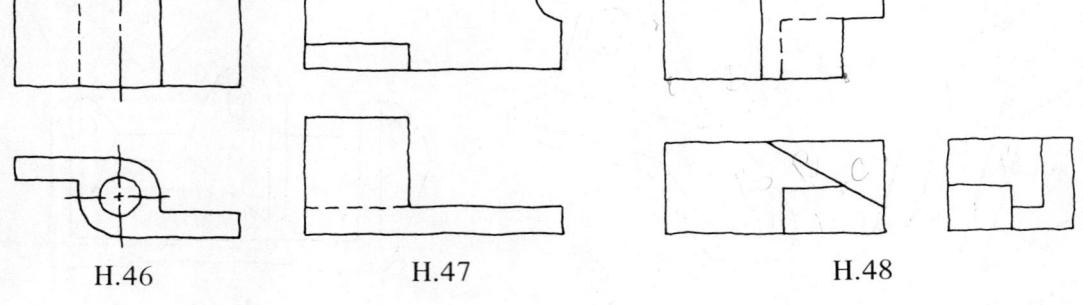

H.48

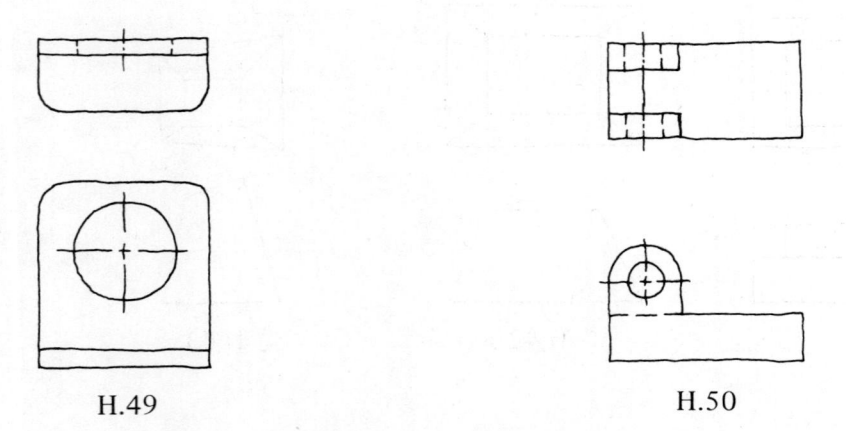

H.49

H.50

H.51

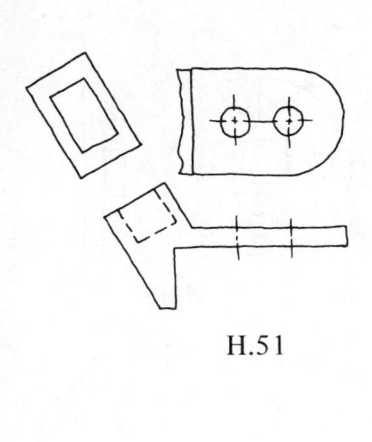

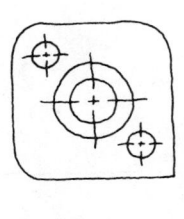

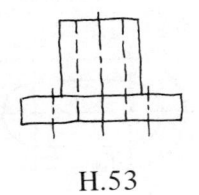

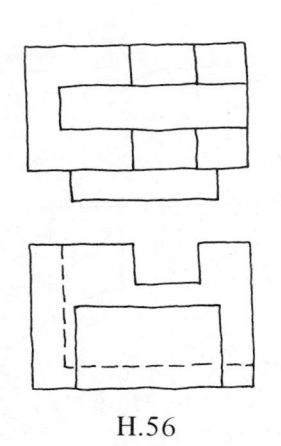

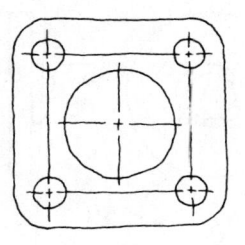

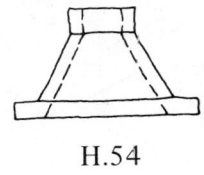

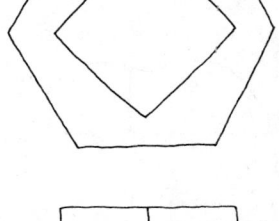

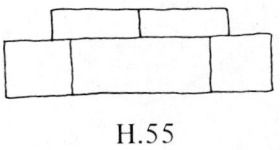

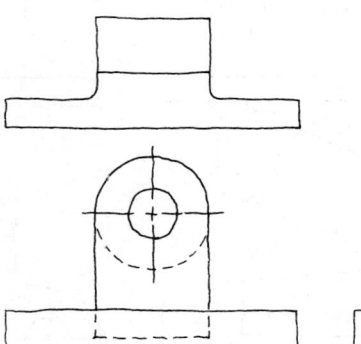

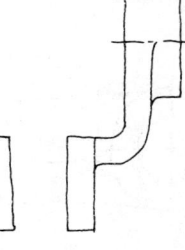

H.52

H.53

H.54

H.55

H.56

H.57

235

H.58

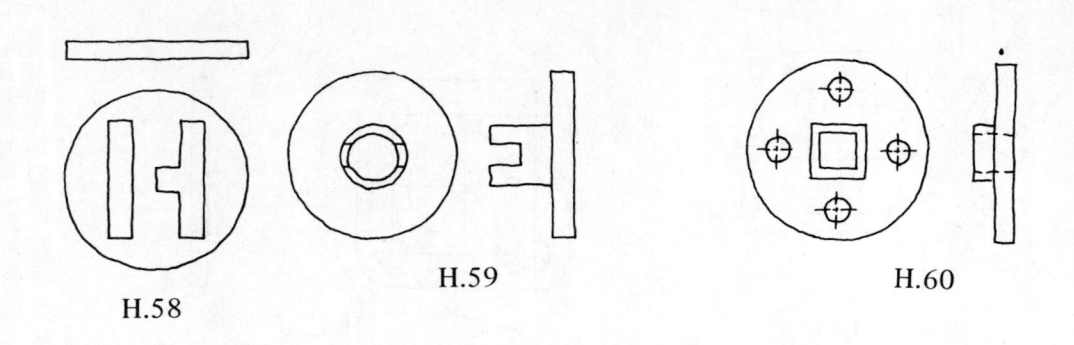

H.59

H.60

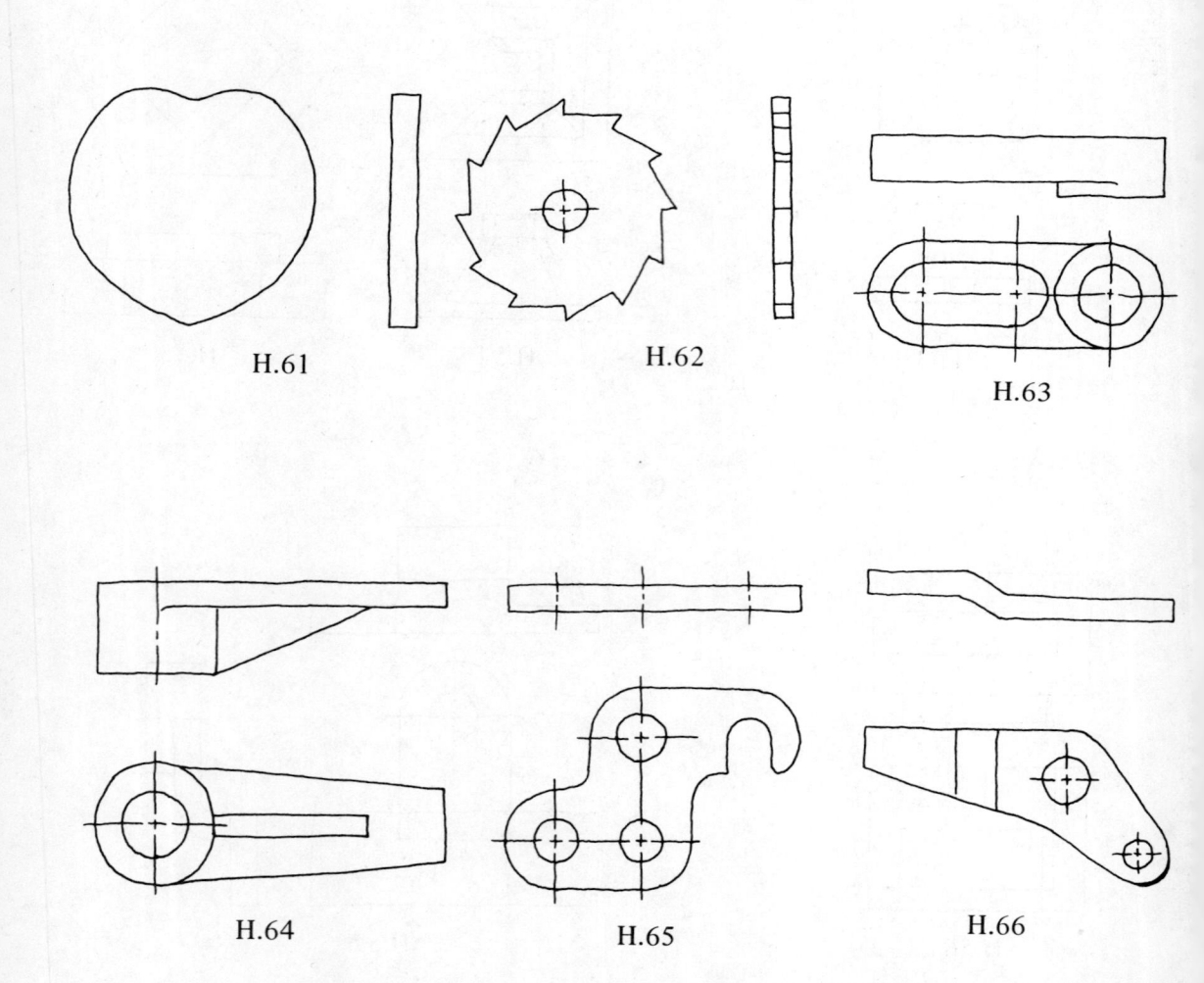

H.61

H.62

H.63

H.64

H.65

H.66

CHOOSE THICKNESS

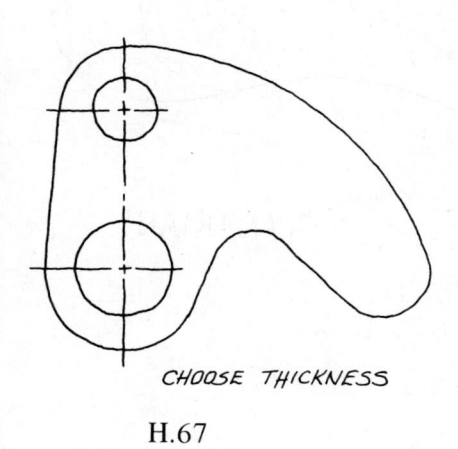

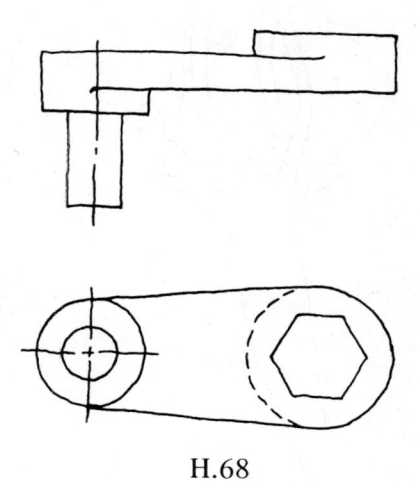

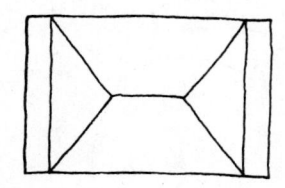

H.67

H.68

A GOOD ONE FOR
PERSPECTIVE

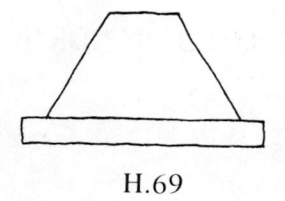

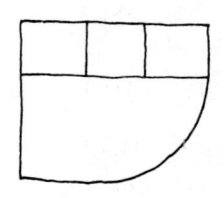

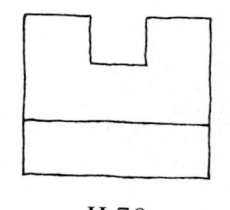

H.69

H.70

237

HYDRA

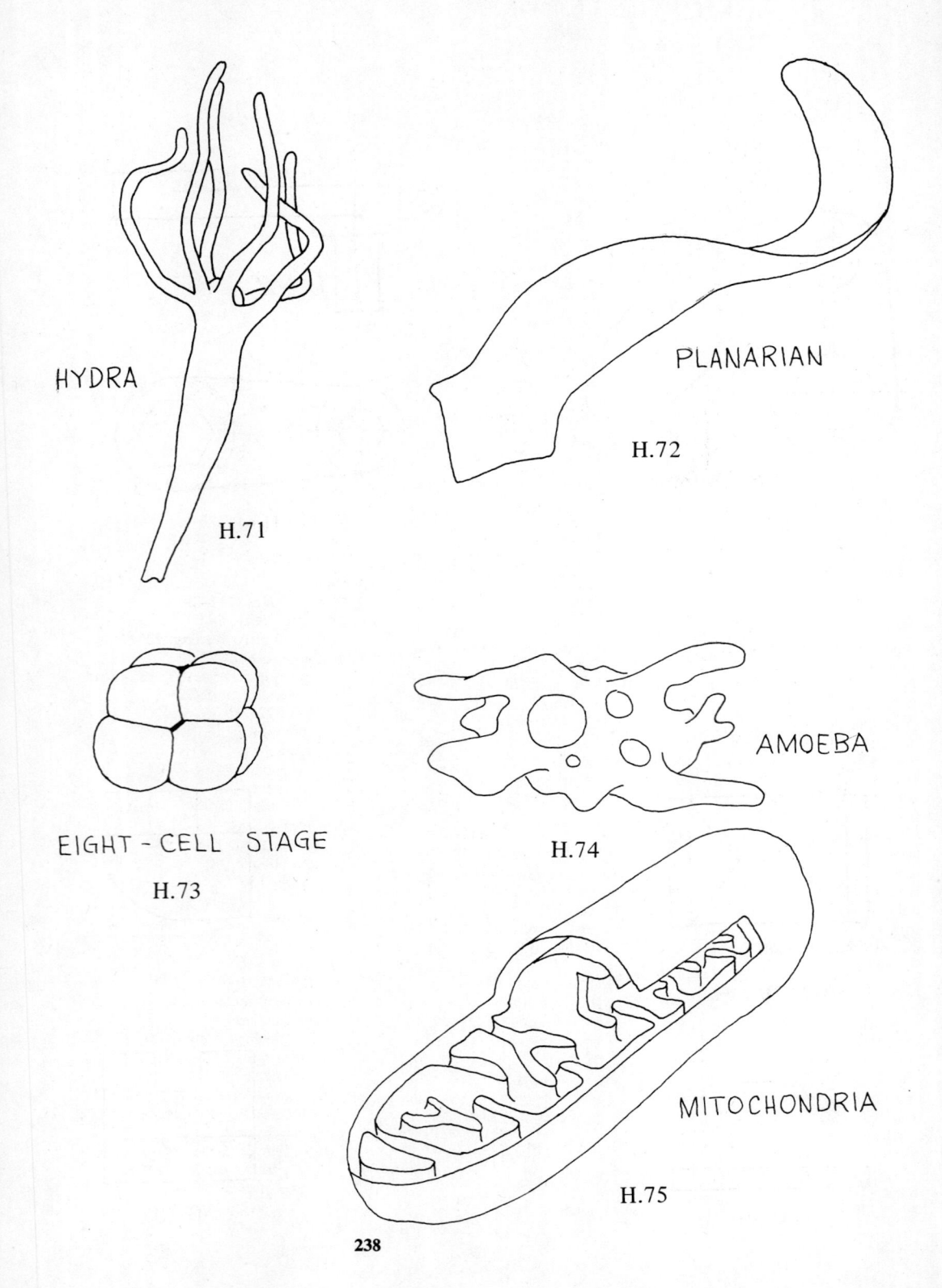

H.71

PLANARIAN

H.72

EIGHT - CELL STAGE

H.73

AMOEBA

H.74

MITOCHONDRIA

H.75

Index

A

Acetate toning sheets, 170–75
Angles:
    for axes in dimetric, 34–38
    for axes in isometric, 13
    for axes in oblique, 62
    for axes in trimetric, 43–50
    construction in axonometric, 18, 19
    in perspective, 78
Architectural drawing, 76
Areas in perspective, 78
Auxiliary views, 5, 6
Axes:
    dimetric, 34
    isometric, 13
    oblique, 62
    trimetric, 43
Axonometric projection:
    definition of, 10
    degrees of difficulty, 11
    dimetric, 30–42 (*see also* Dimetric projection)
    distortion in, 11
    isometric, 11–30 (*see also* Isometric projection)
    from orthographic views, 50–53
    shade in, 103–5
    shadow in, 103–5
    subschemes of, 10
    trimetric, 42–50 (*see also* Trimetric projection)
    true, 50

B

Beam compass, 128
Blueprints, 214
Boldface type, 221
Bottom view, 4
Box construction, 13, 33, 43, 68
Brush, 141
Burnishing tool, 141

C

Cabinet drawing, 64, 105
Calligraphic type, 221
Camera lucida, 136
Cast off, 221
Cavalier drawing, 64, 105
Center line layout, 15, 38, 47, 68, 69
Circles:
    in dimetric, 39
    guides for, 134
    with instruments, 127–29
    in isometric, 21
    in oblique, 70
    in perspective, 78
    in trimetric, 47
Circle template, 134
Circular protractor, 141
Cleaning fluid, 141
Clear tape, 140
Cold type, 220
Communications media, 143, 144
Compasses, 127–29
Composition, 221
Computer typesetting, 221
Conic section, 22
Construction of scales, 13, 43–45
Conversion table, 226
Copy, 221
Crow quill pens, 121
Curves:
    in axonometric, 19–21
    French, 130
    irregular, 130
    in isometric, 19–21
    logarithmic spiral, 140
    in oblique, 66
    ship, 130

D

Depth, 5, 165
Diagonal method, 25, 71
Dimensioning:
    aligned convention, 29, 30, 72
    in isometric, 28, 29
    in oblique, 71, 72
    pictorial drawings, 29, 30, 71, 72
    unidirectional convention, 29, 30, 72
Dimetric axes, 34
Dimetric projection:
    asymmetrical, 32, 104
    axes angles, 34–38
    axes scales, 34–38

Dimetric projection (*cont.*)
  box construction, 33
  center line layout, 38
  circles, 39
  construction of, 38
  definition of, 30, 31
  determining axes angles, 36
  determining axes scales, 35, 36
  ellipses, 39–42
  as orthographic, 31
  from orthographic views, 53
  points of view in, 32–35
  position of axes, 34–38
  problems, 58
  shade in, 104
  shadow in, 104
  symmetrical, 32, 104
  theory of, 31
Direction of light:
  construction in dimetric, 104
  construction in isometric, 103, 104
  construction in oblique, 105
  construction in perspective, 105–8
  construction in trimetric, 104, 105
  conventional, 99, 103, 104, 105
  forty-five degree, 99
  in isometric, 103, 104
  true, 100
Distant light source, 98
Dividers, proportional, 140
Double-backed tape, 141
Drafting film, 189
Drafting machine, 133
Drawing, definition of, 1
Drawings:
  audience for, 147, 148
  axonometric, 10–54
  biological, 176–80, 182–84, 187
  criteria for, 145–49
  descriptive, 145
  dimetric, 30–42
  formula approach, 156–61
  freehand, 151
  hand stippled, 175–80
  ink wash, 186–88
  isometric, 11–30
  mechanical, 151
  oblique, 60–73
  orthographic, 1–7
  perspective, 75–90
  pictorial, 2, 10–90
  pride in, 148
  projection slide, 197–207
  realistic, 147
  references for, 7, 91, 161–64, 192–96
  reproduction of, 211–14
  scratchboard, 185
  semifreehand, 151
  shade for, 98

Drawings (*cont.*)
  shadow for, 95
  shop, 2
  sizing for journals, 156–60
  stipple board, 181–84
  styles of, 151–61
  tint screen, 189–92
  trimetric, 42–50
  using Leroy lettering, 122, 123, 155–61, 200, 201
  using typeset lettering, 155, 158, 160, 206
  for youngsters, 147, 148
Drop compass, 128
Drop folio, 221
Drop outs, 189

E

Electric eraser, 132
Electrostatic copying, 213
Ellipse:
  as conic section, 22
  construction of, 23, 24, 25, 71
  definition of, 22
  diagonal method for construction, 25, 71
  in dimetric, 39–42
  foci, 23
  focus, 23
  four-center construction method, 23, 71
  graphical determination of in dimetric, 39, 40
  guides, 25, 135
  in isometric, 22–27
  major axis, 23
  mathematical definition of, 23
  minor axis, 23
  as orthographic projection, 22
  parts of, 22, 23
  point-by-point construction method, 24, 70, 71
  protractor, 141
  selection of in dimetric, 39–42
  selection of in trimetric, 47–49
  using guides, 25
Ellipse guides:
  alignment of, 26
  angle, 25, 135
  in dimetric, 39–41
  in isometric, 25
  in trimetric, 47–50
  uses of, 25, 26
Ellipse template, 135
Ellipse wheel, 49
Equipment:
  blue lead pencil, 131
  camera lucida, 136

Equipment (*cont.*)
  circle template, 134
  crow quill pens, 121
  cut out templates, 134, 135
  drafting machine, 133
  electric eraser, 132
  ellipse template, 135
  ellipse wheel, 49
  erasers, 132
  ink, 136
  ink dryer, 138
  irregular curves, 130
  KOH-I-NOOR compasses, 128, 129
  lamps, 138
  lead compass, 127
  lead holder, 131
  Leroy lettering guides, 122
  Leroy standard pens, 120
  Letterguide templates, 126
  lettering devices, 122–27
  logarithmic spiral curve, 140
  mechanical pencil, 131
  miscellaneous items, 140–42
  nibs-type inking compass, 128
  Osmiroid pens, 120
  pantograph, 140
  paper, 136
  Pelikan Graphos pens, 119
  pencil pointers, 131
  pencils, 131
  price of, 112
  proportional dividers, 140
  reducing lens, 138
  reservoir pens, 113–18, 120
  ship curves, 130
  Speedball pens, 119
  stencil lettering, 127
  straight edge, 133
  T square, 133
  technical fountain pens, 113–18
  triangles, 129
  ultrasonic cleaner, 136
  visualizer, 137
Erasers, 132
Eye level in perspective, 80

F

Fold lines, 5
Folio, 221
Four-centered ellipse, 23, 24, 71
Freehand drawing, 151–54
Front view, 4, 5

G

Glossary of typographic terms, 221

Graduated screens, 173
Graduated tones, 173

H

Half tone board, 181
Half tone negative, 181, 212
Hand-set type, 219
Hand stipple (*see* Stipple)
Height, 4
Horizon, 80
Illustration (*see* Pictorial illustration)

I

Ink, 136
Ink dryer, 138
Ink wash, 186–88
 as continuous tone copy, 186
 examples, 186–88
 materials, 186
Instruments (*see* Equipment)
International prefixes, 225, 226
Irregular curves, 130
Isometric axes, 13
Isometric drawing, 12
Isometric lines, 13
Isometric planes, 14
Isometric projection:
 angles, 18, 19
 angle of tilt, 11
 box construction, 13
 center line layout, 15
 choosing axes for, 13
 circles, 21
 construction of curves, 20
 conventions for dimensioning, 29, 30
 curved surfaces, 19
 definition of, 11
 definition of axes, 13
 dimensioning, 28
 ellipses, 22–28 (*see also* ellipse)
 from orthographic views, 51–53
 inclined surfaces, 15, 16, 17
 intersection of curves with curves, 20
 intersection of curves with planes, 20
 measurements for, 12
 oblique surfaces, 15, 16, 17
 offset measurements for angles, 19
 as orthographic, 11
 position of axes, 12
 problems, 56–58
 projected axes in, 13
 scale for, 12
 section views, 17
 sectioning planes, 18

Isometric projection (*cont.*)
 spheres, 28
 symmetry in constructing curves, 21
 theory of, 11, 12
 true measure angles, 18

K

Knife, 141
KOH-I-NOOR compasses, 128, 129

L

Lamps, 139
Lead compass, 127
Lead hardness, 131
Leroy lettering guides, 122
Leroy scribers, 123–26
 adjustable, 124
 fixed, 124
 large, 126
 slant-height control, 124, 125
 used with Letterguide, 126
Leroy sets, 122
Leroy standard pens, 120
Lettering:
 to attract attention, 217
 boldface, 221
 for display, 217
 formula approach, 156–60
 freehand, 153
 Greek alphabet, 224
 guide to sizing of, 156–60, 200, 201
 instruments for, 122–27
 Leroy, 122, 155, 200, 201
 lower case, 158, 159
 methods of setting, 219
 pens, 113–21, 156, 158
 sans serif, 222
 serifs, 222
 sizing of, 156–60
 stencil, 127
 typeset, 155, 158, 160
 typographic methods, 219–21
 upper case, 158, 159
Lettering devices, 122–27
Light for shadows, 98–100, 103–8
 advantage of 45°, 99
 determining directions for, 99–101
 directions of, 98–100
 for pictorial drawings, 103–8
 rays oblique to *PP*, 107, 108
 rays parallel to *PP*, 106
 sources, 98
Line copy, 211, 215
Line widths, 115, 116, 156–60, 200, 201

Lines in shade, 101
Lines in shadow, 101
Linotype, 219
Litho film, 215
Lithography, 215
Local light source, 98
Logarithmic spiral curve, 140
Ludlow, 220

M

Masking tape, 140
Materials (*see* Equipment)
Measurements:
 in dimetric, 38
 in isometric, 12, 13, 19
 in oblique, 63
 in orthographic, 4, 5
 in perspective, 80
 in trimetric, 43–45
Metric units, 226
Monotype, 220
Multiple view drawing (*see* Orthographic projection)
Multiview drawing (*see* Orthographic projection)
Mylar (*see* Drafting film)

N

Nibs-type inking compass, 128
Nonisometric lines, 13
Nonisometric planes, 14

O

Oblique drawing (*see* Oblique projection)
Oblique projection, 60–74
 advantage of, 61
 angles, 70
 axis angles, 62
 axis scales, 63
 box construction, 68
 cabinet, 64
 cavalier, 64
 center line layout, 68, 69
 circles, 70, 71
 clinographic scheme, 72
 construction of curves, 66, 67
 construction methods, 68
 in crystallography, 72
 definition of, 60
 dimensioning, 72
 distortion in, 63
 ellipse construction, 71

242 / Index

Oblique projection (*cont.*)
  emphasis of faces, 62
  geometry involved, 61
  length of lines, 63
  offset measurements, 66, 69
  as orthographic, 60
  positioning objects in, 64, 65
  problems, 73, 74
  rules for, 62, 64, 65, 72
  section views, 71
  shadow in, 105
  side view featured, 62
  symmetry in constructing curves, 67
  theory of, 60
  top view featured, 62
  true measure angles, 70
Offset construction method:
  for dimetric, 38
  for drawing angles, 19
  for isometric, 19, 21
  for oblique, 66, 69, 70
  for transferring dimensions, 19, 21, 38, 66, 69, 70
Offset printing, 213
Oil stone, 141
Orthographic projection:
  in constructing a dimetric, 52
  in constructing an isometric, 51
  in constructing a trimetric, 53
  definition of, 3
  hidden lines, 6
  lines of sight, 3
  questions about, 7, 8
  references for, 7
  views, 4, 5
Orthographic views, 4, 5
  alignment, 4
  auxiliary, 5, 6
  sectional, 6
  standard, 4, 5
  transfer of dimensions among, 5
Osmiroid pens, 120
Overlays, 170–75
Ozalid copying, 214

P

Paint brush, 141
Pantagraph, 140
Paper, 136
Paper cutter, 141
Pelikan Graphos pens, 119
Pencil pointers, 131
Pencils, 131
Pens:
  cleaning fluid, 141
  crow quill, 121
  Faber-Castell TG, 117, 118

Pens (*cont.*)
  Faber-Castell 990, 116
  Gillott, 121
  Graphos, 119
  important features, 113
  Leroy reservoir, 114, 115
  Leroy standard, 120
  line weight, 113–16
  Osmiroid, 120
  Rapidograph, 115
  reservoir type, 113–18
  for sketching, 119–21
  Speedball, 119
  technical fountain, 113–18
  ultrasonic cleaner, 136
  uses of, 114, 119–21
Percentage protractor, 141
Perspective:
  angles, 78
  in architecture, 76
  areas, 78
  common method, 83, 86
  compared to orthographic, 77
  concepts, 77–81
  cone of rays, 83
  convergence of projectors, 77
  dimunition, 79
  distortion, 76
  horizons, 80, 81
  locating vanishing points, 84, 86
  location of horizon, 80, 81
  measurements, 80
  one-point, 83–86
  projectors, 77
  realism, 75
  references, 91
  relationship of size to *SP*, 78
  shapes, 78
  sizes, 78
  station point, 77
  systems, 81–90
  terminology, 77–81
  three-point, 89, 90
  true measure, 80
  two-point, 86–88
  uses of, 76, 77
  vanishing point, 81
  viewing angle, 79
Photo lettering, 220
Photo typesetting, 220
Pica, 223
Pica scale, 141, 223
Pictorial illustration:
  definition of, 10
  dimetric, 30–42
  isometric, 11–30
  media for, 165–91
  medical, 188
  oblique, 60–73

Pictorial illustration (*cont.*)
  perspective, 75–90
  references for, 91, 161–64, 192–96
  shade in, 102–8
  shadow in, 102–8
  trimetric, 42–54
  types of, 10, 30, 42, 60, 75
  using hand stippling, 175–80
  using ink wash, 186–88
  using stipple board, 181–84
Point, 223
Pounce, 140
Powers of ten, 225, 226
Price of, 112
Projection:
  definition of, 1
  dimetric, 30–42 (*see also* Dimetric projection)
  isometric, 11–30 (*see also* Isometric projection)
  oblique, 60–73 (*see also* Oblique projection)
  orthographic, 3–7 (*see also* Orthographic projection)
  perspective, 75–90 (*see also* Perspective)
  trimetric, 42–50 (*see also* Trimetric projection)
Projection slides, 197–207
  choosing format, 205
  color, 202–4
  dark slides, 207
  detail, 205
  duplicates, 205
  format, 197, 198
  lantern, 197
  lettering for, 200, 201, 206
  overhead, 197
  scaling for, 199–201
  sizes, 197
  35 mm, 197
  titles, 206
  typewriter copy, 206
Proportional dividers, 140
Protractor, circular, 40
Protractor, ellipse, 141
Publications, 227

R

Rapidograph pens, 115
Reducing lens, 138
Reducing screen patterns, 172, 173
Reproduction processes, 211–14
  blueprint, 214
  continuous tone, 211, 212
  electrostatic, 213
  halftone, 212

Reproduction processes (*cont.*)
   high contrast, 211
   offset printing, 213
   Ozalid, 214
   photographic, 211, 212
   Xerox, 213
Reservoir pens, 113–18, 120
Ross board, 181
Rub-on screens, 170

S

Scales, 142
Scissors, 141
Scratchboard, 185
   examples, 185
   materials, 185
   references, 195
Screen patterns, 171–73
Semifreehand drawing, 151
Shade:
   definition of, 98
   example, 96–98
   in dimetric, 104
   in isometric, 103
   in multiple view drawings, 101, 102
   in oblique, 105
   in perspective, 105, 106
   in pictorial drawings, 102–8
   references, 109
   in trimetric, 104
Shading:
   acetate sheets, 170–75
   hand stipple, 175–80
   highlights, 169
   ink wash, 186–88
   methods, 166
   the problem, 165
   for realism, 166
   rulings, 166, 168–70
   spheres, 166, 167
   stipple board, 181–84
   surface texture, 166
   tint screen, 189–92
Shadow:
   construction of, 102
   definition of, 96
   in dimetric, 104
   direction of light, 98–100, 103–8
   examples, 96–98
   importance of, 94, 95
   in isometric, 97, 103
   methods in pictorial, 102, 103
   in oblique, 105
   on parallel surfaces, 96
   in perspective, 105–8
   in pictorial drawings, 102–8
   planes that cast shadows, 101

Shadow (*cont.*)
   principles in, 100, 101
   references, 109
   in trimetric, 104, 105
   use of vanishing points, 106–8
Ship curves, 130
Slides (*see* Projection slides)
Speedball pens, 119
Stencil lettering, 127
Stipple, 175–80
   definition, 175
   examples, 176–80
   fields of use, 176
   procedure, 176
   references, 195, 196
   steps, 176
Stipple board, 181–84
   advantage of, 181
   examples, 181–84
   as line copy, 181
   materials used, 181
   other names for, 181
   references, 192, 193
Stippled drawings, 175–80
Straight edge, 133
Style of drawings, 144, 151, 154

T

T square, 133
Tape, 140, 141
Tape dispenser, 141
Technical fountain pens:
   line thickness, 113, 115, 116, 200, 201
   line weights, 113, 115, 116, 200, 201
   manufacturers of, 114–18
   operating principle, 114
   use of, 114
Technical terms, 227–29
   abbreviations, 227, 228
   symbols, 227, 228
   use by agencies, 229
Tint Screens:
   cost, 190
   examples, 190, 191
   procedure, 189, 190
   references, 194, 195
   sub-illustrations, 189
   use of drafting film, 189
   use of register marks, 189
Toning sheets, 170–75
Tools (*see* Equipment)
Top view, 4, 5, 62
Tracing paper (*see* Equipment)
Triangle (instrument), 129
   length of, 129
   types needed, 130
   use of, 129

Trimetric projection:
   advantage of, 42
   angles, tabulation of, 48
   axes angles, 43–50
   axes scales, 43–50
   box construction, 43
   center line layout, 47
   construction of scales, 43–45
   definition of, 42
   determining angle ellipses, 48
   determining axes angles, 45, 46
   determining axes scales, 43–50
   disadvantage of, 42
   ellipses, 47–50
   ellipses, selection of, 48
   ellipse wheel, use of, 49
   emphasis of faces, 45, 46
   geometry of, 43
   from orthographic views, 54
   points of view in, 50
   position of axes, 43
   problems, 48, 59
   scales, tabulation of, 48
True axonometric projection:
   advantage of, 50
   construction of, 51, 52
   in dimetric, 53
   in isometric, 52
   theory of, 50, 51
   in trimetric, 54
Tweezers, 141
Type (*see* Typography)
Type font, 221
Typesetting (*see* Typography)
Typography, 217–23
   glossary, 221, 222
   measures, 223
   nomenclature of typeface, 218
   scales, 223
   typefaces, 217

U

Ultrasonic cleaner, 136
Unidirectional dimensioning, 29, 72

V

Vanishing points, 81, 84, 86
Views:
   arrangement of, 5
   auxiliary, 5, 6
   cutaway, 6, 17, 18, 71
   minimum number of, 4
   normal, 5, 12
   orthographic, 3–5

244 / Index

Views (*cont.*)
   position of, 5, 12, 32, 50, 64
   projection of, 4, 5
   section, 6, 17, 18, 71
   to select depth, 5
   to select height, 4
   to select width, 5

Visual communications, 143–49
Visualizer, 137

W

White dot screens, 173
Wooden pencils, 131

X–Z

X-Acto knife, 141
Zip-a-tone, 170
Zip-a-tone patterns, 170
Zip-a-tone screens, 172